# ESSENTIALS OF NANOTECHNOLOGY

## PRINCIPLES AND APPLICATIONS

PRABHAKAR REDDY VEERAREDDY &
MURALIDHAR RAO AKKALADEVI

# Contents

# Preface

The field of nanotechnology is rapidly evolving, presenting unprecedented opportunities and challenges across various scientific domains. Among its most promising applications are those in the medical and pharmaceutical sciences, where nanotechnology is revolutionizing drug delivery systems, diagnostic techniques, and therapeutic interventions. The intricate science of nanoscale materials and their unique properties require a comprehensive understanding that spans multiple disciplines, making it a vital area of study for students, researchers, and professionals.

**"Essentials of Nanotechnology: Principles and Applications"** is conceived with the aim of providing a thorough and accessible resource for B.Pharm students and other learners who aspire to master the fundamentals and advancements in nanotechnology. This book is designed to bridge the gap between foundational concepts and cutting-edge applications, offering an integrated approach to the study of nanomaterials and their biomedical applications.

**The contents of this book are meticulously structured into ten chapters, each delving into key aspects of nanotechnology.** We start with an introduction to the fundamental concepts, history, and unique properties of nanomaterials, laying a solid foundation for understanding their significance. The subsequent chapters are dedicated to the synthesis methods of various nanomaterials, including gold, magnetic, and polymeric nanoparticles, as well as self-assembly structures like liposomes and micelles.

Chapters on biomedical applications provide insights into how nanotechnology is transforming in vitro diagnostics, imaging, and targeting techniques. We also explore specialized topics such as pulmonary and nasal drug delivery systems, cardiovascular and localized drug delivery, highlighting the versatility and potential of nanocarriers in clinical applications.

The final chapters focus on the critical aspects of characterization, drug release, and stability studies of nanomaterials, equipping readers with the knowledge to evaluate and ensure the efficacy and safety of nanotechnology-based products.

**This book is the culmination of extensive research and academic experience by the authors, Prabhakar Reddy Veerareddy and Muralidhar**

**Rao Akkaladevi, who bring a wealth of knowledge and insight into the complexities of nanotechnology.** Our objective is to provide a single, comprehensive reference that students can rely on for in-depth understanding and practical knowledge, eliminating the need to consult multiple sources.

We hope that "Essentials of Nanotechnology: Principles and Applications" will serve as an indispensable resource for students and professionals, fostering a deeper appreciation and mastery of this transformative field. As the landscape of nanotechnology continues to evolve, we trust that this book will inspire and equip the next generation of scientists and innovators to explore and expand the horizons of nanoscience.

**Prabhakar Reddy Veerareddy**
**Muralidhar Rao Akkaladevi**
**10-05-2024**
**HYDERABAD**
**INDIA**

Essentials Of Nanotechnology

*PRINICIPLES AND APPLICATIONS*

• ix •

*BY*

*Prabhakar Reddy Veerareddy*

**Head, University college of Pharmaceutical Sciences**

**Palamuru University**

**Mahabubnagar, Telangana, India**

&

**Dr. A. Muralidhar Rao**

**Principal, St.Mary's College of Pharmacy, Secunderabad**

**Published by Notion Press**

*Notion Press, Inc.*
*800, West EI Camino Real #180,*
*California USA 94040*

*Notion Press Media Pvt Ltd,*
*#7, Red Cross Road,*
*Egmore, Chennai, Tamil Nadu 600008*

• x •

*Email ID: publish@notionpress.com*

*Phone Number: +91 44 46315631*

# CHAPTER ONE

# INTRODUCTION TO NANOTECHNOLOGY

## *1: Introduction to Nanotechnology*

Nanotechnology is defined as the science, engineering, and application of materials and devices with dimensions and tolerances in the nanometer scale, typically ranging from 1 to 100 nanometers. At this scale, unique physical, chemical, and biological properties emerge, which differ significantly from those observed in bulk materials. These properties can be exploited to create novel devices and systems with enhanced functionalities.

**Nanoscale Dimensions:**

Nanotechnology operates at the nanoscale, where materials exhibit quantum mechanical effects and increased surface area-to-volume ratios. This scale is critical because as materials are reduced to nanoscale dimensions, their surface atoms become more significant relative to the total number of atoms, leading to enhanced reactivity and novel physical properties.

**Quantum Effects:**

At the nanoscale, quantum effects become pronounced. For example, the electronic, optical, and magnetic properties of nanoparticles can differ dramatically from their bulk counterparts due to quantum confinement. This phenomenon occurs when the dimensions of a particle are reduced to a size comparable to the wavelength of electrons, leading to discrete energy levels and altered electron behavior.

**Surface Area and Reactivity:**

The increased surface area-to-volume ratio of nanoparticles enhances their reactivity, making them highly effective in catalysis and other chemical processes. This property is particularly important in applications such as drug delivery, where the large surface area allows for more efficient interaction with biological targets.

**Applications of Nanotechnology:**

Nanotechnology has a broad range of applications across various fields, including medicine, electronics, energy, and environmental science. In medicine, nanotechnology is used to develop targeted drug delivery systems, imaging agents, and diagnostic tools. In electronics, it enables the production of smaller, faster, and more efficient devices. Energy applications include the development of more efficient solar cells and batteries, while environmental applications involve the creation of advanced filtration systems and sensors.

**Interdisciplinary Nature:**

Nanotechnology is inherently interdisciplinary, combining principles from physics, chemistry, biology, and engineering. This convergence of disciplines allows for the development of innovative solutions to complex problems and the creation of multifunctional materials and devices.

**Historical Context and Evolution:**

The concept of nanotechnology was first introduced by physicist Richard Feynman in his famous 1959 lecture, "There's Plenty of Room at the Bottom." Feynman envisioned the possibility of manipulating individual atoms and molecules to create nanoscale structures. The term "nanotechnology" was later popularized by K. Eric Drexler in the 1980s, who proposed the idea of molecular manufacturing.

## 1.1 Definition of Nanotechnology

**Definition and Scope:**

Nanotechnology is defined as the branch of science and engineering dedicated to designing, producing, and using structures, devices, and systems by manipulating atoms and molecules at nanoscale dimensions, approximately 1 to 100 nanometers. This field encompasses a variety of scientific disciplines, including physics, chemistry, biology, and materials science, and is characterized by the unique properties that materials exhibit at these tiny scales. The scope of nanotechnology is vast, with applications ranging from medicine and electronics to energy and environmental science, providing innovative solutions to complex problems and advancing technology in unprecedented ways.

**Scale and Size (Nanoscale Dimensions):**

The term "nanoscale" refers to dimensions that are in the range of nanometers (one billionth of a meter). At these dimensions, materials begin to exhibit properties and behaviors that differ significantly from those observed in their bulk counterparts. For example, nanoparticles have a much larger surface area-to-volume ratio compared to bulk materials, leading to increased reactivity and the potential for novel chemical and physical interactions. This large surface area also enhances catalytic activity, making nanoparticles highly effective in various industrial processes. Additionally, quantum mechanical effects become prominent at the nanoscale, influencing the optical, electrical, and magnetic properties of materials. These effects can result in phenomena such as quantum confinement, where the electronic properties of nanoparticles are size-dependent, enabling the creation of materials with tunable optical and electronic characteristics.

**Comparison with Microscale and Macroscale:**

Understanding the nanoscale involves comparing it with the microscale and macroscale dimensions to appreciate the unique advantages and challenges posed by nanotechnology. At the macroscale (millimeters and larger), materials exhibit properties that are well understood and predictable based on classical physics. For instance, the strength, electrical conductivity, and thermal properties of a bulk material are typically uniform and can be easily measured and utilized in various applications.

In contrast, the microscale (ranging from micrometers to millimeters) still adheres largely to classical physics but begins to show increased surface effects due to a higher surface area-to-volume ratio. Microscale devices, such as microelectromechanical systems (MEMS), leverage these properties to create precise mechanical movements and electronic functions. However, the behavior of materials at this scale remains relatively predictable and consistent with bulk properties.

At the nanoscale, however, materials display entirely new properties due to quantum mechanical effects and significant surface interactions. For instance, gold, which is inert and non-reactive in its bulk form, exhibits remarkable catalytic properties when reduced to nanoscale dimensions. Similarly, bulk silicon, a semiconductor widely used in electronics, can exhibit different optical properties at the nanoscale, enabling the development of silicon-based photonic devices.

These comparisons highlight the transformative potential of nanotechnology. By manipulating materials at the atomic and molecular levels, scientists and engineers can design structures with specific properties tailored for unique applications, such as targeted drug delivery systems, advanced imaging techniques, and highly efficient energy storage devices. However, working at the nanoscale also presents challenges, including the need for precise fabrication techniques, rigorous characterization methods, and thorough understanding of nanoscale interactions to ensure safety and effectiveness in practical applications.

## 1.2 History of Nanotechnology

### 1.2.1 Early Beginnings and Milestones

**Ancient Use of Nanomaterials (Lycurgus Cup, Damascus Steel):**

The history of nanotechnology can be traced back to ancient times, long before the term "nanotechnology" was coined. One of the earliest known uses of nanomaterials is found in the Lycurgus Cup, a Roman glass chalice from the $4^{th}$ century AD. This remarkable artifact changes color from green to red when light passes through it, a phenomenon attributed to the presence of nanoscale particles of gold and silver dispersed within the glass matrix. These nanoparticles interact with light through a process called surface plasmon resonance, demonstrating an early, albeit unintentional, application of nanotechnology.

Another historical example is the production of Damascus steel, renowned for its exceptional strength, toughness, and distinctive wavy patterns. Used in the manufacturing of swords and blades from around the $3^{rd}$ century AD, Damascus steel's unique properties were the result of complex microstructural features, including carbon nanotubes and carbide nanowires embedded within the iron matrix. These nanostructures contributed to the material's superior mechanical characteristics, illustrating the advanced, albeit empirical, manipulation of materials at the nanoscale by ancient blacksmiths.

**Richard Feynman's Vision (1959 Talk "There's Plenty of Room at the Bottom"):**

The conceptual foundation of modern nanotechnology was laid by physicist Richard Feynman in his seminal 1959 lecture, "There's Plenty of Room at the Bottom." In this visionary talk, Feynman outlined the possibility of manipulating and controlling individual atoms and molecules to create new materials and devices with unprecedented precision. He speculated on the potential of building machines and instruments at the nanoscale, predicting the advent of techniques that could assemble structures atom by atom. Feynman's ideas, though theoretical at the time, inspired generations of scientists and researchers to explore the possibilities of nanotechnology, setting the stage for future breakthroughs in the field.

## *1.2.2 Evolution and Key Developments in the Field*

**Discovery of Fullerenes (1985):**

A significant milestone in the evolution of nanotechnology was the discovery of fullerenes in 1985 by scientists Harold Kroto, Richard Smalley, and Robert Curl. Fullerenes are a form of carbon characterized by a spherical structure composed of hexagonal and pentagonal arrangements of carbon atoms. The most well-known fullerene, C60, resembles a soccer ball and is often referred to as a "buckyball." The discovery of fullerenes opened up new avenues for research in nanomaterials, leading to the exploration of other carbon-based nanostructures, such as carbon nanotubes and graphene, which have exceptional mechanical, electrical, and thermal properties.

**Development of Scanning Tunneling Microscope (STM) and Atomic Force Microscope (AFM):**

The development of the Scanning Tunneling Microscope (STM) in 1981 by Gerd Binnig and Heinrich Rohrer at IBM's Zurich Research Laboratory marked a pivotal advancement in nanotechnology. The STM enabled scientists to visualize and manipulate individual atoms on a surface, providing unprecedented insight into atomic-scale phenomena. This groundbreaking invention earned Binnig and Rohrer the Nobel Prize in Physics in 1986 and spurred the development of other high-resolution imaging techniques.

Following the STM, Binnig, along with Calvin Quate and Christoph Gerber, invented the Atomic Force Microscope (AFM) in 1986. The AFM allowed researchers to image and measure the forces between atoms on a surface with remarkable precision, further expanding the capabilities of nanoscale investigation. These instruments revolutionized the study of nanomaterials, facilitating the characterization and manipulation of matter at the atomic level, and played a crucial role in the advancement of nanotechnology research.

**Milestones in Nanotechnology Research (Formation of National Nanotechnology Initiative):**

The formal establishment of nanotechnology as a distinct scientific field gained momentum with the formation of the National Nanotechnology Initiative (NNI) in 2000. The NNI, launched by the U.S. government, aimed to coordinate federal research and development efforts in nanotechnology, promoting interdisciplinary collaboration and investment in the field. The initiative significantly increased funding for nanotechnology research, leading to numerous breakthroughs and innovations across various domains, including medicine, electronics, and materials science.

Since the inception of the NNI, the field of nanotechnology has witnessed remarkable progress, with researchers developing novel nanomaterials, advanced fabrication techniques, and practical applications. The impact of nanotechnology continues to grow, driving advancements in areas such as drug delivery, renewable energy, and environmental protection. The ongoing exploration of the nanoscale realm promises to unlock new possibilities and transform industries, cementing nanotechnology's role as a cornerstone of modern science and technology.

## 1.3 Unique Properties of Nanomaterials

### 1.3.1 Nanoscale Effects

**Quantum Effects (Quantum Confinement):**

At the nanoscale, materials exhibit unique properties that differ significantly from their bulk counterparts due to quantum effects. One of the most notable phenomena is quantum confinement, which occurs when the dimensions of a material are reduced to the nanometer scale, typically below 10 nanometers. In this regime, the motion of electrons is restricted, and their energy levels become discrete rather than continuous. This quantization of energy levels alters the electronic, optical, and magnetic properties of the material. For instance, semiconductor nanoparticles, also known as quantum dots, exhibit size-dependent optical properties. As the size of the quantum dot decreases, the energy gap between the valence and conduction bands increases, resulting in a shift of the emission color from red to blue. This tunable photoluminescence makes quantum dots highly valuable in applications such as bioimaging, light-emitting diodes (LEDs), and solar cells.

## *Surface Area to Volume Ratio:*

Another critical factor contributing to the unique properties of nanomaterials is the significantly high surface area to volume ratio. As the particle size decreases, a larger fraction of atoms or molecules resides on the surface compared to those in the bulk. This high surface area enhances the reactivity and interaction of nanomaterials with their environment, making them exceptionally effective as catalysts. For example, gold nanoparticles exhibit remarkable catalytic activity for reactions such as CO oxidation, which bulk gold does not typically catalyze. The increased surface area also improves the performance of nanomaterials in applications like drug delivery, where a larger surface facilitates the adsorption and controlled release of therapeutic agents. Additionally, in the field of energy storage, nanomaterials are used to develop electrodes for batteries and supercapacitors with enhanced charge storage capacity and faster charge-discharge cycles due to their high surface area.

### Optical Properties (Surface Plasmon Resonance):

Nanomaterials exhibit distinctive optical properties that arise from the interaction of light with their surface electrons. One such phenomenon is surface plasmon resonance (SPR), which occurs when the collective oscillation of surface electrons in metal nanoparticles, such as gold and silver, resonates with the incident light frequency. This resonance leads to strong absorption and scattering of light, resulting in intense colors that depend on the size, shape, and dielectric environment of the nanoparticles. For example, gold nanoparticles can appear red or blue depending on their size and the surrounding medium. SPR is exploited in various applications, including biosensing, where changes in the local refractive index around the nanoparticles can be detected with high sensitivity. Additionally, SPR enhances the local electromagnetic field, which is utilized in techniques such as surface-enhanced Raman scattering (SERS) for ultra-sensitive molecular detection. The unique optical properties of nanomaterials also enable advancements in photothermal therapy, where nanoparticles are used to convert absorbed light into heat for targeted cancer treatment.

The exploration of these nanoscale effects has paved the way for numerous technological advancements and continues to be a vibrant area of research in nanoscience and nanotechnology.

## *1.3.2 Physical Properties*

**Mechanical Strength (Nanotubes and Nanowires):**

Nanomaterials such as carbon nanotubes (CNTs) and nanowires exhibit exceptional mechanical properties compared to their bulk counterparts. Carbon nanotubes, for example, have remarkable tensile strength and stiffness due to their strong $sp^2$ carbon-carbon bonds and unique tubular structure. Single-walled carbon nanotubes (SWCNTs) can have tensile strengths up to 100 times greater than steel at one-sixth the weight. This makes CNTs highly valuable for reinforcing composite materials, leading to the development of lightweight and high-strength materials used in aerospace, automotive, and sports equipment industries. Similarly, nanowires, particularly those made from metals like silver and gold, exhibit superior mechanical strength and flexibility. Their small size and high aspect ratio allow them to withstand significant deformation without breaking, making them suitable for applications in flexible electronics and nanoscale devices.

**Thermal Conductivity:**

Nanomaterials also demonstrate unique thermal properties. For instance, carbon nanotubes and graphene exhibit extremely high thermal conductivity. The thermal conductivity of graphene can reach up to 5000 W/m·K, significantly higher than that of conventional materials like copper, which has a thermal conductivity of about 400 W/m·K. This extraordinary thermal conductivity is attributed to the strong carbon-carbon bonds and efficient phonon transport within the graphene lattice. Such properties make these nanomaterials ideal for thermal management applications, including heat sinks, thermal interface materials, and components in electronic devices where efficient heat dissipation is critical. On the other hand, certain nanomaterials can be engineered to exhibit low thermal conductivity, making them suitable for thermoelectric applications where heat-to-electricity conversion is desired.

**Electrical Conductivity:**

Nanomaterials also exhibit diverse electrical properties, which can be tailored for various applications. For example, graphene and carbon nanotubes possess excellent electrical conductivity, making them promising candidates for next-generation electronic devices, conductive coatings, and transparent electrodes. Graphene, a single layer of carbon atoms arranged in a hexagonal lattice, has a high carrier mobility, allowing for fast electron transport and minimal resistive losses. This makes it ideal for applications in high-speed transistors and flexible electronics. Similarly, silver nanowires are used to create highly conductive and flexible transparent electrodes for touchscreens, OLEDs, and solar cells. In contrast, certain nanomaterials can be designed to be semiconducting or insulating, enabling their use in a wide range of electronic components, from transistors to sensors. The ability to manipulate electrical conductivity at the nanoscale opens up new possibilities for the development of advanced materials and devices with tailored electrical properties for specific applications.

## *1.3.3 Chemical Properties*

**Reactivity and Catalytic Activity:**

Nanomaterials exhibit unique chemical properties due to their high surface area-to-volume ratio and the presence of a significant fraction of atoms on their surface. This enhanced surface reactivity is particularly advantageous in catalysis, where nanomaterials can significantly increase the rate of chemical reactions. For example, gold nanoparticles, which are inert in their bulk form, become highly active catalysts at the nanoscale. They are widely used in catalyzing reactions such as carbon monoxide oxidation and hydrogenation processes. Similarly, titanium dioxide ($TiO_2$) nanoparticles are employed in photocatalysis for environmental applications, including the degradation of pollutants in water and air. The enhanced catalytic activity of nanomaterials is attributed to the increased number of active sites, which provide more opportunities for reactant molecules to interact with the catalyst surface. Additionally, the ability to tune the size, shape, and composition of nanocatalysts allows for the optimization of catalytic performance for specific reactions, making them highly versatile in various industrial and environmental applications.

**Stability and Environmental Interactions:**

The stability of nanomaterials is a critical factor in their practical applications, influencing their performance and longevity. Nanomaterials can exhibit different stability profiles compared to their bulk counterparts, often requiring careful consideration of environmental interactions such as exposure to air, moisture, and various chemical environments. For instance, silver nanoparticles are prone to oxidation and aggregation, which can reduce their effectiveness in applications such as antimicrobial coatings and conductive inks. To enhance their stability, surface modifications or the use of stabilizing agents are commonly employed. In environmental contexts, the interactions of nanomaterials with biological systems and ecosystems are of significant concern. Their small size and high reactivity can lead to unexpected behaviors, such as bioaccumulation and potential toxicity to organisms. Therefore, understanding and managing the environmental impact of nanomaterials is crucial for their safe and sustainable use. This involves studying their degradation pathways, persistence in different environments, and potential for causing adverse effects on human health and the environment.

**Surface Functionalization:**

Surface functionalization of nanomaterials involves the deliberate modification of their surface properties to achieve specific functionalities and improve their performance in various applications. This process can include the attachment of organic molecules, polymers, or other nanoparticles to the surface of the nanomaterial, providing control over properties such as solubility, stability, biocompatibility, and targeted interactions. For example, functionalizing the surface of gold nanoparticles with thiol-containing ligands can enhance their stability and facilitate their use in biomedical applications, such as drug delivery and imaging. Similarly, functionalizing carbon nanotubes with carboxyl or amine groups can improve their dispersion in solvents and polymers, making them more effective in composite materials and sensors. Surface functionalization can also be tailored to create specific interactions with biological molecules, enabling the development of targeted drug delivery systems, biosensors, and diagnostic tools. The ability to precisely control the surface chemistry of nanomaterials through functionalization is a powerful tool that expands their applicability across diverse fields, from medicine and electronics to environmental science and materials engineering.

## *1.3.4 Biological Properties*

**Biocompatibility and Toxicity:**

The biological properties of nanomaterials are critical considerations for their use in medical and biotechnological applications. Biocompatibility refers to the ability of nanomaterials to perform their intended function without eliciting adverse reactions in biological systems. This property is essential for applications such as drug delivery, implants, and medical diagnostics. For instance, nanoparticles made from biocompatible materials like lipids, polymers (e.g., PLGA), and certain metals (e.g., gold) are commonly used in drug delivery systems due to their ability to be safely metabolized or excreted by the body. However, the small size and high surface reactivity of nanomaterials can also pose risks of toxicity. Potential toxic effects can arise from oxidative stress, inflammation, and cellular damage, depending on the material composition, size, shape, and surface charge. Therefore, thorough in vitro and in vivo studies are conducted to assess the safety profile of nanomaterials before their clinical application. Strategies to enhance biocompatibility include surface functionalization with biocompatible molecules, encapsulation within biocompatible matrices, and careful control over the physicochemical properties of the nanomaterials.

**Interaction with Biological Systems:**

Nanomaterials interact with biological systems in unique ways due to their nanoscale dimensions, which allow them to interact with cells, tissues, and biological molecules at a molecular level. These interactions can be leveraged for various biomedical applications, but they also necessitate a detailed understanding to avoid unintended effects. For example, nanoparticles can cross biological barriers, such as the blood-brain barrier, which is typically impermeable to larger molecules. This property is advantageous for delivering drugs to specific sites within the brain but requires careful design to prevent neurotoxicity. The surface properties of nanomaterials play a crucial role in their interactions with proteins and cells, influencing processes like cellular uptake, biodistribution, and immune response. Functionalizing the surface with targeting ligands, such as antibodies or peptides, can enhance the specificity of interactions with target cells or tissues, improving the efficacy and safety of nanomaterial-based therapies. Understanding the mechanisms of nanoparticle-cell interactions helps in designing nanomaterials that can navigate the complex biological environment efficiently and safely.

**Applications in Drug Delivery and Imaging:**

Nanomaterials have revolutionized the fields of drug delivery and medical imaging, offering new possibilities for targeted therapies and advanced diagnostic techniques. In drug delivery, nanoparticles can be engineered to encapsulate therapeutic agents, protecting them from degradation and improving their solubility and bioavailability. Targeted drug delivery systems can be designed by attaching ligands that specifically bind to receptors on diseased cells, ensuring that the drug is delivered precisely to the site of action while minimizing side effects. For example, liposomes and polymeric nanoparticles are widely used to deliver chemotherapeutic agents directly to cancer cells, reducing the impact on healthy tissues. In medical imaging, nanomaterials such as quantum dots and gold nanoparticles provide enhanced contrast and specificity. Quantum dots, with their unique optical properties, enable multiplexed imaging, allowing simultaneous visualization of multiple targets within a biological sample. Gold nanoparticles enhance contrast in imaging techniques like computed tomography (CT) and photoacoustic imaging, providing high-resolution images of tissues and organs. These advanced imaging capabilities facilitate early diagnosis, monitoring of disease progression, and evaluation of therapeutic responses, contributing to more effective and personalized medical care.

## 1.4 Classification of Nanomaterials

### 1.4.1 Fullerenes

**Structure and Synthesis (Buckminsterfullerene, C60):**
Fullerenes are a distinct class of carbon-based nanomaterials characterized by their unique molecular structure, resembling a hollow sphere, ellipsoid, or tube. The most well-known fullerene is Buckminsterfullerene (C60), named after architect Buckminster Fuller due to its resemblance to the geodesic domes he designed. The structure of C60 consists of 60 carbon atoms arranged in a pattern of 12 pentagons and 20 hexagons, forming a truncated icosahedron similar to a soccer ball. This spherical arrangement gives fullerenes remarkable stability and unique chemical properties. The synthesis of fullerenes typically involves methods such as arc discharge, laser ablation, and chemical vapor deposition (CVD). In the arc discharge method, an electric arc is generated between two

graphite electrodes in an inert atmosphere, causing the carbon atoms to vaporize and condense into fullerene molecules. Laser ablation involves using a high-powered laser to vaporize a graphite target, leading to the formation of fullerenes upon cooling. Chemical vapor deposition involves the thermal decomposition of hydrocarbon gases over a catalyst, resulting in the formation of fullerenes on the substrate. These synthesis techniques enable the production of fullerenes with varying sizes and properties, suitable for diverse applications.

**Properties and Applications (Drug Delivery, Electronics):**

Fullerenes exhibit a range of unique properties that make them suitable for various applications in drug delivery and electronics. Their spherical structure and ability to encapsulate other molecules allow fullerenes to serve as carriers for drug delivery systems. The interior cavity of fullerenes can encapsulate therapeutic agents, protecting them from degradation and facilitating targeted delivery to specific sites within the body. Additionally, the surface of fullerenes can be functionalized with various chemical groups to enhance their solubility, biocompatibility, and targeting capabilities. In drug delivery, fullerenes have shown potential for delivering anticancer drugs, antiviral agents, and other therapeutic molecules, demonstrating improved efficacy and reduced side effects compared to conventional delivery methods.

In the field of electronics, fullerenes exhibit remarkable electronic properties, including high electron affinity, excellent electron mobility, and the ability to form conductive films. These properties make fullerenes suitable for use in organic photovoltaics, organic light-emitting diodes (OLEDs), and field-effect transistors (FETs). In organic photovoltaics, fullerenes are used as electron acceptors in bulk heterojunction solar cells, improving the efficiency of light absorption and charge separation. In OLEDs, fullerenes enhance the electron transport layer, contributing to the overall performance and efficiency of the devices. In field-effect transistors, fullerene-based materials provide high electron mobility, enabling the development of high-performance electronic components with potential applications in flexible and wearable electronics. The versatility and unique properties of fullerenes continue to drive research and development in these fields, promising advancements in both medical and technological applications.

# 1.4.2 Carbon Nanotubes

**Types (Single-Walled, Multi-Walled):**

Carbon nanotubes (CNTs) are cylindrical nanostructures composed of rolled-up sheets of single-layer carbon atoms (graphene). There are two primary types of carbon nanotubes: single-walled carbon nanotubes (SWCNTs) and multi-walled carbon nanotubes (MWCNTs). Single-walled carbon nanotubes consist of a single graphene sheet rolled into a seamless cylinder with a diameter typically ranging from 0.7 to 2 nanometers. The structure of SWCNTs can vary, leading to different chiralities (zigzag, armchair, or chiral), which influence their electronic properties. Multi-walled carbon nanotubes consist of multiple concentric graphene cylinders nested within one another, with diameters ranging from 2 to 100 nanometers. The interlayer spacing in MWCNTs is approximately 0.34 nanometers, similar to the spacing between graphene layers in graphite. The presence of multiple walls in MWCNTs provides enhanced mechanical strength compared to SWCNTs, making them suitable for various applications requiring robust materials.

**Synthesis Methods (Arc Discharge, Chemical Vapor Deposition):**

The synthesis of carbon nanotubes can be achieved through several methods, with arc discharge and chemical vapor deposition (CVD) being the most common. The arc discharge method involves generating a high-current electric arc between two graphite electrodes in an inert gas atmosphere (typically helium or argon). The intense heat produced by the arc vaporizes the carbon from the electrodes, which then condenses to form carbon nanotubes. This method is efficient for producing high-quality CNTs but often requires purification to remove amorphous carbon and metallic impurities.

Chemical vapor deposition (CVD) is another widely used method for synthesizing CNTs. In CVD, a hydrocarbon gas (such as methane, ethylene, or acetylene) is introduced into a reaction chamber containing a substrate coated with a metal catalyst (such as iron, cobalt, or nickel). The substrate is heated to a high temperature (typically 600-1200°C), causing the hydrocarbon gas to decompose and deposit carbon atoms on the catalyst particles. These carbon atoms then nucleate and grow into carbon nanotubes. CVD allows for better control over the growth process, enabling the production of CNTs with specific properties and alignment. Variations of CVD, such as plasma-enhanced CVD (PECVD) and floating catalyst CVD, further enhance the synthesis capabilities, allowing for the production of CNTs with tailored characteristics for specific applications.

**Properties and Applications (Conductivity, Strength, Sensors):**

Carbon nanotubes possess a unique combination of properties that make them suitable for a wide range of applications. One of the most notable properties of CNTs is their exceptional electrical conductivity. Depending on their chirality, SWCNTs can exhibit metallic or semiconducting behavior, making them useful for electronic applications such as transistors, conductive films, and interconnects in integrated circuits. The high electron mobility in CNTs also makes them attractive for use in field-effect transistors (FETs) and other nanoelectronic devices.

In addition to their electrical properties, carbon nanotubes are renowned for their extraordinary mechanical strength and stiffness. CNTs have a tensile strength approximately 100 times greater than steel, with a density one-sixth that of steel. This remarkable strength, combined with their lightweight nature, makes CNTs ideal for reinforcing composite materials in aerospace, automotive, and construction industries. The incorporation of CNTs into polymers, metals, and ceramics can significantly enhance the mechanical properties of these materials, leading to the development of advanced composites with superior performance characteristics.

Carbon nanotubes also find applications in sensor technology due to their high surface area, chemical stability, and sensitivity to various analytes. CNT-based sensors can detect gases, biomolecules, and other chemical substances at very low concentrations, making them valuable for environmental monitoring, medical diagnostics, and industrial process control. The functionalization of CNT surfaces with specific chemical groups or biomolecules further enhances their selectivity and sensitivity, enabling the development of highly specific sensors for various applications. The unique properties of carbon nanotubes continue to drive research and innovation, promising new advancements in multiple fields.

## 1.4.3 Quantum Dots

**Structure and Composition (Semiconductor Nanocrystals):**

Quantum dots (QDs) are nanoscale semiconductor particles that typically range from 2 to 10 nanometers in diameter. These nanocrystals are composed of semiconductor materials such as cadmium selenide (CdSe), cadmium sulfide (CdS), indium phosphide (InP), and lead sulfide (PbS). The core of a quantum dot is often surrounded by a shell made of another semiconductor material, such as zinc sulfide (ZnS), to enhance its optical properties and stability. The core-shell structure helps to passivate the surface of the quantum dot, reducing surface defects that can act as non-radiative recombination centers. This passivation improves the quantum yield of the QDs, making them more efficient at emitting light when excited. The unique structure of quantum dots allows for tunable electronic and optical properties by simply changing their size, which is a direct consequence of quantum confinement effects.

**Optical Properties (Size-Dependent Emission):**

One of the most remarkable features of quantum dots is their size-dependent optical properties. When the size of a quantum dot decreases, the energy gap between the valence band and the conduction band increases, resulting in a shift in the emission wavelength towards the blue end of the spectrum (higher energy). Conversely, larger quantum dots have a smaller energy gap, leading to red-shifted (lower energy) emission. This phenomenon, known as quantum confinement, enables precise control over the emission color of QDs by adjusting their size during synthesis. Quantum dots exhibit high photostability, narrow emission spectra, and broad absorption spectra, making them highly efficient light emitters. These properties are particularly advantageous for applications requiring bright and stable fluorescence, such as bioimaging, displays, and light-emitting devices.

**Applications (Bioimaging, Displays, Solar Cells):**

Quantum dots have found widespread applications across various fields due to their unique optical and electronic properties. In bioimaging, QDs are used as fluorescent probes for imaging cellular and molecular processes. Their high brightness, resistance to photobleaching, and size-tunable emission make them superior to traditional organic dyes and fluorescent proteins. Quantum dots can be conjugated with antibodies, peptides, or other biomolecules to target specific cells or tissues, allowing for high-resolution imaging and tracking of biological events in real-time.

In the field of displays, quantum dots are employed in the production of QLED (quantum dot light-emitting diode) displays. These displays offer several advantages over conventional LCD and OLED displays, including higher brightness, better color accuracy, and lower power consumption. The ability to precisely control the emission wavelength of QDs enables the creation of displays with a wide color gamut and enhanced visual quality. Quantum dot-enhanced displays are used in televisions, monitors, and mobile devices, providing vivid and lifelike colors.

Quantum dots also hold great promise in solar cell technology. QD-based solar cells have the potential to achieve higher efficiencies than traditional silicon-based solar cells due to their tunable bandgap and ability to utilize a broader spectrum of sunlight. By optimizing the size and composition of QDs, researchers can design solar cells that efficiently absorb and convert sunlight into electricity. Additionally, quantum dots can be incorporated into tandem solar cells, where multiple layers of QDs with different bandgaps are stacked to capture different portions of the solar spectrum, further enhancing the overall efficiency.

The unique properties of quantum dots continue to drive research and development in various applications, paving the way for new technologies and innovations in fields ranging from medicine to energy and consumer electronics.

## 1.4.4 Other Nanomaterials

**Nanowires and Nanorods:**
Nanowires and nanorods are elongated nanostructures with diameters typically less than 100 nanometers and lengths that can extend to several micrometers. These structures exhibit a high aspect ratio, meaning they are much longer than they are wide. Nanowires and nanorods can be composed of various materials, including metals (such as gold and silver), semiconductors (like silicon and zinc oxide), and oxides (such as titanium dioxide). Their synthesis methods include vapor-liquid-solid (VLS) growth, template-assisted methods, and solution-phase techniques. The high aspect ratio of nanowires and nanorods imparts unique electrical, optical, and mechanical properties. For instance, metal nanowires are excellent conductors of electricity and are used in applications such as transparent conductive films, sensors, and interconnects in nanoelectronic devices. Semiconductor nanowires and nanorods, on the other hand, find applications in photodetectors, light-emitting diodes (LEDs), and photovoltaic devices due to their superior charge transport properties and size-dependent bandgap.

**Nanoclays:**

Nanoclays are naturally occurring or synthetically produced layered mineral silicates that possess nanometer-scale thickness and micrometer-scale lateral dimensions. They include materials such as montmorillonite, kaolinite, and hectorite. The unique structure of nanoclays consists of stacked silicate layers held together by weak van der Waals forces, which allows them to be easily exfoliated into individual nanosheets. Nanoclays are used extensively as fillers in polymer nanocomposites to enhance mechanical, thermal, and barrier properties. They are also employed in coatings, adhesives, and drug delivery systems due to their high surface area, ion-exchange capacity, and ability to intercalate with various molecules. The inclusion of nanoclays in polymers can significantly improve tensile strength, heat resistance, and flame retardancy, making them valuable in automotive, aerospace, and packaging industries.

**Dendrimers:**

Dendrimers are highly branched, tree-like macromolecules with a well-defined, symmetric structure and a high degree of molecular uniformity. They are synthesized through a stepwise, repetitive sequence of reactions, resulting in multiple generations of branching. The core, branches, and surface functional groups of dendrimers can be tailored to achieve specific properties and functionalities. Dendrimers exhibit unique properties such as low polydispersity, high solubility, and a large number of functional end groups. These characteristics make them suitable for a wide range of applications, including drug delivery, gene therapy, imaging, and catalysis. In drug delivery, dendrimers can encapsulate or conjugate with therapeutic agents, allowing for controlled release, targeted delivery, and reduced toxicity. Their highly branched structure also facilitates multivalent interactions with biological targets, enhancing their efficacy in biomedical applications.

**Nanocomposites:**

Nanocomposites are materials that incorporate nanoscale fillers into a matrix to enhance the composite's overall properties. These fillers can include nanoparticles, nanotubes, nanowires, nanoclays, and other nanomaterials. The matrix can be composed of polymers, metals, or ceramics. The incorporation of nanofillers into the matrix can significantly improve mechanical strength, thermal stability, electrical conductivity, and barrier properties. For example, polymer nanocomposites containing carbon nanotubes or graphene exhibit enhanced electrical conductivity and mechanical strength, making them suitable for applications in electronics, aerospace, and automotive industries. Metal matrix nanocomposites can demonstrate improved wear resistance and thermal conductivity, which are beneficial for industrial and structural applications. The interaction between the matrix and the nanofillers at the nanoscale level creates unique properties that are not achievable with traditional composites, leading to advanced materials with superior performance for various applications.

The continuous exploration and development of these and other nanomaterials hold great promise for advancing technology and addressing global challenges in healthcare, energy, environment, and materials science.

# CHAPTER TWO

# SYNTHESIS OF GOLD NANOPARTICLES

## *2.1 Chemical Reduction Methods*

### 2.1.1 Citrate Reduction Method
#### 2.1.1.1 Principle and Mechanism
**Reduction of Gold Ions by Citrate Ions**

The citrate reduction method for synthesizing gold nanoparticles is a well-established chemical reduction technique. This method primarily involves the reduction of gold ions to gold atoms by citrate ions, which act as both reducing and stabilizing agents. The process begins with the dissolution of gold salt, commonly chloroauric acid (HAuCl4), in water. The solution typically has a concentration of 1 mM to ensure an optimal reaction environment. When sodium citrate is added to the solution, it donates electrons to the gold ions, reducing them to elemental gold. This reduction occurs due to the citrate ions undergoing oxidation to form dicarboxyacetone. The reaction is facilitated by heating the mixture to about 100°C, which accelerates the reduction process.

**Formation of Colloidal Gold**

Once the gold ions are reduced, the gold atoms start to nucleate and form small clusters. These clusters subsequently grow into nanoparticles through a process known as Ostwald ripening, where smaller particles dissolve, and their material redeposits onto larger particles. The presence of citrate ions is crucial during this stage, as they adsorb onto the surface of the gold nanoparticles, providing electrostatic stabilization. This prevents the nanoparticles from aggregating and ensures a uniform size distribution. Typically, the nanoparticles formed are spherical and have an average diameter ranging from 10 to 20 nanometers, depending on the concentration of citrate and the reaction conditions. The resulting colloidal gold solution appears wine-red to purple in color, a characteristic due to the surface plasmon resonance effect exhibited by the gold nanoparticles. This method is valued for its simplicity, cost-effectiveness, and the ability to produce nanoparticles with a relatively narrow size distribution.

## 2.1.1.2 Procedure

### Preparation of Gold Salt Solution

The first step in the citrate reduction method involves preparing the gold salt solution. Chloroauric acid ($HAuCl_4$) is commonly used for this purpose due to its high solubility in water and its ability to easily release gold ions. To prepare the solution, 0.01 grams of $HAuCl_4$ is accurately weighed and dissolved in 100 milliliters of deionized water, resulting in a 1 millimolar (mM) gold salt solution. The solution should be stirred gently to ensure complete dissolution of the gold salt. It is important to use deionized water to avoid any impurities that might interfere with the reaction.

### Addition of Citrate Solution and Heating

Once the gold salt solution is prepared, the next step is the addition of the citrate solution. Sodium citrate dihydrate ($Na_3C_6H_5O_7 \cdot 2H_2O$) is typically used as the reducing agent. To prepare the citrate solution, 0.1 grams of sodium citrate is dissolved in 10 milliliters of deionized water, creating a 1% (w/v) solution. The gold salt solution is then brought to a gentle boil, maintained at around 100°C. With continuous stirring, 5 milliliters of the citrate solution is quickly added to the boiling gold salt solution. The mixture is kept at boiling temperature, and the reaction is allowed to proceed for approximately 15 to 20 minutes. During this period, the citrate ions reduce the gold ions to gold atoms, and the nanoparticles begin to form.

### Observation of Color Change and Formation of Nanoparticles

A key indicator of the formation of gold nanoparticles is the distinct color change in the solution. Initially, the gold salt solution is pale yellow. Upon addition of the citrate solution and subsequent heating, the solution gradually changes color, passing through various shades from yellow to colorless, then to grey, and finally to a deep wine-red or purple. This color change is due to the surface plasmon resonance phenomenon, where the collective oscillation of electrons in the gold nanoparticles interacts with light. The final color indicates the successful formation of colloidal gold nanoparticles. The size and uniformity of the nanoparticles can be further analyzed using techniques such as UV-Vis spectroscopy, which typically shows an absorption peak around 520 to 530 nanometers, characteristic of gold nanoparticles. The resulting colloidal suspension can be stored at room temperature in dark conditions to prevent any photodegradation.

## 2.1.1.3 Parameters Affecting Synthesis

### Concentration of Gold Salt

The concentration of gold salt in the solution is a critical parameter that significantly influences the size and distribution of the synthesized gold nanoparticles. Higher concentrations of chloroauric acid (HAuCl4) tend to produce larger nanoparticles, as there are more gold ions available for reduction and subsequent nucleation. Conversely, lower concentrations result in smaller nanoparticles due to limited availability of gold ions. For instance, a 1 millimolar (mM) concentration of HAuCl4 typically yields nanoparticles with an average diameter of around 10 to 20 nanometers. If the concentration is increased to 2 mM, the nanoparticles may grow larger, possibly reaching diameters of 30 to 40 nanometers. It is essential to optimize the concentration of gold salt to achieve the desired nanoparticle size and uniformity.

### Temperature and pH

Temperature plays a pivotal role in the citrate reduction method. The reaction is usually carried out at boiling temperature, around 100°C, to facilitate the reduction of gold ions by citrate ions. Higher temperatures accelerate the reduction process, leading to faster nucleation and growth of gold nanoparticles. However, excessively high temperatures may cause rapid aggregation of nanoparticles, resulting in larger, less uniform particles. On the other hand, lower temperatures slow down the reaction, potentially leading to incomplete reduction of gold ions. The pH of the solution also affects the synthesis process. The citrate reduction method typically operates at a slightly acidic to neutral pH (around pH 6-7). At lower pH values, the reduction rate decreases, and the size of nanoparticles increases due to slower nucleation. At higher pH values, the reduction rate increases, resulting in smaller nanoparticles with narrower size distribution.

## *Stirring Speed*

Stirring speed is another crucial parameter that influences the uniformity and size of gold nanoparticles. Proper stirring ensures homogeneous mixing of the reactants, leading to uniform nucleation and growth of nanoparticles. A moderate stirring speed, typically around 300 to 500 revolutions per minute (rpm), is sufficient to maintain uniformity. If the stirring speed is too low, it can result in uneven distribution of citrate ions, causing heterogeneous nucleation and leading to a broad size distribution of nanoparticles. On the other hand, excessively high stirring speeds can induce shear forces that may disrupt the formation of nanoparticles, leading to irregular shapes and sizes. Therefore, optimizing the stirring speed is essential for achieving monodisperse gold nanoparticles with desired characteristics.

## *2.1.2 Role of Stabilizing Agents*

## *2.1.2.1 Importance of Stabilizers*

## *Prevention of Aggregation*

Stabilizing agents play a crucial role in the synthesis of gold nanoparticles by preventing aggregation, which is a common challenge in colloidal nanoparticle synthesis. Gold nanoparticles have a high surface energy, making them prone to agglomeration due to van der Waals forces. Stabilizers, such as citrate ions in the citrate reduction method, adsorb onto the surface of the nanoparticles and provide electrostatic repulsion between the particles. This repulsion counteracts the attractive forces that would otherwise cause the nanoparticles to stick together. For example, in a typical synthesis, the addition of citrate not only reduces gold ions but also coats the nanoparticles, creating a negatively charged layer around each particle. This negative charge generates repulsive forces between the nanoparticles, thereby preventing aggregation. As a result, the nanoparticles remain uniformly dispersed in the solution, maintaining their colloidal stability over time.

## *Control over Particle Size*

Stabilizing agents also play a vital role in controlling the size of the gold nanoparticles. By influencing the nucleation and growth processes, stabilizers can determine the final size and size distribution of the nanoparticles. During the reduction process, the presence of stabilizers like citrate ions affects the rate at which gold ions are reduced and subsequently nucleate to form nanoparticles. A higher concentration of stabilizer typically results in the formation of smaller nanoparticles. This is because the stabilizer molecules adsorb onto the growing nanoparticle surfaces, limiting the availability of gold ions for further growth. For instance, in the citrate reduction method, varying the amount of sodium citrate can produce nanoparticles with different average diameters. A higher citrate-to-gold ratio generally yields smaller particles, whereas a lower ratio results in larger particles. Moreover, stabilizers can provide a steric barrier around the nanoparticles, preventing them from coming too close to each other and thus controlling their size. The ability to fine-tune the particle size by adjusting the concentration of stabilizing agents is essential for applications where specific nanoparticle sizes are required, such as in medical imaging, drug delivery, and catalysis.

## *2.1.2.2 Common Stabilizing Agents*

## *Citrate Ions*

Citrate ions are among the most widely used stabilizing agents in the synthesis of gold nanoparticles, particularly in the citrate reduction method.

Sodium citrate acts as both a reducing and a stabilizing agent. When added to a gold salt solution, citrate ions reduce gold ions to gold atoms, which then nucleate to form nanoparticles. Concurrently, citrate ions adsorb onto the surface of the newly formed nanoparticles, imparting a negative charge. This negative charge creates electrostatic repulsion between nanoparticles, preventing aggregation and ensuring colloidal stability. The concentration of citrate can be adjusted to control the size of the nanoparticles. Typically, a higher concentration of citrate leads to smaller nanoparticles due to increased electrostatic stabilization, while a lower concentration results in larger particles. The simplicity and effectiveness of citrate make it a preferred choice in many nanoparticle synthesis protocols.

## *Polyvinylpyrrolidone (PVP)*

Polyvinylpyrrolidone (PVP) is another common stabilizing agent used in the synthesis of gold nanoparticles. PVP is a non-ionic polymer that stabilizes nanoparticles through steric hindrance. When PVP is added to a gold nanoparticle synthesis reaction, it adsorbs onto the surface of the nanoparticles, forming a protective layer. This polymer layer prevents the nanoparticles from coming into close contact with each other, thus avoiding aggregation. PVP is particularly effective in controlling the size and shape of nanoparticles. For example, it can be used to synthesize not only spherical nanoparticles but also anisotropic shapes like nanorods and nanowires. The molecular weight of PVP can be varied to fine-tune the stabilization and particle size. Higher molecular weight PVP generally provides better stabilization due to the thicker polymer layer formed around the nanoparticles. PVP-stabilized gold nanoparticles are widely used in applications such as drug delivery and catalysis due to their excellent stability and biocompatibility.

## *Thiol Compounds*

Thiol compounds, characterized by the presence of a sulfur-hydrogen (–SH) group, are highly effective stabilizing agents for gold nanoparticles. The strong affinity of sulfur for gold allows thiol molecules to form a stable, covalent bond with the gold surface. This strong binding results in a highly stable monolayer that protects the nanoparticles from aggregation. Common thiol compounds used in nanoparticle stabilization include thiol-terminated polyethylene glycol (PEG-SH), alkanethiols, and thiolated organic acids. Thiol-terminated PEG, for example, not only stabilizes gold nanoparticles but also enhances their biocompatibility and reduces non-specific binding in biological environments. The use of thiol compounds allows for precise control over the surface chemistry of gold nanoparticles, making them suitable for functionalization with various biomolecules for targeted drug delivery and diagnostic applications. Additionally, the length and functional groups of thiol compounds can be tailored to achieve the desired stabilization and functionality of the nanoparticles.

## *2.1.2.3 Mechanism of Stabilization*

### *Electrostatic Stabilization*

Electrostatic stabilization is a mechanism wherein the surface of gold nanoparticles is coated with ions that impart a charge, creating repulsive forces between the particles. This repulsion prevents the nanoparticles from aggregating. In the citrate reduction method, citrate ions adsorb onto the nanoparticle surface, providing a negative charge. This negative charge induces electrostatic repulsion between nanoparticles, ensuring they remain dispersed in the solution. The effectiveness of electrostatic stabilization depends on the concentration of the stabilizing ions and the ionic strength of the solution. For instance, in a typical citrate-stabilized gold nanoparticle synthesis, the addition of sodium citrate results in a uniform layer of negatively charged citrate ions around each nanoparticle. This electrostatic layer creates a repulsive force that counteracts van der Waals forces, preventing the particles from coming close enough to aggregate. The zeta potential, a measure of the surface charge, is often used to assess the stability of electrostatically stabilized nanoparticles. A high zeta potential (either positive or negative) indicates good stability, as it implies strong electrostatic repulsion between particles.

### *Steric Stabilization*

Steric stabilization involves the use of large molecules or polymers that adsorb onto the surface of nanoparticles, creating a physical barrier that prevents them from coming into close contact. Polyvinylpyrrolidone (PVP) and thiol-terminated polyethylene glycol (PEG-SH) are common agents used for steric stabilization. These molecules form a protective layer around each nanoparticle, providing steric hindrance that prevents aggregation. For example, PVP molecules adsorb onto the nanoparticle surface, with the polymer chains extending into the surrounding medium. These extended chains create a physical barrier, preventing other nanoparticles from approaching closely enough to aggregate. The thickness and density of this polymer layer determine the effectiveness of steric stabilization. In the case of PEG-SH, the thiol group binds strongly to the gold surface, while the PEG chains provide steric hindrance. This mechanism is particularly useful in biological applications where nanoparticles need to remain stable in complex environments. Sterically stabilized nanoparticles are less sensitive to changes in ionic strength and pH compared to electrostatically stabilized ones.

## Combination of Both Mechanisms

In many cases, a combination of electrostatic and steric stabilization mechanisms is employed to achieve enhanced stability of gold nanoparticles. This dual approach leverages the advantages of both mechanisms, providing robust protection against aggregation under a wide range of conditions. For instance, citrate ions can provide initial electrostatic stabilization, while a secondary stabilizer like PVP or PEG-SH can add steric stabilization. This combination ensures that nanoparticles remain stable in both low and high ionic strength environments and under varying pH conditions. The dual stabilization mechanism is particularly beneficial in biomedical applications where nanoparticles are exposed to complex biological fluids. In such scenarios, the electrostatic component prevents initial aggregation, while the steric component ensures long-term stability and biocompatibility. For example, gold nanoparticles synthesized with both citrate and PEG-SH exhibit excellent stability in physiological conditions, making them ideal for drug delivery and imaging applications. The combination of these mechanisms results in nanoparticles that are not only stable but also functionalizable for various applications.

## 2.2 Physical Methods

## *2.2.1 Laser Ablation Technique*

## *2.2.1.1 Principle and Mechanism*

**Ablation of Bulk Gold Using Laser Pulses**

The laser ablation technique for synthesizing gold nanoparticles involves the use of high-energy laser pulses to ablate bulk gold targets in a liquid medium. This method is based on the principle that when a high-intensity laser beam is focused on a gold target, the energy from the laser is absorbed by the gold surface, causing rapid heating, melting, and vaporization of the material. The laser pulses typically have durations in the range of nanoseconds to femtoseconds, with energy densities sufficient to induce ablation. During ablation, the gold atoms are ejected from the target surface into the surrounding liquid medium. For instance, using a pulsed Nd:YAG laser with a wavelength of 1064 nm and pulse duration of 10 nanoseconds, the energy density can be adjusted to around 1-10 $J/cm^2$ to achieve efficient ablation. The choice of laser parameters, such as pulse duration, energy, and repetition rate, is critical for controlling the ablation process and the size of the resulting nanoparticles.

## *Formation of Nanoparticles in a Liquid Medium*

The ablated gold atoms released into the liquid medium rapidly cool and condense to form nanoparticles. The liquid medium, which can be water, ethanol, or other solvents, plays a crucial role in stabilizing the nanoparticles and preventing their aggregation. The high-energy laser pulses not only ablate the gold target but also create a plasma plume consisting of gold atoms, ions, and electrons. As the plasma expands and cools, the gold atoms nucleate and grow into nanoparticles. The surrounding liquid quenches the nanoparticles, preventing further growth and stabilizing them. The size and distribution of the nanoparticles can be influenced by several factors, including the laser parameters, the type of liquid medium, and the duration of the ablation process. For example, nanoparticles synthesized in water tend to have a smaller average size compared to those synthesized in organic solvents due to the higher quenching rate in water. Typically, the nanoparticles formed by laser ablation are spherical and can range from a few nanometers to several tens of nanometers in diameter. The resulting colloidal solution is often characterized by its distinctive color, which is due to the surface plasmon resonance of the gold nanoparticles. This method is valued for its ability to produce pure nanoparticles without the need for chemical reducing agents or stabilizers, making it suitable for applications where high purity is essential.

## 2.2.1.2 Procedure

### Setup of Laser Ablation System

The setup of the laser ablation system is a critical step in the synthesis of gold nanoparticles. The primary components of this system include a pulsed laser, a focusing lens, a gold target, and a liquid medium container. The pulsed laser, such as a Nd:YAG ( neodymium-doped yttrium aluminum garnet) laser, is chosen for its high power and ability to deliver energy in short bursts. The gold target, often a high-purity gold disk or foil, is placed at the bottom of a container filled with the liquid medium. The container can be made of quartz or another material that allows the laser beam to pass through without significant absorption. The laser beam is directed through the focusing lens, which concentrates the laser energy onto a small spot on the gold target surface. The position of the gold target and the alignment of the laser beam are adjusted to ensure optimal ablation conditions. The container is usually placed on a motorized stage to enable uniform ablation over the entire surface of the gold target by moving the target in a controlled manner during the laser irradiation process.

### Parameters: Laser Wavelength, Power, and Duration

The parameters of the laser, including wavelength, power, and duration, are crucial for controlling the ablation process and the characteristics of the resulting gold nanoparticles. The wavelength of the laser determines the energy absorption efficiency of the gold target. A commonly used wavelength for gold ablation is 1064 nm, provided by Nd:YAG lasers, which is efficiently absorbed by gold, leading to effective ablation. The laser power, which is the energy delivered per pulse, directly influences the ablation rate and the size of the nanoparticles. For instance, a laser power density of 1-10 $J/cm^2$ is typically used for gold nanoparticle synthesis.

Higher power densities result in more intense ablation, producing smaller nanoparticles due to the increased number of nucleation sites. Conversely, lower power densities produce larger nanoparticles due to fewer nucleation sites and more extensive growth.

The pulse duration, which can range from nanoseconds to femtoseconds, affects the ablation dynamics and the thermal characteristics of the process. Nanosecond pulses (e.g., 10 ns) provide sufficient energy for ablation but also generate significant heat, leading to larger particles and potential thermal damage to the target. Femtosecond pulses (e.g., 100 fs) deliver energy in an ultra-short time frame, minimizing thermal effects and producing smaller, more uniform nanoparticles. The repetition rate of the laser pulses, typically ranging from a few Hz to several kHz, determines the number of pulses per second and, consequently, the total energy delivered to the target. A higher repetition rate increases the ablation efficiency and can lead to a higher yield of nanoparticles. By carefully tuning these laser parameters, researchers can control the size, shape, and distribution of the gold nanoparticles, optimizing them for specific applications such as biomedical imaging, catalysis, and electronic devices.

## 2.2.1.3 Advantages and Disadvantages

### High Purity of Nanoparticles

One of the primary advantages of the laser ablation technique is the high purity of the synthesized nanoparticles. Unlike chemical reduction methods, laser ablation does not require chemical reagents such as reducing or stabilizing agents, which can introduce impurities. The process involves only a high-purity gold target and a clean liquid medium, typically deionized water or an organic solvent. This results in nanoparticles that are free from residual chemicals and by-products, making them ideal for applications requiring high purity, such as in biomedical fields where impurities could cause adverse reactions. The absence of chemical contaminants also simplifies post-synthesis purification processes, reducing the overall complexity and cost of nanoparticle production.

### Control over Size and Shape

The laser ablation technique offers significant control over the size and shape of the synthesized nanoparticles. By adjusting the laser parameters such as wavelength, power, pulse duration, and repetition rate, researchers can finely tune the characteristics of the nanoparticles. For instance, shorter pulse durations (femtoseconds) and higher laser powers typically produce smaller and more uniform nanoparticles due to rapid nucleation and limited growth time. Additionally, the type of liquid medium and its properties, such as viscosity and boiling point, can influence the cooling rate and stabilization of the nanoparticles, further affecting their size and shape. This level of control is particularly beneficial for applications that require specific nanoparticle sizes and shapes, such as targeted drug delivery systems, where the size and shape of the nanoparticles can influence their biological interactions and efficacy.

## High Equipment Cost

Despite its advantages, the laser ablation technique has notable disadvantages, primarily related to the high cost of equipment. The setup requires a high-power pulsed laser, such as an Nd:YAG laser, which can be expensive to purchase and maintain. Additionally, the optical components, such as focusing lenses and precision alignment systems, add to the overall cost. The need for a cleanroom environment to prevent contamination and the requirement for precise control systems to ensure consistent ablation further increase the operational expenses. These high initial and maintenance costs can be prohibitive for some research labs and small-scale production facilities, limiting the widespread adoption of the technique. Moreover, the process's scalability can be challenging due to the equipment's complexity and the time-intensive nature of producing large quantities of nanoparticles. Thus, while laser ablation provides high purity and control over nanoparticle synthesis, the associated costs and operational requirements can be significant drawbacks.

## 2.2.2 Vapor Deposition Methods

## 2.2.2.1 Physical Vapor Deposition (PVD)

**Evaporation and Condensation of Gold Vapor**

Physical Vapor Deposition (PVD) is a method used to produce thin films and nanoparticles by evaporating a material in a vacuum and allowing it to condense on a substrate. For gold nanoparticles, the process begins with the evaporation of bulk gold in a high-vacuum chamber. The gold is heated to its boiling point, around 2856°C, using techniques such as thermal evaporation, where a high current is passed through a resistive heating element containing gold, or electron beam evaporation, where an electron beam is focused on the gold target to induce localized heating. The high vacuum (typically below 10^-6 Torr) is essential to minimize contamination and to ensure that the evaporated gold atoms travel in a straight path from the source to the substrate without colliding with gas molecules.

**Formation of Thin Films and Nanoparticles**

Once the gold vapor is generated, it travels through the vacuum chamber and condenses onto a cooler substrate placed at a certain distance from the evaporation source. The substrate could be anything from a silicon wafer to a glass slide, depending on the desired application. The cooling rate and the distance between the evaporation source and the substrate are critical parameters that determine whether the deposited material forms a continuous thin film or discrete nanoparticles.

For thin film formation, the substrate temperature and deposition rate are controlled to allow the gold atoms to spread and coalesce, forming a uniform layer. The thickness of the thin film can be precisely controlled by monitoring the deposition time and the rate of evaporation. This control is achieved using a quartz crystal microbalance, which measures the mass of the deposited material in real-time, ensuring uniformity and reproducibility.

For nanoparticle formation, the deposition conditions are adjusted so that the gold atoms do not have enough time to diffuse and coalesce into a continuous film. Instead, they nucleate and grow into small clusters or nanoparticles. This can be achieved by reducing the substrate temperature or increasing the deposition rate, leading to the formation of discrete nanoparticles. The size and distribution of these nanoparticles can be further controlled by varying the substrate temperature, the deposition rate, and the type of substrate material. For instance, lower substrate temperatures tend to result in smaller nanoparticles due to reduced mobility of the gold atoms on the substrate surface.

PVD is advantageous for its ability to produce high-purity thin films and nanoparticles with precise control over thickness and composition. However, it requires sophisticated equipment and a high vacuum environment, making it a relatively expensive and complex technique. This method is widely used in electronics, optics, and materials science for creating coatings and nanostructures with specific properties.

## 2.2.2.2 Chemical Vapor Deposition (CVD)

### Decomposition of Gold-Containing Precursors

Chemical Vapor Deposition (CVD) is a process in which volatile gold-containing precursors are introduced into a reaction chamber and decomposed to form a thin film or nanoparticles on a substrate. The CVD process for gold typically involves gold precursors such as dimethylgold(III) acetylacetonate (Me2Au(acac)) or gold(III) chloride (AuCl3). These precursors are selected for their ability to volatilize at relatively low temperatures, facilitating their transport in the gas phase. The precursor is vaporized in a heated chamber and carried into the reaction zone by an inert carrier gas, such as argon or nitrogen. Upon reaching the heated substrate, the precursor molecules undergo thermal decomposition or reduction, releasing gold atoms. For example, Me2Au(acac) decomposes at temperatures between 150°C and 300°C, making it suitable for low-temperature CVD processes. The decomposition can be further promoted by the presence of reducing gases such as hydrogen, which helps in reducing the gold ions to elemental gold.

### Deposition on Substrate

As the gold-containing precursor decomposes, gold atoms are deposited onto the substrate, forming a thin film or nanoparticles depending on the deposition conditions. The substrate is usually heated to a temperature that facilitates the decomposition of the precursor and the subsequent deposition of gold. The temperature and other process parameters, such as the flow rate of the precursor and carrier gases, the chamber pressure, and the duration of deposition, are carefully controlled to achieve the desired film or nanoparticle characteristics.

For thin film deposition, the substrate temperature is maintained within a specific range that allows the gold atoms to diffuse and form a continuous, uniform layer. The thickness of the film can be controlled by adjusting the deposition time and the concentration of the precursor in the gas phase. The use of substrates with high surface energy, such as silicon or sapphire, can promote better adhesion and uniformity of the gold film.

For nanoparticle synthesis, the deposition conditions are adjusted to promote nucleation and growth of discrete gold particles rather than a continuous film. This can be achieved by lowering the substrate temperature or by using substrates with specific surface treatments that favor the formation of isolated nanoparticles. The size and distribution of the nanoparticles can be controlled by varying the precursor concentration, the deposition temperature, and the deposition time. For example, using a lower precursor concentration and a higher substrate temperature may lead to smaller and more uniformly distributed nanoparticles.

CVD is highly advantageous for producing high-purity gold films and nanoparticles with excellent control over thickness, composition, and morphology. It allows for uniform coating on complex substrate geometries and is scalable for industrial applications. However, the process requires precise control of deposition parameters and specialized equipment, making it more complex and costly compared to some other deposition methods. CVD is widely used in microelectronics, optics, and materials science for fabricating thin films and nanostructures with specific properties and applications.

## 2.2.2.3 Comparison of PVD and CVD

**Process Conditions and Equipment**

**Physical Vapor Deposition (PVD)** and **Chemical Vapor Deposition (CVD)** are two prominent methods for depositing thin films and synthesizing nanoparticles, each with distinct process conditions and equipment requirements.

**PVD Process Conditions and Equipment**

PVD involves the physical transfer of material from a source to a substrate through processes like evaporation or sputtering. The equipment for PVD typically includes a vacuum chamber, a high-energy source for material evaporation (such as an electron beam or resistive heater for thermal evaporation), and a substrate holder. The process is carried out under high vacuum conditions, often below 10^-6 Torr, to minimize contamination and ensure a straight-line path for the evaporated atoms. The substrate temperature can be controlled to influence the film morphology, but it is generally lower than in CVD processes. PVD is known for its ability to produce high-purity films and is widely used for coatings in optics, electronics, and decorative applications.

**CVD Process Conditions and Equipment**

CVD, on the other hand, involves the chemical reaction of volatile precursors in the gas phase, leading to the deposition of material on a substrate. The equipment for CVD includes a reaction chamber, gas delivery system for the precursors, and a heating system to maintain the substrate at the required temperature. The process can be conducted at atmospheric or low pressure, depending on the specific CVD technique used. Temperatures in CVD are typically higher than in PVD, often ranging from 300°C to 1000°C, to facilitate the decomposition of precursors and the deposition of the desired material. CVD allows for excellent conformity over complex geometries and precise control over film composition and thickness, making it ideal for microelectronics and advanced materials.

## Applications and Limitations

### Applications of PVD

PVD is widely used in industries where high-purity, dense, and adherent coatings are required. Common applications include the production of thin films for semiconductor devices, hard coatings for cutting tools, decorative coatings for consumer goods, and optical coatings for lenses and mirrors. The ability to control film thickness and composition with high precision makes PVD suitable for applications demanding stringent material properties.

**Limitations of PVD**

Despite its advantages, PVD has limitations such as line-of-sight deposition, which can make it challenging to coat complex shapes uniformly. The process also requires high vacuum conditions, adding to the operational complexity and cost. Additionally, PVD is less suitable for depositing materials that require chemical reactions to achieve the desired phase or composition.

**Applications of CVD**

CVD is extensively used in the fabrication of high-performance materials and devices. It is a key process in the semiconductor industry for producing high-quality silicon, silicon dioxide, and other thin films. CVD is also used for coating turbine blades with thermal barrier coatings, producing diamond films, and synthesizing carbon nanotubes. Its ability to conformally coat intricate structures makes it invaluable for applications in microelectronics, MEMS devices, and advanced materials research.

**Limitations of CVD**

However, CVD has its own set of challenges. The need for high temperatures can limit the choice of substrate materials and lead to thermal stresses. The process often involves toxic or hazardous precursors, necessitating stringent safety measures. The equipment and operational costs are higher compared to PVD, and controlling the stoichiometry and uniformity of complex compounds can be challenging.

## *2.3.1 Plant Extracts*

## *2.3.1.1 Principles and Mechanism*

**Reduction of Gold Ions by Phytochemicals**

Biological synthesis of gold nanoparticles using plant extracts is a green chemistry approach that leverages the natural reducing and stabilizing agents found in plants. The principles of this method are grounded in the use of phytochemicals, such as flavonoids, alkaloids, terpenoids, and phenolic compounds, which are capable of reducing gold ions ($Au^{3+}$) to elemental gold ($Au^0$). These phytochemicals are abundant in various plant extracts and serve as both reducing and capping agents. The process begins with the preparation of a gold salt solution, typically using chloroauric acid ($HAuCl_4$). The plant extract, containing the phytochemicals, is then added to this solution.

Upon mixing, the phytochemicals interact with the gold ions, initiating a reduction reaction. For instance, flavonoids, which possess hydroxyl and carbonyl groups, can donate electrons to the gold ions, reducing them to gold atoms. This reduction process occurs at room temperature and under mild conditions, making it an environmentally friendly alternative to traditional chemical reduction methods that often require harsh chemicals and high temperatures. The phytochemicals not only reduce the gold ions but also stabilize the resulting gold nanoparticles, preventing their aggregation by capping their surface. This dual role of reduction and stabilization is key to the successful synthesis of gold nanoparticles using plant extracts.

## Formation of Nanoparticles

The formation of gold nanoparticles through biological synthesis involves several steps, including nucleation, growth, and stabilization. Once the gold ions are reduced to gold atoms by the phytochemicals, these atoms begin to nucleate, forming small clusters. The nucleation phase is rapid and is followed by a growth phase where additional gold atoms are reduced and deposit onto the existing clusters, leading to the formation of nanoparticles. The size and shape of the nanoparticles are influenced by the concentration of the gold salt, the type of plant extract used, and the reaction conditions, such as pH and temperature.

During the growth phase, the phytochemicals continue to play a crucial role by stabilizing the surface of the nanoparticles, preventing them from agglomerating. This stabilization is achieved through the adsorption of phytochemicals onto the nanoparticle surface, which creates a protective layer around each particle. This layer imparts a negative charge to the nanoparticles, resulting in electrostatic repulsion that keeps the particles dispersed in the solution.

The entire process can be monitored by observing the color change of the solution, which occurs due to the surface plasmon resonance (SPR) of gold nanoparticles. Typically, the solution changes from pale yellow to ruby red or purple, indicating the formation of gold nanoparticles. The reaction progress can be further confirmed using techniques such as UV-Vis spectroscopy, which shows a characteristic absorption peak around 520-530 nm corresponding to the SPR of gold nanoparticles.

## 2.3.1.3 Procedure and Optimization

## Preparation of Plant Extract

The preparation of the plant extract is the initial and crucial step in the biological synthesis of gold nanoparticles. This process involves selecting a suitable plant and obtaining its parts, such as leaves, stems, flowers, or fruits, depending on the specific phytochemicals required. The chosen plant material is thoroughly washed with distilled water to remove any dirt and contaminants. After cleaning, the plant material is chopped into small pieces and subjected to drying, either under shade or using an oven at a low temperature to preserve the phytochemicals. Once dried, the plant material is ground into a fine powder using a mortar and pestle or a mechanical grinder.

The powdered plant material is then subjected to extraction using a solvent, typically water or an ethanol-water mixture. The extraction process involves boiling the plant material in the solvent for a specific duration, usually ranging from 10 to 60 minutes, depending on the plant type and the desired phytochemicals. After boiling, the mixture is allowed to cool, and the plant extract is filtered using Whatman filter paper or a fine sieve to remove any solid residues. The resulting filtrate, which contains the phytochemicals, is collected and stored at 4°C until further use.

## Mixing with Gold Salt Solution

The next step involves the reduction of gold ions to gold nanoparticles by mixing the prepared plant extract with a gold salt solution. Typically, chloroauric acid ($HAuCl_4$ ) is used as the gold salt. A specific volume of the gold salt solution is prepared at a desired concentration, usually ranging from 0.5 mM to 10 mM, depending on the required nanoparticle size and concentration. The plant extract is then added to the gold salt solution in a specific ratio, such as 1:1 or 1:2 (v/v). The mixture is stirred continuously at room temperature to ensure uniform mixing and to facilitate the reduction reaction.

During this process, the reduction of gold ions to gold nanoparticles occurs, and the solution undergoes a color change, typically from yellow to ruby red or purple, indicating the formation of gold nanoparticles. The reaction is monitored over time, and the extent of nanoparticle formation can be analyzed using UV-Vis spectroscopy, which shows an absorption peak around 520-530 nm, characteristic of gold nanoparticles.

## Parameters Affecting Synthesis

Several parameters influence the synthesis of gold nanoparticles using plant extracts, and optimizing these parameters is essential for obtaining nanoparticles with desired characteristics.

1. **Concentration of Gold Salt**: The concentration of the gold salt solution plays a significant role in determining the size and yield of the gold nanoparticles. Higher concentrations of gold salt can lead to the formation of larger nanoparticles due to increased availability of gold ions for reduction. Conversely, lower concentrations tend to produce smaller nanoparticles. Optimal concentrations typically range from 0.5 mM to 10 mM, depending on the specific requirements.

2. **Volume Ratio of Plant Extract to Gold Salt Solution**: The volume ratio of the plant extract to the gold salt solution affects the efficiency of the reduction process and the stabilization of the nanoparticles. An optimal ratio ensures complete reduction of gold ions and adequate capping of the nanoparticles by phytochemicals. Commonly used ratios include 1:1, 1:2, or 2:1 (v/v), with the exact ratio depending on the concentration of phytochemicals in the extract.

3. **pH of the Reaction Mixture**: The pH of the reaction mixture significantly impacts the reduction kinetics and the stability of the synthesized nanoparticles. Acidic or neutral pH conditions may slow down the reduction process, while slightly alkaline conditions (pH 7-9) are often favorable for rapid reduction and stabilization. Adjusting the pH using dilute NaOH or HCl solutions can optimize the synthesis process.

4. **Temperature**: The temperature of the reaction mixture influences the rate of the reduction reaction and the size of the nanoparticles. Room temperature reactions are common, but slight heating (40-60°C) can enhance the reduction rate and result in smaller, more uniform nanoparticles. However, excessive heating should be avoided as it can lead to aggregation.

5. **Reaction Time**: The duration of the reaction affects the completion of the reduction process and the growth of nanoparticles. Shorter reaction times may result in incomplete reduction, while longer times ensure complete reduction and stabilization. Typical reaction times range from 30 minutes to several hours, depending on the other parameters.

By carefully optimizing these parameters, high-quality gold nanoparticles with desired size, shape, and stability can be synthesized using plant extracts, making this method a sustainable and eco-friendly alternative to conventional chemical synthesis methods.

## 2.3.2.2 Fungal Synthesis

**Reduction by Fungal Biomass**

Fungal synthesis of gold nanoparticles is a promising biological method that utilizes fungal biomass for the reduction of gold ions to elemental gold. This method exploits the unique metabolic pathways and the presence of reductive enzymes and proteins in fungi, which facilitate the conversion of gold ions ($Au^{3+}$) into gold nanoparticles ($Au^0$). The process begins with the cultivation of fungi in an appropriate growth medium, typically a nutrient broth or agar, under controlled conditions. Once the fungal biomass is obtained, it is harvested and washed thoroughly with distilled water to remove any residual medium components.

The washed fungal biomass is then suspended in distilled water or an aqueous gold salt solution, such as chloroauric acid ($HAuCl_4$). The interaction between the fungal biomass and the gold salt solution initiates the reduction process. Fungal cells possess various biomolecules, including enzymes like nitrate reductase, proteins, and polysaccharides, which act as reducing agents. These biomolecules facilitate the reduction of gold ions by donating electrons, resulting in the formation of gold atoms. The reduction reaction can be carried out under ambient conditions, making it a cost-effective and environmentally friendly approach.

During the reduction process, the fungal biomass not only reduces the gold ions but also acts as a stabilizing agent, capping the formed nanoparticles and preventing their aggregation. This dual functionality of the fungal biomass is crucial for obtaining stable and well-dispersed gold nanoparticles. The entire process can be monitored by observing the color change of the solution, which typically transitions from yellow to ruby red or purple, indicating the formation of gold nanoparticles. The reaction progress and the characteristics of the synthesized nanoparticles can be further confirmed using techniques such as UV-Vis spectroscopy, which shows a characteristic absorption peak around 520-530 nm.

**Examples: Fusarium, Penicillium**

Several fungal species have been explored for their ability to synthesize gold nanoparticles, with **Fusarium** and **Penicillium** being among the most studied.

**Fusarium spp.**

Fusarium species are filamentous fungi known for their efficient production of gold nanoparticles. In the case of Fusarium oxysporum, the fungal biomass is incubated with an aqueous solution of chloroauric acid. The enzymes and proteins present in Fusarium oxysporum, such as nitrate reductase, play a significant role in reducing gold ions. The gold nanoparticles synthesized using Fusarium spp. are typically spherical and range in size from 5 to 50 nm. The nanoparticles exhibit excellent stability and are well-dispersed in the solution, making them suitable for various applications, including biomedical and catalytic fields.

**Penicillium spp.**

Penicillium species, another group of filamentous fungi, have also demonstrated the capability to reduce gold ions and synthesize gold nanoparticles. For instance, Penicillium chrysogenum, when exposed to a gold salt solution, facilitates the reduction of gold ions through its extracellular enzymes and metabolites. The gold nanoparticles produced by Penicillium spp. are generally spherical and can range from 10 to 100 nm in size, depending on the specific conditions and parameters of the synthesis process. These nanoparticles are stabilized by proteins and other capping agents secreted by the fungal biomass, ensuring their stability and preventing aggregation.

The use of fungal biomass for the synthesis of gold nanoparticles offers several advantages, including the ease of cultivation, scalability, and the potential for large-scale production. Moreover, this method is environmentally friendly, as it avoids the use of toxic chemicals and harsh conditions typically associated with conventional chemical synthesis methods. The biocompatibility and stability of the nanoparticles synthesized using fungi further enhance their potential for various applications, such as drug delivery, imaging, and environmental remediation.

## 2.3.2.3 Procedure and Cultivation

**Cultivation of Microorganisms**

The cultivation of microorganisms, particularly fungi, is the first critical step in the synthesis of gold nanoparticles. This process begins with the selection of a suitable fungal species, such as **Fusarium oxysporum** or **Penicillium chrysogenum**. The chosen fungal strain is typically obtained from culture collections or isolated from natural sources. The fungal spores or mycelial fragments are inoculated into a nutrient-rich growth medium, such as potato dextrose broth or Sabouraud dextrose broth, which provides the essential nutrients required for fungal growth.

The inoculated medium is then incubated under optimal conditions, usually at a temperature range of 25-30°C and with a pH of around 6-7. The incubation period varies depending on the fungal species but generally ranges from 5 to 7 days. During this period, the fungi grow and proliferate, forming a dense biomass. The growth is monitored visually by observing the turbidity or through microscopic examination. Once a sufficient biomass is achieved, the fungal cultures are harvested by filtering through Whatman filter paper or using centrifugation at 4000-6000 rpm for 10-15 minutes to separate the biomass from the growth medium. The harvested biomass is washed several times with distilled water to remove any residual media components and is then ready for the nanoparticle synthesis process.

**Incubation with Gold Salts**

The next step involves the reduction of gold ions to form nanoparticles, which is achieved by incubating the prepared fungal biomass with a gold salt solution. Typically, chloroauric acid ($HAuCl_4$) is used as the gold salt. A specific concentration of the gold salt solution, often ranging from 0.5 mM to 5 mM, is prepared in distilled water. The fungal biomass is then added to this solution in a ratio that allows for efficient interaction between the gold ions and the fungal reducing agents. Common ratios range from 1:10 to 1:50 (biomass to gold salt solution).

The mixture is stirred gently and incubated at room temperature or slightly elevated temperatures (25-35°C) to facilitate the reduction process. During this incubation period, the gold ions are reduced to elemental gold by the reductive enzymes, proteins, and other metabolites present in the fungal biomass. The reaction progress is monitored by observing the color change of the solution, which indicates the formation of gold nanoparticles. A transition from a yellowish to a ruby red or purple color is typically observed. The reduction process can take anywhere from a few hours to several days, depending on the fungal species and the concentration of the gold salt.

**Recovery of Nanoparticles**

Once the gold nanoparticles are formed, they need to be recovered and purified for further use. The recovery process involves several steps to ensure the nanoparticles are free from any residual fungal biomass or other impurities. The initial recovery is usually done by centrifugation. The reaction mixture is centrifuged at high speeds (10,000-15,000 rpm) for 20-30 minutes. This process separates the nanoparticles, which form a pellet at the bottom of the centrifuge tube, from the supernatant containing unreacted gold ions and other soluble components.

The nanoparticle pellet is then washed multiple times with distilled water to remove any remaining impurities. The washing involves resuspending the pellet in distilled water, followed by repeated centrifugation. In some cases, additional washing with ethanol or other solvents may be performed to ensure thorough purification. After washing, the purified gold nanoparticles are collected and dried. Drying can be done using a vacuum desiccator or by lyophilization (freeze-drying), which helps to preserve the nanoparticles in a stable form.

The size, shape, and dispersion of the recovered nanoparticles can be characterized using various analytical techniques such as transmission electron microscopy (TEM), scanning electron microscopy (SEM), dynamic light scattering (DLS), and UV-Vis spectroscopy. These techniques help confirm the successful synthesis and provide detailed information about the nanoparticle properties, which are essential for their intended applications in fields such as medicine, electronics, and environmental science.

The procedure for fungal synthesis of gold nanoparticles, encompassing cultivation, incubation with gold salts, and recovery, demonstrates an eco-friendly and sustainable approach to nanoparticle production, leveraging the natural capabilities of fungi to reduce and stabilize metal ions.

## 2.3.3.2 Challenges

**Control over Size and Shape**

One of the significant challenges in the biological synthesis of gold nanoparticles, including using plant and fungal extracts, is achieving precise control over the size and shape of the nanoparticles. The size and shape of nanoparticles are critical parameters that influence their physical, chemical, and biological properties, impacting their suitability for various applications. In the case of biological synthesis, the reduction process is often influenced by the natural variability of the biological materials used, such as the concentration and composition of phytochemicals in plant extracts or the metabolic state of fungal cultures. This variability can lead to inconsistent and heterogeneous nanoparticle sizes and shapes.

Achieving uniformity in nanoparticle synthesis requires careful optimization of several factors, including the concentration of the gold salt, the volume ratio of biological extract to gold salt solution, the pH, temperature, and reaction time. Additionally, the intrinsic properties of the biological material, such as the specific types of reducing and stabilizing agents present, play a crucial role. Despite efforts to standardize these conditions, biological systems' inherent variability often leads to batch-to-batch differences in nanoparticle characteristics. Advanced techniques, such as surface functionalization and the use of additional stabilizing agents, are being explored to improve control over nanoparticle size and shape, but this remains a complex and ongoing area of research.

**Scale-Up and Standardization**

Scaling up the biological synthesis of gold nanoparticles from laboratory-scale to industrial-scale production presents several challenges. One of the primary issues is maintaining consistency and reproducibility across large batches. Biological systems, such as plants and fungi, can exhibit significant variability in their biochemical composition due to factors like growing conditions, harvest time, and genetic differences. This variability can lead to inconsistencies in the reduction and stabilization processes, affecting the quality and properties of the nanoparticles produced at a larger scale.

Standardization of the biological synthesis process is essential to address these challenges. This involves developing robust protocols that minimize variability and ensure uniform production conditions. Automation and process control technologies can be employed to monitor and adjust parameters in real-time, enhancing consistency. Additionally, sourcing biological materials from standardized and controlled environments can help reduce variability. Despite these efforts, achieving complete standardization remains difficult due to the complex nature of biological systems. Ongoing research is focused on developing more reliable and scalable methods for biological nanoparticle synthesis, including genetic engineering of microorganisms to produce more consistent reducing agents.

**Stability and Storage**

Ensuring the stability and long-term storage of biologically synthesized gold nanoparticles is another critical challenge. Nanoparticles tend to aggregate over time, which can alter their size, shape, and functional properties, rendering them less effective or unsuitable for certain applications. Biological synthesis methods often rely on natural stabilizing agents, such as proteins and polysaccharides, which may not provide sufficient long-term stability, especially under varying storage conditions.

To address this, researchers are investigating various strategies to enhance the stability of gold nanoparticles. One approach is to use additional synthetic stabilizing agents, such as polyethylene glycol (PEG), which can provide a steric barrier to prevent aggregation. Another approach involves optimizing the concentration and composition of the natural stabilizers used during synthesis to improve their effectiveness. The storage conditions, including temperature, pH, and the presence of light or oxygen, also play a significant role in maintaining nanoparticle stability. Ideal storage conditions typically involve low temperatures and inert atmospheres to minimize oxidation and aggregation.

Developing reliable methods for the long-term storage of gold nanoparticles is crucial for their practical applications. This includes formulating nanoparticles in stable dispersions or as dry powders using techniques like freeze-drying or spray-drying. Ensuring the nanoparticles can be easily redispersed without loss of functionality is essential for their use in various fields, such as medicine, catalysis, and electronics. Despite ongoing advancements, achieving optimal stability and storage conditions for biologically synthesized gold nanoparticles remains an area of active research and development.

# CHAPTER THREE

# SYNTHESIS OF MAGNETIC NANOPARTICLES

## 3.1 Co-Precipitation Method

### 3.1.1 Basic Principles and Procedure

The co-precipitation method is one of the most widely used techniques for the synthesis of magnetic nanoparticles, particularly iron oxide nanoparticles such as magnetite ($Fe_3O_4$) and maghemite ($\gamma$-$Fe_2O_3$). This method involves the simultaneous precipitation of iron ions from aqueous solutions by the addition of a base under an inert atmosphere. The basic principle relies on the controlled chemical reduction and oxidation of ferrous ($Fe^{2+}$) and ferric ($Fe^{3+}$) ions in solution to form magnetic iron oxide nanoparticles.

The typical procedure for the co-precipitation method begins with the preparation of a solution containing the desired stoichiometric ratio of $Fe^{2+}$ and $Fe^{3+}$ ions. This is usually achieved by dissolving iron salts, such as ferrous sulfate ($FeSO_4$) and ferric chloride ($FeCl_3$), in distilled water. The ratio of $Fe^{2+}$ to $Fe^{3+}$ is critical, with the ideal ratio for magnetite formation being 1:2. The resulting solution is then mixed thoroughly to ensure homogeneity.

Next, a base, commonly ammonium hydroxide ($NH_4OH$) or sodium hydroxide ($NaOH$), is added dropwise to the iron ion solution while continuously stirring. The addition of the base increases the pH of the solution, leading to the co-precipitation of iron hydroxides. The reaction is typically conducted under an inert atmosphere, such as nitrogen or argon, to prevent oxidation of $Fe^{2+}$ ions to $Fe^{3+}$ ions, which can affect the composition and properties of the resulting nanoparticles.

As the pH rises, the iron ions undergo hydrolysis and subsequently form iron oxide nanoparticles. The reaction is represented by the following simplified equations:

$$Fe^{2+} + 2OH^- \rightarrow Fe(OH)_2$$
$$2Fe^{3+} + 6OH^- \rightarrow 2Fe(OH)_3$$
$$Fe(OH)_2 + 2Fe(OH)_3 \rightarrow Fe_3O_4 + 4H_2O$$

The nanoparticles formed are then allowed to age for a specific period, during which they grow and crystallize. The resulting nanoparticles are magnetically separated from the reaction mixture using a magnet or by centrifugation. They are then washed several times with distilled water and ethanol to remove any unreacted ions and impurities. Finally, the nanoparticles are dried under vacuum or in an oven at a moderate temperature.

## 3.1.2 Factors Affecting Particle Size

The size and size distribution of magnetic nanoparticles synthesized via the co-precipitation method are influenced by several factors, including the concentration of iron salts, the pH of the solution, the temperature of the reaction, and the rate of base addition.

**Concentration of Iron Salts**

The initial concentration of $Fe^{2+}$ and $Fe^{3+}$ ions in the solution plays a significant role in determining the size of the nanoparticles. Higher concentrations of iron salts generally lead to the formation of larger nanoparticles due to increased nucleation rates and the availability of more ions for particle growth. Conversely, lower concentrations tend to produce smaller nanoparticles with narrower size distributions.

**pH of the Solution**

The pH of the reaction mixture is another critical factor that affects the size and morphology of the nanoparticles. The pH determines the extent of hydrolysis and the subsequent precipitation of iron hydroxides. A higher pH typically results in the formation of smaller nanoparticles, as the rapid precipitation leads to a greater number of smaller nuclei. However, very high pH values can lead to the formation of non-magnetic by-products, such as goethite ($\alpha$-FeOOH) and lepidocrocite ($\gamma$-FeOOH).

**Temperature of the Reaction**

The temperature at which the co-precipitation reaction is carried out also influences the size and properties of the nanoparticles. Higher temperatures generally promote faster nucleation and growth rates, leading to larger nanoparticles with improved crystallinity. However, excessively high temperatures can cause aggregation and coarsening of the nanoparticles, resulting in broader size distributions.

**Rate of Base Addition**

The rate at which the base is added to the iron ion solution affects the nucleation and growth processes. Slow addition of the base ensures a controlled increase in pH, leading to uniform nucleation and smaller, monodisperse nanoparticles. Rapid addition, on the other hand, can result in a sudden increase in pH, causing uncontrolled nucleation and the formation of larger, polydisperse nanoparticles.

## 3.2 Thermal Decomposition

### 3.2.1 High-Temperature Synthesis

The thermal decomposition method, specifically high-temperature synthesis, is a robust technique for producing magnetic nanoparticles with well-defined sizes and shapes. This method involves the thermal decomposition of organometallic precursors in the presence of stabilizing agents at elevated temperatures, typically ranging from 200°C to 400°C. The controlled high-temperature environment facilitates the formation of highly crystalline nanoparticles with narrow size distributions and enhanced magnetic properties.

The high-temperature synthesis begins with the selection of suitable organometallic precursors, such as iron pentacarbonyl ($Fe(CO)_5$), iron acetylacetonate ($Fe(acac)_3$), or iron oleate. These precursors are dissolved in organic solvents, such as octadecene or benzyl ether, which have high boiling points and provide a stable reaction medium. The solution is then mixed with surfactants or stabilizing agents like oleic acid, oleylamine, or trioctylphosphine oxide (TOPO). These stabilizers play a crucial role in controlling the growth and preventing the aggregation of nanoparticles by providing a steric or electrostatic barrier around the particles.

The reaction mixture is heated gradually to the desired decomposition temperature under an inert atmosphere, usually nitrogen or argon, to prevent oxidation of the iron precursor and to ensure a reducing environment. The heating rate is critical; a slow and controlled increase in temperature promotes uniform nucleation and growth of the nanoparticles. The decomposition of the organometallic precursor occurs at elevated temperatures, leading to the formation of iron or iron oxide nanoparticles. The typical reaction can be represented by the following equation for iron pentacarbonyl:

**$Fe(CO)_5 \rightarrow Fe + 5CO$ (at high temperature)**

In the presence of a controlled amount of oxygen or other oxidizing agents, the iron nanoparticles can be partially oxidized to form iron oxide nanoparticles:

**$2Fe + O_2 \rightarrow 2FeO$**

As the reaction proceeds, the nanoparticles grow to the desired size. The stabilizing agents adsorbed on the surface of the nanoparticles prevent them from aggregating and ensure a uniform size distribution. The reaction time, temperature, and concentration of precursors and stabilizers are key factors that influence the size, shape, and magnetic properties of the synthesized nanoparticles.

Once the reaction is complete, the mixture is cooled to room temperature, and the nanoparticles are separated from the reaction medium. This is typically achieved by adding a non-polar solvent, such as hexane, to precipitate the nanoparticles. The precipitated nanoparticles are then collected by centrifugation or magnetic separation. The collected nanoparticles are washed several times with solvents like ethanol or acetone to remove any residual organic compounds and unreacted precursors.

The final product is highly crystalline magnetic nanoparticles with a uniform size and shape. The size, morphology, and crystalline structure of the nanoparticles are characterized using techniques such as transmission electron microscopy (TEM), X-ray diffraction (XRD), and dynamic light scattering (DLS). These nanoparticles exhibit superior magnetic properties, making them suitable for various applications, including magnetic resonance imaging (MRI), drug delivery, magnetic data storage, and catalysis.

High-temperature synthesis via thermal decomposition offers several advantages, including the ability to produce highly crystalline nanoparticles with precise control over size and shape. However, it also presents challenges, such as the need for high temperatures, which require specialized equipment and careful handling to ensure safety and reproducibility. Despite these challenges, thermal decomposition remains a valuable method for synthesizing high-quality magnetic nanoparticles for advanced technological applications.

## 3.3 Hydrothermal and Solvothermal Methods

### 3.3.1 Synthesis in Aqueous Media

The hydrothermal method is a versatile and efficient technique for synthesizing magnetic nanoparticles in aqueous media. This method involves the use of water as the solvent under high temperature and pressure conditions, typically in a sealed autoclave. The hydrothermal synthesis allows for the controlled crystallization and growth of nanoparticles, resulting in products with uniform sizes, shapes, and high purity.

The process begins with the preparation of an aqueous solution containing the desired metal salts. For the synthesis of iron oxide nanoparticles, common precursors include ferric chloride ($FeCl_3$), ferrous chloride ($FeCl_2$), and ferric nitrate ($Fe(NO_3)_3$). These salts are dissolved in deionized water to form a homogeneous solution. The pH of the solution is adjusted using a base such as sodium hydroxide (NaOH) or ammonium hydroxide ($NH_4$ OH), which helps control the hydrolysis and precipitation processes.

The reaction mixture is then transferred into a stainless steel autoclave, which is capable of withstanding high temperatures and pressures. The autoclave is sealed and heated to a temperature typically ranging from 120°C to 220°C. The pressure inside the autoclave can reach several atmospheres due to the vapor pressure of water at elevated temperatures. These conditions facilitate the dissolution and recrystallization of the metal salts, promoting the formation of highly crystalline nanoparticles.

During the hydrothermal process, the metal ions undergo hydrolysis, leading to the formation of metal hydroxides. These hydroxides then dehydrate and crystallize into metal oxide nanoparticles. For instance, the hydrothermal synthesis of magnetite ($Fe_3O_4$) nanoparticles can be represented by the following simplified reaction:

$$3Fe(OH)_2 + Fe(OH)_3 \rightarrow Fe_3O_4 + 4H_2O \text{ (at high temperature and pressure)}$$

The high temperature and pressure conditions enhance the solubility and reactivity of the precursors, resulting in the rapid nucleation and growth of nanoparticles. The use of surfactants or capping agents, such as polyethylene glycol (PEG) or citric acid, can further control the size and morphology of the nanoparticles by preventing agglomeration and providing steric stabilization.

The duration of the hydrothermal treatment, typically ranging from a few hours to several days, also affects the size and crystallinity of the nanoparticles. Longer reaction times generally lead to larger and more crystalline particles due to Ostwald ripening, where smaller particles dissolve and redeposit onto larger particles.

After the reaction is complete, the autoclave is cooled to room temperature, and the nanoparticles are collected by centrifugation or magnetic separation. The collected nanoparticles are washed several times with water and ethanol to remove any unreacted precursors and residual capping agents. The final product is dried under vacuum or in an oven at a moderate temperature.

The hydrothermal synthesis in aqueous media offers several advantages, including the use of water as a green solvent, the ability to produce highly crystalline nanoparticles with controlled sizes and shapes, and the potential for scaling up the process for industrial production. Additionally, the method can be easily modified to incorporate dopants or functionalize the nanoparticles for specific applications.

However, the hydrothermal method also presents challenges, such as the need for specialized high-pressure equipment and the potential for batch-to-batch variability. Despite these challenges, the hydrothermal synthesis remains a popular and effective method for producing high-quality magnetic nanoparticles for a wide range of applications, including biomedical imaging, drug delivery, environmental remediation, and magnetic storage devices.

## 3.3.2 Non-Aqueous Media Synthesis

The solvothermal method, a variant of hydrothermal synthesis, involves the use of non-aqueous solvents under high temperature and pressure conditions to produce magnetic nanoparticles. This approach leverages the unique properties of organic solvents, such as high boiling points and the ability to dissolve metal precursors that are insoluble in water, to achieve better control over particle size, shape, and crystallinity.

The non-aqueous media synthesis begins with the selection of suitable metal precursors and organic solvents. Common precursors for the synthesis of magnetic nanoparticles include iron acetylacetonate $(Fe(acac)_3$ ), iron oleate, and iron pentacarbonyl $(Fe(CO)_5)$. These precursors are dissolved in organic solvents like benzyl ether, octadecene, or oleylamine. The choice of solvent is crucial as it affects the solubility of the precursors, the reaction kinetics, and the final properties of the nanoparticles.

The reaction mixture, consisting of the metal precursor and solvent, is often combined with surfactants or capping agents such as oleic acid, oleylamine, or trioctylphosphine oxide (TOPO). These agents serve multiple roles, including stabilizing the growing nanoparticles, controlling their size and shape, and preventing agglomeration. The mixture is then transferred into a sealed autoclave or a high-pressure reaction vessel.

The vessel is heated to a temperature typically ranging from 150°C to 350°C, depending on the boiling point of the solvent and the thermal stability of the precursors. The high temperature facilitates the decomposition of the metal precursors and the subsequent nucleation and growth of nanoparticles. For example, the thermal decomposition of iron pentacarbonyl in an organic solvent can be represented as:

**$Fe(CO)_5 \rightarrow Fe + 5CO$ (at high temperature)**

In the presence of a controlled amount of oxygen or another oxidizing agent, iron nanoparticles can be partially or fully oxidized to form iron oxide nanoparticles. The reactions can be represented as:

**$2Fe + O_2 \rightarrow 2FeO$**

**$4Fe + 3O_2 \rightarrow 2Fe_2O_3$**

The use of non-aqueous solvents allows for precise control over the reaction environment, leading to the formation of nanoparticles with uniform size and shape. The high boiling points of organic solvents enable the synthesis to be conducted at elevated temperatures, promoting the formation of highly crystalline nanoparticles. Additionally, the presence of surfactants ensures that the nanoparticles remain stable and do not aggregate during the synthesis process.

Once the reaction is complete, the vessel is cooled to room temperature. The nanoparticles are then separated from the reaction mixture using techniques such as centrifugation or magnetic separation. The collected nanoparticles are washed with organic solvents like ethanol or acetone to remove any residual precursors and surfactants. The final product is typically dried under vacuum or in an oven at a moderate temperature.

Non-aqueous media synthesis offers several advantages over aqueous synthesis, including the ability to produce highly crystalline nanoparticles with precise control over size and shape. The use of organic solvents and surfactants enhances the stability of the nanoparticles and prevents agglomeration. Additionally, the solvothermal method can be easily adapted to incorporate various dopants or functional groups, enabling the production of tailored nanoparticles for specific applications.

However, this method also presents challenges, such as the need for high-pressure equipment and the handling of potentially hazardous organic solvents. The cost of solvents and surfactants can also be a consideration, particularly for large-scale production. Despite these challenges, non-aqueous media synthesis remains a valuable technique for producing high-quality magnetic nanoparticles with diverse applications in fields such as biomedicine, catalysis, and magnetic storage.

## 3.4 Microemulsion Technique

### 3.4.1 Formation within Microemulsion Droplets

The microemulsion technique is an innovative and efficient method for synthesizing magnetic nanoparticles, leveraging the unique properties of microemulsions. Microemulsions are thermodynamically stable colloidal dispersions of water and oil, stabilized by surfactants and often co-surfactants. These dispersions form nanometer-sized droplets that serve as nanoreactors for the controlled synthesis of nanoparticles.

The process begins with the preparation of a microemulsion system. A typical microemulsion consists of an aqueous phase, an oil phase, a surfactant, and sometimes a co-surfactant. For the synthesis of magnetic nanoparticles, the aqueous phase usually contains the metal precursors, such as ferric chloride ($FeCl_3$) and ferrous chloride ($FeCl_2$) for iron oxide nanoparticles. The oil phase can be composed of hydrocarbons like hexane or cyclohexane. Common surfactants used in microemulsions include sodium dodecyl sulfate (SDS), cetyltrimethylammonium bromide (CTAB), and nonionic surfactants like Triton X-100. Co-surfactants such as butanol or ethanol may also be added to enhance the stability and reduce the interfacial tension of the microemulsion.

The formation of microemulsions involves mixing the components in specific ratios to achieve the desired phase behavior. Upon gentle stirring, the surfactant molecules arrange themselves at the oil-water interface, creating nanometer-sized droplets of the aqueous phase dispersed within the oil phase, or vice versa. These droplets act as confined reaction environments, where the size and shape of the droplets can be precisely controlled by adjusting the surfactant concentration and the ratio of the components.

Once the microemulsion system is prepared, the synthesis of magnetic nanoparticles is initiated by introducing a reducing agent into the system. Common reducing agents include sodium borohydride ($NaBH_4$), hydrazine ($N_2H_4$), or ammonium hydroxide ($NH_4OH$). The reducing agent can be added directly to the microemulsion or pre-dispersed in either the aqueous or oil phase, depending on the desired reaction dynamics.

As the reducing agent comes into contact with the metal precursors within the microemulsion droplets, a reduction reaction occurs, leading to the nucleation and growth of metal or metal oxide nanoparticles. For example, the reduction of iron salts can be represented by the following reaction:

$$2Fe^{3+} + Fe^{2+} + 8OH^- \rightarrow Fe_3O_4 + 4H_2O$$

The confined environment of the microemulsion droplets ensures that the nucleation and growth processes are limited to the nanometer scale, resulting in nanoparticles with uniform sizes and shapes. The surfactant molecules surrounding the droplets also act as stabilizing agents, preventing the nanoparticles from aggregating and ensuring a narrow size distribution.

After the reaction is complete, the microemulsion is destabilized to recover the nanoparticles. This can be achieved by adding a large volume of a non-solvent, such as ethanol or acetone, which causes the microemulsion to break down and precipitate the nanoparticles. The precipitated nanoparticles are then collected by centrifugation or magnetic separation, washed multiple times with ethanol or water to remove any residual surfactants and unreacted precursors, and finally dried under vacuum or in an oven.

The microemulsion technique offers several advantages, including the ability to produce highly uniform nanoparticles with controlled sizes and shapes, as well as the flexibility to tune the properties of the nanoparticles by modifying the composition and conditions of the microemulsion system.

Additionally, the use of mild reaction conditions and the scalability of the process make it an attractive method for the large-scale production of magnetic nanoparticles.

However, the method also presents challenges, such as the need for precise control over the microemulsion composition and the potential for surfactant contamination in the final product. Despite these challenges, the microemulsion technique remains a powerful and versatile approach for the synthesis of high-quality magnetic nanoparticles for various applications, including biomedical imaging, drug delivery, and magnetic storage systems.

### 3.4.2 Benefits and Applications

The microemulsion technique offers numerous benefits and diverse applications, making it a highly regarded method for synthesizing magnetic nanoparticles. The unique environment provided by microemulsion droplets allows for precise control over particle size, shape, and uniformity, which arc crucial for various technological and biomedical applications.

## *Benefits of the Microemulsion Technique*

**Controlled Size and Shape:** The microemulsion technique provides exceptional control over the size and shape of nanoparticles. The nanoreactor-like environment of the microemulsion droplets ensures uniform nucleation and growth, leading to nanoparticles with narrow size distributions and well-defined morphologies. By adjusting the surfactant concentration, the oil-to-water ratio, and the type of reducing agent, researchers can finely tune the characteristics of the nanoparticles.

**High Purity and Stability:** The surfactants used in microemulsions stabilize the nanoparticles, preventing agglomeration and enhancing their colloidal stability. This leads to the production of highly pure nanoparticles with consistent properties. The method also allows for the synthesis of nanoparticles at relatively low temperatures, reducing the risk of unwanted side reactions and contamination.

**Versatility:** The microemulsion technique is versatile and can be adapted to synthesize a wide range of magnetic nanoparticles, including iron oxides (magnetite, $Fe_3O_4$, and maghemite, $\gamma$-$Fe_2O_3$), as well as other magnetic materials like cobalt ferrite ($CoFe_2O_4$) and nickel ferrite ($NiFe_2O_4$). The method is also compatible with various surfactants and co-surfactants, allowing for the customization of nanoparticle properties.

**Scalability:** The microemulsion technique can be scaled up for industrial production, making it suitable for large-scale manufacturing of magnetic nanoparticles. The process can be conducted in batch or continuous modes, providing flexibility for different production needs.

**Applications of Microemulsion-Synthesized Magnetic Nanoparticles**

**Biomedical Imaging:** Magnetic nanoparticles synthesized via the microemulsion technique are widely used in biomedical imaging, particularly in magnetic resonance imaging (MRI). The uniform size and high magnetic properties of these nanoparticles enhance the contrast in MRI scans, allowing for improved diagnosis and monitoring of diseases such as cancer and neurological disorders.

**Drug Delivery:** The high surface area and stability of microemulsion-synthesized magnetic nanoparticles make them ideal candidates for drug delivery systems. These nanoparticles can be functionalized with various ligands and drugs, enabling targeted delivery to specific tissues or cells. The magnetic properties also allow for the external control of drug release using magnetic fields.

**Magnetic Hyperthermia:** In cancer treatment, magnetic nanoparticles can be used for magnetic hyperthermia, a technique where an alternating magnetic field induces localized heating in the tumor tissue. The precise control over size and shape provided by the microemulsion technique ensures the efficient heating and destruction of cancer cells without damaging surrounding healthy tissue.

**Environmental Remediation:** Magnetic nanoparticles are used in environmental remediation to remove contaminants from water and soil. The high surface area and reactivity of microemulsion-synthesized nanoparticles enhance their ability to adsorb heavy metals, organic pollutants, and other hazardous substances. The magnetic properties allow for easy separation and recovery of the nanoparticles after treatment.

**Magnetic Storage:** The uniform size and high crystallinity of microemulsion-synthesized magnetic nanoparticles make them suitable for use in magnetic storage devices. These nanoparticles are used in the fabrication of high-density magnetic tapes and hard drives, where they provide enhanced data storage capacity and stability.

**Catalysis:** Magnetic nanoparticles are employed as catalysts in various chemical reactions due to their high surface area and active sites. The microemulsion technique allows for the production of nanoparticles with controlled surface properties, improving their catalytic efficiency in reactions such as hydrogenation, oxidation, and Fischer-Tropsch synthesis.

The microemulsion technique stands out for its ability to produce high-quality magnetic nanoparticles with tailored properties. Its applications span across fields such as medicine, environmental science, data storage, and catalysis, demonstrating its significant impact on advancing technology and improving quality of life.

# CHAPTER FOUR

# SYNTHESIS OF POLYMERIC NANOPARTICLES

## 4.1 Emulsion Polymerization

### 4.1.1 Oil-in-Water Emulsions

**Introduction to Oil-in-Water Emulsions:**

Oil-in-water (O/W) emulsions are a fundamental technique in the synthesis of polymeric nanoparticles. In this system, oil droplets containing monomer, initiator, and sometimes a crosslinker are dispersed within an aqueous phase, which contains an emulsifier or surfactant. The surfactant stabilizes the emulsion by reducing the interfacial tension between the oil and water phases and preventing the coalescence of the oil droplets. This method is widely used due to its ability to produce nanoparticles with controlled size, uniformity, and high surface area.

**Mechanism of Emulsion Polymerization:**

1. **Initiation:**

   - The polymerization process begins with the formation of free radicals, which can be initiated by thermal, redox, or photochemical means. Common initiators include water-soluble initiators like potassium persulfate (KPS) or oil-soluble initiators like benzoyl peroxide.
   - The free radicals generated in the aqueous phase migrate to the monomer-loaded oil droplets or micelles stabilized by the surfactant.

1. **Propagation:**

   - The free radicals initiate the polymerization of monomers within the oil droplets, leading to the formation of polymer chains. This process continues with the addition of monomer units to the growing polymer chains.
   - The polymerization within the droplets causes the monomer concentration to decrease, and more monomer diffuses from the surrounding aqueous phase into the droplets to sustain the polymerization process.

3. **Stabilization:**

   - The surfactant molecules adsorb onto the surface of the growing polymer particles, providing steric or electrostatic stabilization to prevent aggregation.
   - The presence of surfactants ensures the formation of stable, uniformly sized nanoparticles.

4. **Termination:**

   - The polymerization reaction eventually terminates through various mechanisms such as combination, disproportionation, or chain transfer. This results in the formation of polymeric nanoparticles with the desired properties.

**Advantages of Oil-in-Water Emulsion Polymerization:**

- **Controlled Particle Size:** The size of the polymeric nanoparticles can be precisely controlled by adjusting the concentration of surfactant, monomer, and initiator, as well as the reaction conditions.
- **High Surface Area:** The method produces nanoparticles with a high surface area, which is beneficial for applications requiring enhanced interaction with the surrounding environment, such as drug delivery and catalysis.
- **Versatility:** This technique is versatile and can be used to synthesize a wide range of polymeric materials, including homopolymers, copolymers, and functionalized polymers.

# *Applications of Oil-in-Water Emulsion Polymerization:*

## 1. Drug Delivery:

- Polymeric nanoparticles synthesized via O/W emulsion polymerization are widely used as drug carriers. They can encapsulate therapeutic agents within their core, protecting them from degradation and facilitating controlled release.
- The surface of these nanoparticles can be functionalized with targeting ligands to achieve site-specific delivery, improving the efficacy and reducing the side effects of the drugs.

## 2. Biomedical Imaging:

- Functionalized polymeric nanoparticles can serve as contrast agents in various imaging modalities, including magnetic resonance imaging (MRI), fluorescence imaging, and computed tomography (CT).
- The high surface area and tunable properties of these nanoparticles enhance the contrast and resolution of imaging techniques, aiding in accurate diagnosis and monitoring of diseases.

## 3. Environmental Applications:

- Polymeric nanoparticles are used in water purification systems to remove contaminants such as heavy metals, organic pollutants, and microorganisms.
- Their high surface area and reactivity enable efficient adsorption and degradation of pollutants, contributing to environmental remediation efforts.

## 4. Catalysis:

- The high surface area of polymeric nanoparticles synthesized via O/W emulsion polymerization makes them excellent candidates for catalytic applications.

- These nanoparticles can be functionalized with catalytic active sites, providing a platform for various chemical reactions, including oxidation, reduction, and polymerization processes.

## Challenges and Considerations:

- **Stability:** Ensuring the long-term stability of the nanoparticles in suspension can be challenging, as aggregation and sedimentation may occur over time. The choice of surfactant and stabilization method is crucial to maintaining stability.
- **Scalability:** Scaling up the emulsion polymerization process from laboratory to industrial scale requires careful optimization of reaction conditions and equipment to ensure consistent quality and properties of the nanoparticles.
- **Toxicity and Biocompatibility:** For biomedical applications, it is essential to thoroughly assess the toxicity and biocompatibility of the polymeric nanoparticles to ensure their safety for clinical use.

Oil-in-water emulsion polymerization is a robust and versatile technique for synthesizing polymeric nanoparticles with controlled size, uniformity, and high surface area. Its applications span various fields, including drug delivery, biomedical imaging, environmental remediation, and catalysis, making it a valuable method in the field of nanotechnology. The continued development and optimization of this technique will further enhance its capabilities and expand its applications in science and industry.

## 4.1.2 Water-in-Oil Emulsions

## Introduction to Water-in-Oil Emulsions:

Water-in-oil (W/O) emulsions are another crucial method in the synthesis of polymeric nanoparticles. In this system, water droplets containing monomers, initiators, and other reactants are dispersed within a continuous oil phase that contains surfactants. The surfactants stabilize the emulsion by reducing the interfacial tension between the water and oil phases and preventing the coalescence of the water droplets. This technique is particularly useful for producing nanoparticles with hydrophilic cores and hydrophobic shells, which can be advantageous for various applications, including drug delivery and encapsulation of water-soluble substances.

## *Mechanism of Emulsion Polymerization:*

1. **Initiation:**

   - The polymerization process begins with the formation of free radicals, typically initiated within the water droplets. Common initiators for W/O emulsion polymerization include water-soluble initiators such as ammonium persulfate (APS) or redox initiator systems.
   - The free radicals generated within the water phase initiate the polymerization of monomers contained in the dispersed water droplets.

2. **Propagation:**

   - The free radicals propagate the polymerization reaction by continuously adding monomer units to the growing polymer chains within the water droplets.
   - As the polymerization proceeds, the concentration of monomers within the water droplets decreases, and more monomers diffuse from the oil phase into the water droplets to sustain the reaction.

3. **Stabilization:**

   - The surfactants adsorbed at the interface between the water droplets and the oil phase provide steric or electrostatic stabilization, preventing the aggregation of the growing polymer nanoparticles.
   - The stabilization ensures the formation of uniform nanoparticles with controlled size and morphology.

4. **Termination:**

- The polymerization reaction terminates through various mechanisms such as combination, disproportionation, or chain transfer, leading to the formation of stable polymeric nanoparticles.
- The resulting nanoparticles are dispersed within the continuous oil phase, stabilized by the surfactant molecules.

## *Advantages of Water-in-Oil Emulsion Polymerization:*

- **Encapsulation of Hydrophilic Substances:** The W/O emulsion system is particularly suitable for encapsulating hydrophilic substances, such as drugs, proteins, and enzymes, within the aqueous core of the nanoparticles. This provides protection and controlled release of the encapsulated substances.
- **Control Over Particle Size:** The size of the polymeric nanoparticles can be precisely controlled by adjusting the concentration of surfactant, the ratio of water to oil, and the reaction conditions.
- **Versatility:** This technique is versatile and can be used to synthesize a wide range of polymeric materials, including homopolymers, copolymers, and functionalized polymers.

## *Applications of Water-in-Oil Emulsion Polymerization:*

1. **Drug Delivery:**

   - Polymeric nanoparticles synthesized via W/O emulsion polymerization are widely used as drug carriers for delivering hydrophilic drugs. The hydrophilic core can encapsulate water-soluble drugs, protecting them from degradation and enabling controlled release.
   - The surface of these nanoparticles can be functionalized with targeting ligands to achieve site-specific delivery, improving the efficacy and reducing the side effects of the drugs.

2. **Encapsulation of Biomolecules:**

- The W/O emulsion technique is effective for encapsulating biomolecules such as proteins, peptides, and nucleic acids, preserving their biological activity and stability.
- These encapsulated biomolecules can be used in various biomedical applications, including vaccines, gene therapy, and tissue engineering.

3. **Cosmetics and Personal Care:**

- Polymeric nanoparticles produced through W/O emulsion polymerization are used in cosmetics and personal care products to encapsulate active ingredients, such as vitamins, antioxidants, and moisturizers, enhancing their stability and controlled release.
- These nanoparticles provide improved texture, spreadability, and efficacy of cosmetic formulations.

4. **Food Industry:**

- In the food industry, W/O emulsion polymerization is used to encapsulate flavors, nutrients, and bioactive compounds, protecting them from degradation and ensuring controlled release during consumption.
- This technique improves the stability, shelf life, and sensory properties of food products.

**Challenges and Considerations:**

- **Stability:** Ensuring the long-term stability of the nanoparticles in the continuous oil phase can be challenging, as aggregation and coalescence may occur over time. The choice of surfactant and stabilization method is crucial to maintaining stability.
- **Scalability:** Scaling up the W/O emulsion polymerization process from laboratory to industrial scale requires careful optimization of reaction conditions and equipment to ensure consistent quality and properties of the nanoparticles.
- **Toxicity and Biocompatibility:** For biomedical and food applications, it is essential to thoroughly assess the toxicity and biocompatibility of the polymeric nanoparticles and the surfactants used to ensure their safety

for human use.

Water-in-oil emulsion polymerization is a versatile and effective technique for synthesizing polymeric nanoparticles with hydrophilic cores and controlled size. Its applications span various fields, including drug delivery, encapsulation of biomolecules, cosmetics, personal care, and the food industry. The continued development and optimization of this technique will further enhance its capabilities and expand its applications in science and industry.

## 4.2 Nanoprecipitation

## 4.2.1 Mechanism and Process

### Introduction to Nanoprecipitation:

Nanoprecipitation, also known as solvent displacement or the solvent injection method, is a straightforward and efficient technique for synthesizing polymeric nanoparticles. This method involves the precipitation of a polymer from an organic solvent into an aqueous phase, leading to the formation of nanoparticles. Nanoprecipitation is particularly advantageous due to its simplicity, mild processing conditions, and ability to produce nanoparticles with controlled size and narrow size distribution.

### Mechanism of Nanoprecipitation:

1. **Preparation of Polymer Solution:**

   - The process begins by dissolving the polymer in a suitable organic solvent that is miscible with water but a nonsolvent for the polymer. Commonly used solvents include acetone, ethanol, and tetrahydrofuran (THF).
   - The choice of polymer and solvent depends on the desired properties of the nanoparticles and their intended application.

2. **Injection into Aqueous Phase:**

- The organic solution containing the dissolved polymer is rapidly injected into an aqueous phase containing a surfactant or stabilizer. The aqueous phase acts as a nonsolvent for the polymer, causing it to precipitate.
- The surfactant or stabilizer adsorbs onto the surface of the forming nanoparticles, preventing aggregation and providing steric or electrostatic stabilization.

3. **Formation of Nanoparticles:**

- Upon injection, the rapid diffusion of the solvent into the aqueous phase leads to supersaturation of the polymer, resulting in its precipitation and the formation of nanoparticles.
- The size of the nanoparticles is influenced by factors such as the concentration of the polymer, the rate of injection, the solvent-to-water ratio, and the type and concentration of the surfactant or stabilizer.

4. **Stabilization and Collection:**

- The surfactant or stabilizer ensures that the nanoparticles remain dispersed and stable in the aqueous phase.
- The nanoparticles are then collected by methods such as centrifugation, filtration, or dialysis to remove any excess solvent and unprecipitated polymer.

## *Advantages of Nanoprecipitation:*

- **Simplicity and Mild Conditions:** Nanoprecipitation is a simple process that can be carried out under mild conditions without the need for high temperatures or complex equipment.
- **Control Over Particle Size:** The technique allows for precise control over the size of the nanoparticles by adjusting parameters such as polymer concentration, solvent-to-water ratio, and injection rate.

- **High Encapsulation Efficiency:** Nanoprecipitation can achieve high encapsulation efficiency for hydrophobic drugs, making it suitable for drug delivery applications.
- **Scalability:** The process can be easily scaled up for large-scale production of nanoparticles, making it suitable for industrial applications.

## *Applications of Nanoprecipitation:*

1. **Drug Delivery:**

   - Nanoprecipitation is widely used to produce polymeric nanoparticles for drug delivery. The technique allows for the encapsulation of hydrophobic drugs within the polymer matrix, enhancing their solubility, stability, and bioavailability.
   - The surface of the nanoparticles can be functionalized with targeting ligands to achieve site-specific delivery, improving therapeutic efficacy and reducing side effects.

2. **Controlled Release Systems:**

   - Polymeric nanoparticles produced by nanoprecipitation can be designed to provide controlled release of encapsulated drugs or bioactive agents. The release rate can be tailored by modifying the polymer composition, particle size, and surface properties.
   - This controlled release capability is beneficial for applications in cancer therapy, where sustained drug release can improve treatment outcomes.

3. **Biomedical Imaging:**

   - Functionalized nanoparticles can serve as contrast agents for various imaging modalities, such as magnetic resonance imaging (MRI), fluorescence imaging, and computed tomography (CT).
   - The high surface area and tunable properties of these nanoparticles enhance the contrast and resolution of imaging techniques, aiding in

accurate diagnosis and monitoring of diseases.

4. **Nutraceuticals and Food Industry:**

- Nanoprecipitation is used to encapsulate nutraceuticals and bioactive compounds, improving their stability, solubility, and bioavailability in functional foods and dietary supplements.
- The encapsulated nanoparticles can protect sensitive ingredients from degradation and ensure controlled release during digestion.

## *Challenges and Considerations:*

- **Solvent Selection:** The choice of solvent is critical for the success of the nanoprecipitation process. The solvent must be miscible with water and capable of dissolving the polymer without affecting its properties.
- **Stability:** Ensuring the long-term stability of the nanoparticles in suspension can be challenging, as aggregation and sedimentation may occur over time. The choice of surfactant or stabilizer is crucial to maintaining stability.
- **Toxicity and Biocompatibility:** For biomedical applications, it is essential to thoroughly assess the toxicity and biocompatibility of the polymeric nanoparticles and the solvents used to ensure their safety for clinical use.

Nanoprecipitation is a versatile and efficient technique for synthesizing polymeric nanoparticles with controlled size and high encapsulation efficiency. Its applications span various fields, including drug delivery, controlled release systems, biomedical imaging, and the food industry. The continued development and optimization of this technique will further enhance its capabilities and expand its applications in science and industry.

## *4.2.2 Advantages and Limitations*

## *Advantages of Nanoprecipitation:*

1. **Simplicity and Efficiency:**

   - **Ease of Process:** Nanoprecipitation is a straightforward technique that requires relatively simple equipment and processes. The method involves dissolving the polymer in a solvent, followed by the injection of this solution into an aqueous phase containing a surfactant.
   - **Rapid Production:** The process is rapid and can produce nanoparticles within minutes, making it suitable for quick production and testing of formulations.

2. **Mild Conditions:**

   - **Low Energy Requirement:** The technique operates under mild conditions, typically at room temperature, without the need for high energy input, such as heating or high-pressure systems.
   - **Preservation of Sensitive Compounds:** The mild conditions help preserve the integrity of sensitive compounds, including proteins, peptides, and nucleic acids, which can be easily degraded by harsh processing conditions.

3. **Control Over Particle Size:**

   - **Tunability:** The size of the nanoparticles can be precisely controlled by adjusting the concentration of the polymer, the solvent-to-water ratio, the rate of solvent injection, and the type and concentration of surfactants.
   - **Narrow Size Distribution:** Nanoprecipitation typically yields nanoparticles with a narrow size distribution, which is crucial for applications requiring uniform particle sizes, such as drug delivery and diagnostics.

4. **High Encapsulation Efficiency:**

   - **Effective Encapsulation:** The technique can achieve high encapsulation efficiency for hydrophobic drugs and bioactive compounds, enhancing their solubility, stability, and bioavailability.
   - **Protection of Active Ingredients:** Encapsulating active ingredients within nanoparticles protects them from degradation by

environmental factors, such as light, oxygen, and enzymatic activity.

5. **Scalability:**

- **Industrial Scale-Up:** Nanoprecipitation can be easily scaled up for large-scale production of nanoparticles, making it suitable for industrial applications in pharmaceuticals, cosmetics, and food industries.
- **Batch-to-Batch Consistency:** The reproducibility and consistency of the nanoprecipitation process ensure high-quality production, which is essential for commercial manufacturing.

**Limitations of Nanoprecipitation:**

1. **Solvent Selection:**

- **Solvent Restrictions:** The choice of solvent is critical, as it must be capable of dissolving the polymer without affecting its properties and must be miscible with water to facilitate precipitation.
- **Toxicity Concerns:** Some organic solvents used in nanoprecipitation may pose toxicity concerns, necessitating thorough removal and purification steps to ensure the safety of the final product.

2. **Stability Issues:**

- **Aggregation and Sedimentation:** Ensuring the long-term stability of nanoparticles in suspension can be challenging, as they may aggregate or sediment over time. The choice and concentration of surfactants or stabilizers are crucial for maintaining stability.
- **Environmental Sensitivity:** Nanoparticles synthesized by nanoprecipitation may be sensitive to environmental conditions, such as pH, temperature, and ionic strength, which can affect their stability and performance.

3. **Limited Encapsulation of Hydrophilic Compounds:**

- **Hydrophobic Bias:** Nanoprecipitation is particularly effective for encapsulating hydrophobic compounds, but it may not be as efficient for hydrophilic drugs or bioactive agents, limiting its versatility for certain applications.

- **Need for Modifications:** Additional modifications or alternative techniques may be required to effectively encapsulate hydrophilic compounds, adding complexity to the process.

4. **Batch Variability:**

- **Reproducibility Challenges:** Although nanoprecipitation can be scaled up, maintaining consistency between batches can be challenging, especially when transferring the process from the laboratory to an industrial scale.
- **Quality Control:** Ensuring strict quality control measures is essential to achieve reproducible results and maintain the desired properties of nanoparticles across different production batches.

5. **Removal of Solvent Residues:**

- **Purification Steps:** Complete removal of residual organic solvents is essential to ensure the safety and efficacy of the final product, particularly for biomedical applications. This requires additional purification steps, such as dialysis, evaporation, or filtration.
- **Process Complexity:** The need for thorough purification can add complexity and time to the overall production process, potentially increasing costs.

## 4.3 Interfacial Polymerization

## 4.3.1 Synthesis at Liquid Interfaces

### Introduction to Interfacial Polymerization:

Interfacial polymerization is a versatile technique used for the synthesis of polymeric nanoparticles and nanocapsules. This method involves polymerization at the interface between two immiscible liquid phases, typically an aqueous phase and an organic phase. The process relies on the reaction of monomers dissolved in each phase, forming a polymeric membrane at the interface. This technique is widely used due to its ability to produce nanoparticles with controlled size and morphology, as well as the capability to encapsulate a variety of active agents.

## *Mechanism of Interfacial Polymerization:*

1. **Preparation of Liquid Phases:**

   - Two immiscible liquid phases are prepared: an aqueous phase and an organic phase. Each phase contains monomers that can react at the interface. Commonly used monomers include diacid chlorides and diamines for polyamide synthesis, or diisocyanates and diols for polyurethane synthesis.
   - Surfactants or emulsifiers are often added to stabilize the interface and prevent coalescence of the dispersed droplets.

2. **Formation of the Interface:**

   - The aqueous phase is typically dispersed in the organic phase, or vice versa, creating an emulsion. The interface between the two phases is where the polymerization reaction occurs.
   - The monomers from each phase diffuse to the interface, where they react to form a polymeric membrane. This membrane grows as the polymerization continues, forming a shell around the dispersed phase.

3. **Polymerization Reaction:**

   - The monomers react rapidly at the interface, leading to the formation of a polymeric layer. The nature of the polymer formed depends on the specific monomers and reaction conditions used.
   - For example, the reaction between a diacid chloride (in the organic phase) and a diamine (in the aqueous phase) forms a polyamide (nylon) at the interface.

4. **Encapsulation and Particle Formation:**

- The growing polymeric membrane can encapsulate the dispersed phase, forming nanocapsules. If no core material is encapsulated, the process results in the formation of solid nanoparticles.
- The thickness and properties of the polymeric shell can be controlled by adjusting the concentration of monomers, the reaction time, and the conditions at the interface.

## *Advantages of Interfacial Polymerization:*

- **Encapsulation Efficiency:** This method is highly efficient for encapsulating active agents, such as drugs, pesticides, or nutrients, within a polymeric shell. The encapsulated agents are protected from degradation and can be released in a controlled manner.
- **Controlled Particle Size and Morphology:** The size and morphology of the nanoparticles or nanocapsules can be precisely controlled by adjusting the process parameters, such as the concentration of monomers, the type of surfactant, and the stirring speed.
- **Versatility:** Interfacial polymerization can be used to synthesize a wide variety of polymers, including polyamides, polyurethanes, polyesters, and polyureas, by selecting appropriate monomers.

## *Applications of Interfacial Polymerization:*

1. **Drug Delivery:**

- Polymeric nanocapsules synthesized via interfacial polymerization are widely used in drug delivery systems. The encapsulated drugs are protected from degradation and can be released in a controlled manner, improving therapeutic efficacy and reducing side effects.
- The surface of these nanocapsules can be functionalized with targeting ligands to achieve site-specific delivery, enhancing the precision of drug delivery.

## 2. Agriculture:

- In agriculture, interfacial polymerization is used to encapsulate pesticides, herbicides, and fertilizers. The encapsulation protects these active agents from environmental degradation and allows for their controlled release, enhancing efficacy and reducing environmental impact.
- Encapsulated agrochemicals can be designed to release their active ingredients in response to specific environmental triggers, such as moisture or pH changes, providing targeted and efficient pest and weed control.

## 3. Food Industry:

- Nanocapsules synthesized via interfacial polymerization are used to encapsulate flavors, vitamins, and other bioactive compounds in food products. The encapsulation enhances the stability and bioavailability of these compounds, improving the nutritional value and shelf life of the food products.
- Encapsulation also allows for the controlled release of flavors and nutrients, enhancing the sensory and nutritional properties of the food.

## 4. Cosmetics and Personal Care:

- Interfacial polymerization is used to encapsulate active ingredients in cosmetics and personal care products, such as moisturizers, antioxidants, and UV filters. The encapsulation protects these ingredients from degradation and ensures their controlled release upon application.
- Encapsulated nanoparticles can improve the stability, efficacy, and aesthetic properties of cosmetic formulations.

## *Challenges and Considerations:*

- **Interfacial Stability:** Ensuring the stability of the interface during the polymerization process is critical. The choice of surfactant and the conditions used to stabilize the emulsion play a crucial role in the successful formation of nanoparticles or nanocapsules.
- **Scalability:** Scaling up the interfacial polymerization process from laboratory to industrial scale requires careful optimization to maintain consistent quality and properties of the nanoparticles. The process parameters, such as mixing efficiency and monomer diffusion rates, need to be carefully controlled.
- **Toxicity and Biocompatibility:** For biomedical and food applications, it is essential to thoroughly assess the toxicity and biocompatibility of the polymeric nanoparticles and the monomers used to ensure their safety for human use.

Interfacial polymerization is a versatile and efficient technique for synthesizing polymeric nanoparticles and nanocapsules with controlled size and morphology. Its applications span various fields, including drug delivery, agriculture, food industry, and cosmetics, making it a valuable method in the field of nanotechnology. The continued development and optimization of this technique will further enhance its capabilities and expand its applications in science and industry.

## 4.3.2 Control over Particle Size

### Introduction to Particle Size Control in Interfacial Polymerization:

Controlling the particle size in interfacial polymerization is critical for tailoring the properties of polymeric nanoparticles for specific applications. Particle size can significantly influence the physical, chemical, and biological behavior of nanoparticles, affecting their stability, drug loading capacity, release kinetics, and interaction with biological systems. Achieving precise control over particle size requires an understanding of the factors that influence the polymerization process and the ability to manipulate these factors effectively.

# *Factors Influencing Particle Size:*

1. **Monomer Concentration:**

   - **Higher Monomer Concentration:** Increasing the concentration of monomers in the organic or aqueous phase typically leads to the formation of larger particles. This is because higher monomer concentration results in a higher rate of polymerization, leading to rapid particle growth.
   - **Lower Monomer Concentration:** Conversely, lower monomer concentration tends to produce smaller particles due to slower polymerization rates and reduced particle growth.

2. **Surfactant Concentration and Type:**

   - **Surfactant Concentration:** The concentration of surfactants or emulsifiers is crucial in stabilizing the emulsion and preventing coalescence of the droplets. Higher surfactant concentrations generally lead to smaller particle sizes due to better stabilization and prevention of droplet coalescence.
   - **Type of Surfactant:** The choice of surfactant also affects particle size. Surfactants with higher hydrophilic-lipophilic balance (HLB) values are more effective in stabilizing smaller droplets, leading to the formation of smaller nanoparticles.

3. **Stirring Speed and Mixing Conditions:**

   - **Stirring Speed:** The speed of stirring or mixing during the formation of the emulsion influences the size of the dispersed droplets. Higher stirring speeds create more shear forces, resulting in smaller droplets and, consequently, smaller nanoparticles.
   - **Mixing Efficiency:** Efficient mixing ensures uniform distribution of monomers and surfactants, leading to consistent particle sizes. Inadequate mixing can result in a wide size distribution and larger particles.

4. **Phase Ratio (Oil-to-Water Ratio):**

- **Oil-to-Water Ratio:** The ratio of the organic phase to the aqueous phase impacts the size of the nanoparticles. A higher volume of the organic phase relative to the aqueous phase can lead to larger particles due to the increased availability of monomers for polymerization.

5. **Temperature:**

- **Polymerization Temperature:** The temperature at which polymerization occurs can influence the rate of monomer diffusion and reaction kinetics. Higher temperatures typically increase the rate of polymerization, leading to larger particles. However, excessively high temperatures can cause instability in the emulsion, leading to coalescence and irregular particle sizes.

## *Techniques for Controlling Particle Size:*

1. **Emulsion Stabilization:**

- **Optimizing Surfactant Concentration:** Careful optimization of surfactant concentration ensures effective stabilization of the emulsion, preventing coalescence and achieving uniform particle sizes.
- **Selection of Appropriate Surfactants:** Choosing surfactants with suitable HLB values and properties can enhance emulsion stability and control particle size.

2. **Controlled Addition of Monomers:**

- **Gradual Addition:** Gradually adding monomers to the reaction mixture can help control the rate of polymerization and particle growth, leading to more uniform particle sizes.
- **Pre-emulsion Preparation:** Creating a pre-emulsion by mixing monomers with surfactants before initiating polymerization ensures uniform distribution and better control over particle size.

3. **Adjusting Stirring Speed:**

- **High-Speed Homogenization:** Using high-speed homogenization during the emulsification process can create smaller droplets, leading to the formation of smaller nanoparticles.
- **Ultrasonication:** Ultrasonication can be used to achieve fine emulsions with smaller droplet sizes, resulting in smaller nanoparticles.

4. **Temperature Control:**

- **Maintaining Optimal Temperature:** Carefully controlling the polymerization temperature can help achieve the desired particle size by balancing the rate of polymerization and emulsion stability.

5. **Phase Ratio Adjustment:**

- **Optimizing Oil-to-Water Ratio:** Adjusting the ratio of the organic phase to the aqueous phase can help control the size of the nanoparticles. A balanced phase ratio ensures proper emulsification and polymerization, leading to uniform particle sizes.

**Applications of Controlled Particle Size:**

1. **Drug Delivery:**

- **Optimized Release Profiles:** Controlling the size of polymeric nanoparticles allows for the design of drug delivery systems with optimized release profiles, enhancing therapeutic efficacy and minimizing side effects.
- **Targeted Delivery:** Smaller nanoparticles can penetrate biological barriers more effectively, enabling targeted delivery to specific tissues or cells.

2. **Biomedical Imaging:**

- **Enhanced Imaging Contrast:** Nanoparticles with controlled sizes provide enhanced contrast in imaging techniques such as MRI, fluorescence imaging, and CT, improving diagnostic accuracy.

- **Longer Circulation Time:** Smaller nanoparticles with controlled sizes tend to have longer circulation times in the bloodstream, enhancing their effectiveness as imaging agents.

3. **Environmental Applications:**

- **Efficient Pollutant Removal:** Nanoparticles with optimized sizes can provide a high surface area for adsorption and degradation of pollutants, improving the efficiency of environmental remediation processes.
- **Controlled Release of Agrochemicals:** Nanoparticles with controlled sizes ensure the controlled release of agrochemicals, enhancing their effectiveness and reducing environmental impact.

4. **Cosmetics and Personal Care:**

- **Improved Product Performance:** Nanoparticles with controlled sizes enhance the performance of cosmetic and personal care products by providing better texture, stability, and controlled release of active ingredients.
- **Enhanced Skin Penetration:** Smaller nanoparticles can penetrate the skin more effectively, delivering active ingredients to deeper layers and improving the efficacy of skincare products.

# 4.4 Solvent Evaporation Method

## 4.4.1 Encapsulation of Drugs

### Introduction to Solvent Evaporation Method:

The solvent evaporation method is a widely used technique for the encapsulation of drugs within polymeric nanoparticles. This method involves dissolving both the polymer and the drug in a volatile organic solvent, forming an emulsion, and then evaporating the solvent to produce nanoparticles. The encapsulated drug is protected within the polymer matrix, allowing for controlled and sustained release. This method is particularly useful for hydrophobic drugs that are difficult to deliver in aqueous environments.

**Mechanism of Solvent Evaporation:**

1. **Preparation of the Organic Phase:**

   - The polymer and the drug are dissolved in a suitable volatile organic solvent such as dichloromethane (DCM), chloroform, or ethyl acetate. The choice of solvent depends on the solubility of both the polymer and the drug.
   - This organic solution forms the dispersed phase for the emulsion.

2. **Formation of the Emulsion:**

   - The organic solution is emulsified into an aqueous phase containing a surfactant or emulsifier, such as polyvinyl alcohol (PVA), to stabilize the droplets. This step creates an oil-in-water (O/W) emulsion.
   - The emulsion can be formed using high-speed homogenization, ultrasonication, or mechanical stirring to achieve the desired droplet size.

3. **Solvent Evaporation:**

   - The volatile organic solvent is gradually evaporated under reduced pressure or ambient conditions, leading to the solidification of the polymer around the drug.
   - The evaporation process causes the polymer to precipitate and form solid nanoparticles with the drug encapsulated within the polymer matrix.

4. **Collection and Purification:**

   - After solvent evaporation, the resulting nanoparticles are collected by centrifugation, filtration, or sedimentation. The nanoparticles are then washed to remove any residual surfactant, unencapsulated drug, and organic solvent.

- The purification steps ensure that the final nanoparticle formulation is free from contaminants and is suitable for its intended application.

## *Advantages of the Solvent Evaporation Method:*

1. **High Encapsulation Efficiency:**

   - The solvent evaporation method can achieve high encapsulation efficiency, particularly for hydrophobic drugs. The drug is efficiently trapped within the polymer matrix during the solidification process.

2. **Controlled Particle Size:**

   - The size of the nanoparticles can be controlled by adjusting the concentration of the polymer and drug, the type and concentration of the surfactant, the rate of solvent evaporation, and the homogenization conditions.

3. **Versatility:**

   - This method is versatile and can be used to encapsulate a wide range of drugs, including small molecules, proteins, and peptides. It is also compatible with various biodegradable and biocompatible polymers, such as poly(lactic-co-glycolic acid) (PLGA), polylactic acid (PLA), and polycaprolactone (PCL).

## *Applications of Drug-Loaded Polymeric Nanoparticles:*

1. **Cancer Therapy:**

   - Polymeric nanoparticles encapsulating chemotherapeutic agents can deliver drugs directly to tumor sites, enhancing drug accumulation in cancer cells while minimizing systemic toxicity. The nanoparticles can be engineered to release the drug in response to specific stimuli, such as pH or temperature, providing targeted and controlled drug delivery.

2. **Vaccines:**

- The solvent evaporation method is used to encapsulate antigens within nanoparticles for vaccine delivery. These nanoparticles can enhance the stability and immunogenicity of the antigens, promoting a stronger and more sustained immune response.

3. **Gene Therapy:**

- Nanoparticles can be designed to encapsulate nucleic acids, such as DNA or RNA, protecting them from degradation and facilitating their delivery into target cells. This is particularly important for gene therapy applications, where efficient and safe delivery of genetic material is crucial.

4. **Targeted Drug Delivery:**

- Surface modification of nanoparticles with targeting ligands, such as antibodies, peptides, or small molecules, can direct the nanoparticles to specific cells or tissues. This targeted approach improves the therapeutic index of drugs and reduces off-target effects.

## *Challenges and Considerations:*

1. **Solvent Selection:**

- The choice of solvent is critical for the success of the solvent evaporation method. The solvent must dissolve both the polymer and the drug, and it must be easily removable by evaporation. Solvent toxicity must also be considered, especially for biomedical applications.

2. **Stability:**

- Ensuring the long-term stability of the nanoparticles is essential. The formulation must be stable during storage and upon administration, maintaining its size, shape, and encapsulation efficiency.

3.  **Scalability:**

- Scaling up the solvent evaporation process for industrial production requires careful optimization of parameters to ensure consistency and quality of the nanoparticles. This includes maintaining control over particle size distribution and encapsulation efficiency.

4.  **Biocompatibility:**

- The biocompatibility and biodegradability of the polymer used for encapsulation are crucial, particularly for clinical applications. The polymer should not induce an adverse immune response and should degrade into non-toxic byproducts.

The solvent evaporation method is a robust and versatile technique for encapsulating drugs within polymeric nanoparticles. It offers high encapsulation efficiency, controlled particle size, and the ability to deliver a wide range of therapeutic agents. The continued development and optimization of this method will enhance its applications in drug delivery, gene therapy, vaccines, and other biomedical fields.

## 4.4.2 Factors Affecting Efficiency

### *Introduction to Efficiency in Solvent Evaporation Method:*

The efficiency of the solvent evaporation method in producing polymeric nanoparticles, particularly in terms of drug encapsulation, particle size control, and overall yield, is influenced by a variety of factors. Understanding and optimizing these factors are essential for achieving high-quality nanoparticles with desired characteristics for specific applications. These factors include the choice of solvent, polymer and drug properties, surfactant concentration, stirring speed, solvent evaporation rate, and purification process.

## *Factors Influencing Efficiency:*

1. **Choice of Solvent:**

   - **Solvent Properties:** The solvent must effectively dissolve both the polymer and the drug. Common solvents used include dichloromethane (DCM), chloroform, and ethyl acetate. The solvent should have a low boiling point to facilitate easy evaporation.
   - **Toxicity:** The solvent should be non-toxic or easily removable to ensure the safety of the final product, especially for biomedical applications.

2. **Polymer and Drug Properties:**

   - **Polymer Characteristics:** The molecular weight, crystallinity, and hydrophobicity of the polymer influence the encapsulation efficiency and release profile of the drug. Biodegradable polymers such as poly(lactic-co-glycolic acid) (PLGA), polylactic acid (PLA), and polycaprolactone (PCL) are commonly used.
   - **Drug Solubility:** The solubility of the drug in the organic solvent and its compatibility with the polymer matrix are crucial for achieving high encapsulation efficiency. Hydrophobic drugs are typically more easily encapsulated using this method.

3. **Surfactant Concentration and Type:**

   - **Surfactant Role:** Surfactants or emulsifiers stabilize the oil-in-water emulsion, preventing the coalescence of the droplets. Common surfactants include polyvinyl alcohol (PVA), Tween 80, and sodium dodecyl sulfate (SDS).
   - **Concentration:** The concentration of the surfactant must be optimized to ensure effective stabilization. Insufficient surfactant can lead to larger particle sizes and aggregation, while excess surfactant may result in difficult purification and potential toxicity.

4. **Stirring Speed and Mixing Conditions:**

- **High-Speed Homogenization:** High-speed homogenization or ultrasonication can create smaller and more uniform droplets in the emulsion, leading to smaller nanoparticle sizes.
- **Mixing Efficiency:** Uniform mixing ensures consistent droplet size and distribution, which is essential for producing nanoparticles with narrow size distributions.

## 5. Solvent Evaporation Rate:

- **Evaporation Conditions:** The rate of solvent evaporation affects the formation of nanoparticles. Rapid evaporation can lead to smaller particles but may also cause rapid solidification, potentially trapping residual solvent. Controlled evaporation under reduced pressure can help achieve uniform particle size and complete solvent removal.
- **Temperature and Pressure:** The evaporation process is influenced by temperature and pressure. Higher temperatures and reduced pressures can accelerate solvent evaporation, but must be carefully controlled to avoid destabilizing the emulsion.

## 6. Polymer and Drug Concentration:

- **Polymer Concentration:** Higher polymer concentrations can increase the viscosity of the organic phase, potentially leading to larger particle sizes. Optimizing the polymer concentration is essential for balancing encapsulation efficiency and particle size.
- **Drug Loading:** The amount of drug to be encapsulated affects the encapsulation efficiency and release profile. High drug loading may result in drug crystallization or leakage from the nanoparticles.

## 7. Purification Process:

- **Removal of Residual Solvent:** Thorough purification is necessary to remove residual solvent, surfactant, and unencapsulated drug. Techniques such as centrifugation, dialysis, and filtration are commonly used.
- **Washing and Redispersion:** Multiple washing steps with water or an appropriate buffer can help remove impurities and stabilize the nanoparticles. The nanoparticles must be redispersed in a suitable

medium for storage and use.

## *Optimization Strategies:*

1. **Experimental Design:**

   - **Design of Experiments (DoE):** Using a systematic approach such as DoE can help identify the optimal conditions by evaluating the effects of multiple factors simultaneously.
   - **Response Surface Methodology (RSM):** RSM can be used to model and optimize the process parameters to achieve the desired nanoparticle characteristics.

2. **Process Scale-Up:**

   - **Reproducibility:** Ensuring reproducibility of the process at different scales is crucial for industrial applications. This includes maintaining consistent mixing, solvent evaporation, and purification conditions.
   - **Quality Control:** Implementing stringent quality control measures ensures the consistency and safety of the final product. This includes monitoring particle size, encapsulation efficiency, and residual solvent levels.

3. **Surface Functionalization:**

   - **Targeting Ligands:** Functionalizing the surface of nanoparticles with targeting ligands such as antibodies, peptides, or small molecules can enhance their specificity and efficacy for targeted drug delivery.
   - **Stealth Properties:** Incorporating hydrophilic polymers such as polyethylene glycol (PEG) can improve the circulation time of nanoparticles by reducing opsonization and clearance by the immune system.

# CHAPTER FIVE

# SELF ASSEMBLY STRUCTURES

## 5.1 Liposomes

### *5.1.1 Formation and Hydration*

Liposomes are spherical vesicles consisting of one or more phospholipid bilayers, resembling the structure of cell membranes. They are widely used as drug delivery systems due to their biocompatibility, ability to encapsulate both hydrophilic and hydrophobic substances, and their potential for targeted delivery. The formation and hydration process of liposomes is critical for ensuring their stability and functionality.

**Formation of Liposomes:** The formation of liposomes begins with the preparation of phospholipids, which are amphipathic molecules containing hydrophilic heads and hydrophobic tails. Common phospholipids used in liposome synthesis include phosphatidylcholine (PC), phosphatidylserine (PS), and phosphatidylethanolamine (PE). These phospholipids are initially dissolved in organic solvents such as chloroform or methanol to ensure complete dispersion and homogeneity.

Once the phospholipids are dissolved, the organic solvent is removed through a process called solvent evaporation. This can be achieved using a rotary evaporator, which gently rotates the phospholipid solution under reduced pressure and mild heating, leading to the formation of a thin lipid film on the inner surface of the evaporation flask. This lipid film represents the precursor to liposome formation and is typically dried under vacuum to remove any residual solvent, ensuring purity and safety for subsequent hydration.

**Hydration of the Lipid Film:** The dried lipid film is then hydrated by adding an aqueous buffer solution, typically containing the drug or therapeutic agent to be encapsulated. The hydration process causes the lipid film to swell and peel off, forming multilamellar vesicles (MLVs). The temperature of the hydration buffer is crucial and is usually maintained above the phase transition temperature of the phospholipids to facilitate the formation of flexible and homogeneous liposomes.

Hydration can be enhanced by gentle agitation or vortexing to ensure uniform dispersion of the lipids in the aqueous phase. The resulting MLVs are relatively large and heterogeneous in size, with diameters ranging from a few hundred nanometers to several micrometers. To achieve a more uniform size distribution and enhance the encapsulation efficiency, MLVs can be subjected to further processing techniques.

**Size Reduction and Homogenization:** The large MLVs are often downsized to unilamellar vesicles (ULVs) through mechanical means such as sonication or extrusion. Sonication involves the use of high-frequency sound waves to break down the large vesicles into smaller ones. This process can be performed using a probe sonicator or a bath sonicator, with the duration and intensity of sonication tailored to achieve the desired liposome size.

Extrusion is another common method for size reduction, where the liposome suspension is repeatedly passed through polycarbonate membranes with defined pore sizes using an extruder. This process produces liposomes with a narrow size distribution and improved stability. Extrusion parameters, such as the number of passes and membrane pore size, are critical for controlling the final liposome size.

**Encapsulation Efficiency:** The efficiency of encapsulation, which refers to the amount of drug or therapeutic agent successfully incorporated into the liposomes, is influenced by several factors, including the lipid composition, hydration conditions, and processing techniques. Optimizing these parameters ensures maximum drug loading and retention within the liposomes, enhancing their therapeutic efficacy.

**Stability Considerations:** Liposome stability is an important consideration for their practical application. Stability can be affected by factors such as lipid composition, storage conditions, and the presence of stabilizing agents. Liposomes can be stabilized by incorporating cholesterol into the lipid bilayer, which enhances membrane rigidity and reduces permeability, thereby improving the retention of encapsulated drugs.

The formation and hydration process of liposomes involves the careful preparation of phospholipids, the creation of a thin lipid film, and its hydration to produce multilamellar vesicles. Subsequent size reduction techniques, such as sonication and extrusion, yield uniform and stable liposomes suitable for drug delivery applications. Optimizing these processes ensures high encapsulation efficiency and stability, making liposomes a versatile and effective delivery system in various biomedical fields.

## *5.2 Niosomes*

## 5.2.1 Synthesis Using Non-Ionic Surfactants

Niosomes are non-ionic surfactant-based vesicles similar to liposomes, but they are formed from non-ionic surfactants rather than phospholipids. Niosomes have garnered significant attention in the field of drug delivery due to their stability, biocompatibility, and ability to encapsulate both hydrophilic and hydrophobic drugs. The synthesis of niosomes involves the use of non-ionic surfactants, which play a crucial role in the formation and stability of these vesicles.

**Selection of Non-Ionic Surfactants:** The first step in the synthesis of niosomes is the selection of appropriate non-ionic surfactants. Commonly used non-ionic surfactants include Span (sorbitan esters) and Tween (polysorbates). These surfactants are chosen based on their hydrophilic-lipophilic balance (HLB) values, which determine their ability to form stable vesicles. Surfactants with HLB values between 4 and 8 are typically used for forming stable niosomes.

**Preparation of Surfactant Solution:** The selected surfactants are dissolved in an organic solvent such as chloroform or ethanol. This solution can also include cholesterol, which is often added to improve the stability and rigidity of the niosome bilayer. Cholesterol modulates the fluidity and permeability of the vesicle membrane, enhancing the encapsulation efficiency and stability of the niosomes.

**Formation of Thin Film:** Similar to the preparation of liposomes, the organic solvent containing the surfactants and cholesterol is evaporated using a rotary evaporator. This process creates a thin film of surfactants on the inner surface of the evaporation flask. The evaporation is typically conducted under reduced pressure and mild heating to ensure complete removal of the solvent, resulting in a dry, thin film that is ready for hydration.

**Hydration of the Thin Film:** The dry surfactant film is then hydrated with an aqueous buffer solution. This solution can contain the drug or therapeutic agent intended for encapsulation within the niosomes. The hydration process causes the surfactant film to swell and peel off, forming multilamellar vesicles (MLVs). The temperature of the hydration buffer is maintained above the transition temperature of the surfactants to ensure efficient swelling and dispersion of the film.

**Size Reduction and Homogenization:** The initially formed MLVs are often large and heterogeneous. To achieve a more uniform and smaller size distribution, the MLVs are subjected to size reduction techniques such as sonication or extrusion. Sonication involves the use of high-frequency sound waves to break down the large vesicles into smaller, more uniform vesicles. Extrusion, on the other hand, involves passing the niosome suspension through polycarbonate membranes with defined pore sizes using an extruder. This process produces niosomes with a narrow size distribution and improved stability.

**Optimization of Synthesis Parameters:** Several parameters influence the synthesis and characteristics of niosomes, including the surfactant-to-cholesterol ratio, the hydration temperature, and the duration of sonication or extrusion. The surfactant-to-cholesterol ratio is critical for balancing the fluidity and rigidity of the vesicle membrane. A higher cholesterol content typically results in more stable and rigid niosomes, whereas a lower cholesterol content produces more fluid and permeable vesicles. The hydration temperature must be optimized to ensure efficient swelling and formation of the surfactant film, while the duration and intensity of sonication or extrusion determine the final size and uniformity of the niosomes.

**Encapsulation Efficiency and Stability:** The encapsulation efficiency of niosomes is influenced by the properties of the surfactants, the method of preparation, and the characteristics of the drug being encapsulated. Hydrophilic drugs are encapsulated within the aqueous core of the niosomes, while hydrophobic drugs are incorporated into the surfactant bilayer. The stability of niosomes is also a crucial factor, as it affects the retention of encapsulated drugs and the overall efficacy of the niosome formulation. Stability can be enhanced by optimizing the surfactant composition, the inclusion of cholesterol, and the storage conditions.

The synthesis of niosomes using non-ionic surfactants involves the preparation of a surfactant solution, the formation of a thin film, hydration to form multilamellar vesicles, and subsequent size reduction techniques to achieve uniform and stable vesicles. The optimization of synthesis parameters is essential for maximizing encapsulation efficiency and ensuring the stability of niosomes, making them a versatile and effective drug delivery system.

## 5.2 Niosomes

### *5.2.2 Comparative Advantages*

Niosomes offer several comparative advantages over other types of vesicular drug delivery systems, such as liposomes and polymeric nanoparticles. These advantages make niosomes an attractive option for various biomedical applications, including targeted drug delivery, gene therapy, and vaccine delivery. Understanding the specific benefits of niosomes can help in selecting the most appropriate drug delivery system for different therapeutic needs.

**Stability:** One of the primary advantages of niosomes is their stability. Niosomes are formed from non-ionic surfactants, which are less susceptible to oxidative degradation compared to phospholipids used in liposomes. This inherent stability translates into a longer shelf life and reduced need for special storage conditions, making niosomes a more practical option for commercial pharmaceutical formulations.

**Cost-Effectiveness:** The components required for niosome synthesis, such as non-ionic surfactants and cholesterol, are generally less expensive and more readily available than the phospholipids used in liposomes. This cost-effectiveness is a significant advantage, particularly for large-scale production, where the cost of raw materials can significantly impact the overall production expenses.

**Versatility in Encapsulation:** Niosomes are capable of encapsulating a wide range of therapeutic agents, including hydrophilic, hydrophobic, and amphiphilic drugs. This versatility is due to their unique structure, which includes both an aqueous core and a lipid bilayer. Hydrophilic drugs can be encapsulated within the aqueous core, while hydrophobic drugs can be integrated into the lipid bilayer. This dual encapsulation capability enhances the therapeutic potential of niosomes and broadens their applicability across various treatment modalities.

**Biocompatibility and Non-Immunogenicity:** Niosomes are composed of biocompatible and non-toxic materials, which minimize the risk of adverse reactions when administered in vivo. Additionally, the non-ionic nature of the surfactants used in niosomes reduces the likelihood of eliciting an immune response, making them suitable for repeated administration and long-term therapeutic use. This non-immunogenic property is particularly advantageous in applications such as vaccine delivery and chronic disease treatment.

**Controlled Release and Targeted Delivery:** Niosomes can be engineered to provide controlled release of encapsulated drugs, which can enhance the therapeutic efficacy and reduce the frequency of dosing. By modifying the composition of the surfactant bilayer and incorporating targeting ligands, niosomes can also be designed to achieve targeted delivery to specific tissues or cells. This targeted delivery capability minimizes systemic side effects and maximizes the concentration of the drug at the desired site of action, improving overall treatment outcomes.

**Enhanced Penetration and Absorption:** Niosomes can improve the penetration and absorption of encapsulated drugs through biological membranes. This is particularly beneficial for the delivery of drugs that have poor bioavailability when administered via conventional routes. For example, niosomes can enhance the transdermal delivery of drugs by facilitating their passage through the skin barrier, or improve the oral bioavailability of drugs that are poorly absorbed in the gastrointestinal tract.

**Customizable Size and Surface Properties:** The size and surface properties of niosomes can be easily tailored during the synthesis process. By adjusting parameters such as surfactant concentration, hydration conditions, and processing techniques, niosomes can be produced in various sizes, ranging from nanometers to micrometers. The surface properties of niosomes can also be modified to include polyethylene glycol (PEG) for improved circulation time, or targeting ligands for enhanced specificity. This customization allows for the optimization of niosome formulations to meet specific therapeutic requirements.

**Reduced Toxicity:** Niosomes exhibit lower toxicity compared to other synthetic drug delivery systems, such as polymeric nanoparticles. This is largely due to the biocompatible and non-ionic nature of the surfactants used in their preparation. Reduced toxicity is particularly important for applications involving sensitive tissues or long-term administration, where minimizing adverse effects is crucial for patient safety and compliance.

The comparative advantages of niosomes, including their stability, cost-effectiveness, versatility in encapsulation, biocompatibility, controlled release capabilities, enhanced penetration, customizable properties, and reduced toxicity, make them a promising and versatile platform for drug delivery. These attributes position niosomes as a valuable tool in advancing therapeutic interventions and improving patient outcomes across a range of medical conditions.

## 5.3 Micelles

## 5.3.1 Formation from Amphiphilic Molecules

Micelles are spherical structures formed by the self-assembly of amphiphilic molecules in an aqueous environment. These amphiphilic molecules, also known as surfactants, contain both hydrophilic (water-loving) and hydrophobic (water-fearing) regions. The unique ability of these molecules to arrange themselves in such a way that minimizes unfavorable interactions with water is central to the formation of micelles.

**Amphiphilic Molecules:** Amphiphilic molecules have a dual nature: they possess a hydrophilic head group and one or more hydrophobic tail groups. Common examples of amphiphilic molecules include detergents, soaps, and certain lipids. The hydrophilic head groups can be ionic (charged) or non-ionic (uncharged), while the hydrophobic tails are typically long hydrocarbon chains. This structural arrangement allows these molecules to interact favorably with both aqueous and lipid environments.

**Critical Micelle Concentration (CMC):** The formation of micelles occurs only when the concentration of amphiphilic molecules in solution exceeds a certain threshold known as the critical micelle concentration (CMC). Below the CMC, amphiphilic molecules exist as individual entities dispersed in the solution. However, once the CMC is reached, the molecules spontaneously aggregate to form micelles. The CMC is a characteristic property of each amphiphilic molecule and is influenced by factors such as temperature, ionic strength of the solution, and the presence of additives.

**Self-Assembly Process:** When the concentration of amphiphilic molecules exceeds the CMC, the hydrophobic tails of the molecules aggregate to minimize their exposure to water. Simultaneously, the hydrophilic heads orient themselves towards the aqueous environment, forming a spherical structure with the hydrophobic tails sequestered in the core and the hydrophilic heads forming the outer surface. This arrangement significantly reduces the free energy of the system and is thermodynamically favorable.

**Micelle Structure and Dynamics:** The resulting micelles are typically spherical with a hydrophobic core and a hydrophilic shell. The size of micelles can vary, but they generally range from 2 to 20 nanometers in diameter. The dynamic nature of micelles allows them to rapidly form and dissociate in response to changes in environmental conditions, such as temperature or concentration of the amphiphilic molecules. This dynamic behavior is essential for their function in various applications.

**Types of Micelles:** Depending on the nature of the hydrophilic head groups, micelles can be classified into several types, including ionic micelles (formed from ionic surfactants), non-ionic micelles (formed from non-ionic surfactants), and mixed micelles (formed from a combination of different types of surfactants). Ionic micelles, for example, are formed from surfactants like sodium dodecyl sulfate (SDS), which has a negatively charged head group. Non-ionic micelles, on the other hand, are formed from surfactants like polyethylene glycol (PEG), which has a neutral head group.

**Applications of Micelles:** Micelles have a wide range of applications, particularly in the fields of pharmaceuticals, cosmetics, and detergency. In drug delivery, micelles can encapsulate hydrophobic drugs within their core, enhancing the solubility and bioavailability of the drugs. This property is especially useful for delivering poorly water-soluble drugs. In cosmetics, micelles are used in formulations such as cleansing waters, where they help solubilize and remove dirt, oil, and makeup from the skin. In detergency, micelles play a crucial role in emulsifying oils and greases, making them easier to wash away.

The formation of micelles from amphiphilic molecules is a fundamental process driven by the need to minimize unfavorable interactions between hydrophobic regions and the aqueous environment. The self-assembly of these molecules into micelles above the critical micelle concentration results in stable, dynamic structures that have numerous practical applications in drug delivery, cosmetics, and detergency. The unique properties of micelles, including their ability to encapsulate hydrophobic substances and their responsive behavior to environmental changes, make them an invaluable tool in various scientific and industrial fields.

## 5.4 Aquasomes

### *5.4.1 Structure and Synthesis*

Aquasomes are a unique type of nanoparticulate carrier system characterized by their water-like properties and a three-layered self-assembled structure. These nanocarriers are particularly notable for their ability to deliver bioactive molecules while maintaining their structural integrity and biological activity. The synthesis and structure of aquasomes play a critical role in their effectiveness as drug delivery systems.

**Three-Layered Structure:** The core structure of aquasomes consists of three distinct layers:

1. **Core Particle:** The innermost layer is typically composed of an inorganic ceramic core, often made of materials such as calcium phosphate, hydroxyapatite, or tin oxide. These materials are chosen for their biocompatibility and ability to provide structural stability.
2. **Polymeric Coating:** The core particle is coated with a polyhydroxy oligomer, commonly carbohydrate-based materials like cellobiose, trehalose, or lactose. This coating serves multiple purposes: it protects the core, helps in the adsorption of the bioactive molecules, and mimics the natural environment, which helps preserve the biological activity of the encapsulated molecules.
3. **Bioactive Molecule Layer:** The outermost layer consists of the bioactive molecules to be delivered, such as proteins, peptides, antigens, or nucleic acids. These molecules are adsorbed onto the surface of the coated core through non-covalent interactions, including hydrogen bonding, van der Waals forces, and electrostatic interactions.

**Synthesis of Aquasomes:** The synthesis process of aquasomes involves several key steps to ensure the successful assembly of the three-layered structure.

**Preparation of Core Particle:** The synthesis begins with the preparation of the core particle. For example, if using calcium phosphate as the core material, a typical method involves the co-precipitation of calcium and phosphate ions under controlled conditions to form nanoparticles. These nanoparticles are then collected, washed, and dried to obtain a stable core.

**Polymeric Coating:** The prepared core particles are subsequently coated with the polyhydroxy oligomer. This process can be accomplished through various techniques, such as physical adsorption or covalent attachment. In physical adsorption, the core particles are mixed with a solution containing the polyhydroxy oligomer, allowing the oligomer to adsorb onto the surface of the core particles. This step often involves gentle stirring and incubation to ensure uniform coating.

**Adsorption of Bioactive Molecules:** The coated core particles are then exposed to a solution containing the bioactive molecules. The adsorption process relies on non-covalent interactions between the polyhydroxy oligomer coating and the bioactive molecules. The conditions, such as pH, temperature, and ionic strength, are carefully controlled to facilitate optimal adsorption and maintain the biological activity of the molecules.

**Optimization and Characterization:** The synthesis of aquasomes is optimized by varying parameters such as the concentration of the coating material, the type and concentration of the bioactive molecules, and the adsorption conditions. Characterization techniques such as dynamic light scattering (DLS), scanning electron microscopy (SEM), transmission electron microscopy (TEM), and Fourier-transform infrared spectroscopy (FTIR) are employed to analyze the size, morphology, surface properties, and structural integrity of the synthesized aquasomes.

**Advantages of Aquasomes:** The unique structure and synthesis process of aquasomes confer several advantages, making them highly effective as drug delivery systems. The ceramic core provides structural stability, ensuring that the aquasomes maintain their integrity under physiological conditions. The polyhydroxy oligomer coating mimics the natural environment, protecting the bioactive molecules and preserving their biological activity. Additionally, the non-covalent adsorption of bioactive molecules allows for a high loading capacity and facilitates the release of the molecules in their active form.

**Applications of Aquasomes:** Aquasomes have a wide range of applications in drug delivery, particularly for the delivery of sensitive bioactive molecules such as proteins, peptides, and antigens. Their ability to preserve the biological activity of encapsulated molecules makes them ideal for vaccine delivery, where maintaining the antigenicity of the delivered antigen is crucial. Aquasomes are also used in the delivery of enzymes and therapeutic proteins, where the preservation of enzymatic activity and protein stability is essential for therapeutic efficacy.

The structure and synthesis of aquasomes involve the careful assembly of a three-layered system consisting of a ceramic core, a polyhydroxy oligomer coating, and an outer layer of bioactive molecules. This unique structure provides stability, biocompatibility, and the ability to preserve the biological activity of the encapsulated molecules, making aquasomes a versatile and effective platform for drug delivery applications.

## 5.5 Nanoemulsions

### 5.5.1 High-Energy Methods

Nanoemulsions are submicron-sized emulsions with droplet sizes typically in the range of 20-200 nanometers. They are characterized by their kinetic stability, small droplet size, and potential applications in various fields such as drug delivery, cosmetics, and food industries. The production of nanoemulsions often requires high-energy methods to achieve the desired droplet size and stability. High-energy methods involve the application of mechanical energy to break down larger droplets into nanosized droplets.

**High-Pressure Homogenization:** One of the most commonly used high-energy methods for producing nanoemulsions is high-pressure homogenization. In this process, a coarse emulsion is passed through a narrow valve at extremely high pressures, typically ranging from 100 to 2000 bar. As the emulsion passes through the valve, it experiences intense shear forces, cavitation, and turbulence, which break down the larger droplets into nanosized droplets. The high-pressure homogenization process can be repeated several times to achieve the desired droplet size and distribution. This method is widely used due to its ability to produce nanoemulsions with narrow size distributions and good stability.

**Ultrasonication:** Ultrasonication is another high-energy method used to produce nanoemulsions. In this technique, high-frequency sound waves (typically in the range of 20 kHz to 100 kHz) are applied to the emulsion. The sound waves generate cavitation bubbles in the liquid, which collapse violently, creating intense localized shear forces that break down the droplets into nanosized droplets. Ultrasonication is effective in producing small droplet sizes and can be used for both batch and continuous processing. However, the efficiency of ultrasonication depends on factors such as the power of the ultrasonic device, the duration of sonication, and the properties of the emulsion components.

**Microfluidization:** Microfluidization is a high-energy method that utilizes a microfluidizer, a device that forces the coarse emulsion through microchannels under high pressure (typically 500 to 1500 bar). As the emulsion passes through the microchannels, it is subjected to intense shear forces and impact, which break down the larger droplets into nanosized droplets. Microfluidization is known for producing nanoemulsions with uniform droplet sizes and high stability. The method is scalable and can be used for large-scale production of nanoemulsions.

**High-Shear Mixing:** High-shear mixing involves the use of high-shear mixers or rotor-stator devices to produce nanoemulsions. These mixers generate high shear rates by rapidly rotating a rotor within a stationary stator, creating intense mechanical forces that break down the droplets. High-shear mixing is effective for producing nanoemulsions with relatively small droplet sizes, although it may not achieve the same level of size uniformity and stability as other high-energy methods. This method is often used in combination with other techniques, such as high-pressure homogenization or ultrasonication, to enhance the efficiency of nanoemulsion production.

**Parameters Influencing High-Energy Methods:** Several parameters influence the efficiency and outcome of high-energy methods for nanoemulsion production. These parameters include the type and concentration of emulsifiers, the oil-to-water ratio, the processing conditions (such as pressure, temperature, and duration), and the physical properties of the emulsion components (such as viscosity and interfacial tension). Optimizing these parameters is crucial for achieving the desired droplet size, stability, and functionality of the nanoemulsion.

**Advantages of High-Energy Methods:** High-energy methods offer several advantages in the production of nanoemulsions. They can produce nanoemulsions with very small droplet sizes, which enhances the bioavailability and efficacy of encapsulated active ingredients. The methods are also versatile and can be applied to a wide range of formulations, including those with high viscosity or complex compositions. Additionally, high-energy methods can produce nanoemulsions with good kinetic stability, reducing the risk of phase separation or coalescence over time.

**Applications of Nanoemulsions:** Nanoemulsions produced by high-energy methods have numerous applications across various industries. In pharmaceuticals, nanoemulsions are used for drug delivery, enhancing the solubility and bioavailability of poorly water-soluble drugs. In cosmetics, nanoemulsions are used to deliver active ingredients, such as vitamins and antioxidants, to the skin, providing improved penetration and efficacy. In the food industry, nanoemulsions are used to encapsulate flavors, colors, and nutraceuticals, enhancing the sensory properties and nutritional value of food products.

High-energy methods are essential for the production of nanoemulsions with small droplet sizes and high stability. Techniques such as high-pressure homogenization, ultrasonication, microfluidization, and high-shear mixing utilize intense mechanical forces to break down larger droplets into nanosized droplets. By optimizing the parameters of these methods, it is possible to produce nanoemulsions with desirable properties for a wide range of applications in pharmaceuticals, cosmetics, and the food industry.

## 5.5 Nanoemulsions

## *5.5.2 Low-Energy Methods*

Low-energy methods for producing nanoemulsions rely on the intrinsic physicochemical properties of the system rather than the application of intense mechanical forces. These methods typically involve the spontaneous formation of nanoemulsions through the manipulation of formulation parameters such as surfactant concentration, oil-to-water ratio, and temperature. Low-energy methods are advantageous due to their simplicity, lower energy consumption, and ability to produce nanoemulsions with minimal equipment.

**Phase Inversion Temperature (PIT) Method:** The Phase Inversion Temperature (PIT) method is a widely used low-energy technique for producing nanoemulsions. This method involves the temperature-induced phase inversion of an emulsion. Initially, a coarse emulsion is prepared using an oil, water, and nonionic surfactant mixture. The emulsion is then gradually heated to a temperature known as the phase inversion temperature. At this temperature, the emulsion undergoes a phase inversion from an oil-in-water (O/W) emulsion to a water-in-oil (W/O) emulsion or vice versa. Upon cooling back to room temperature, a fine nanoemulsion with small droplet sizes is formed. The effectiveness of the PIT method depends on the careful selection of surfactants and the precise control of temperature.

**Spontaneous Emulsification:** Spontaneous emulsification, also known as the self-emulsification method, relies on the spontaneous formation of nanoemulsions when two immiscible liquids are mixed in the presence of a surfactant. This method can be carried out at room temperature and involves the addition of the oil phase to the aqueous phase under gentle stirring. The surfactant molecules reduce the interfacial tension between the oil and water, leading to the spontaneous formation of nanosized droplets. Factors such as surfactant concentration, oil-to-water ratio, and the type of oil and surfactant used influence the efficiency and stability of the resulting nanoemulsion.

**Solvent Displacement Method:** The solvent displacement method, also known as the nanoprecipitation method, involves the precipitation of an oil phase from an organic solvent into an aqueous phase containing a surfactant. In this process, the oil phase is dissolved in a water-miscible organic solvent, such as ethanol or acetone. This solution is then rapidly injected into an aqueous phase under stirring. As the organic solvent diffuses into the aqueous phase, the oil phase precipitates out, forming nanosized droplets stabilized by the surfactant molecules. The solvent displacement method is simple and can be performed at ambient temperature, making it suitable for heat-sensitive compounds.

**Emulsion Phase Inversion (EPI) Method:** The Emulsion Phase Inversion (EPI) method involves the gradual addition of water to an oil-surfactant mixture or the addition of oil to a water-surfactant mixture, leading to phase inversion and the formation of a nanoemulsion. This method is based on the change in the curvature of surfactant molecules during the addition process. Initially, the surfactant molecules form a micellar solution in one of the phases. As the addition continues, the curvature of the surfactant molecules changes, leading to the formation of nanosized droplets. The EPI method is effective in producing stable nanoemulsions with uniform droplet sizes.

**Advantages of Low-Energy Methods:** Low-energy methods offer several advantages over high-energy methods. They require less energy input, making them more cost-effective and environmentally friendly. These methods are also relatively simple and can be performed with minimal equipment, making them accessible for various applications. Additionally, low-energy methods are gentle on the components, reducing the risk of degradation of sensitive bioactive molecules.

**Applications of Low-Energy Nanoemulsions:** Nanoemulsions produced by low-energy methods have diverse applications across multiple industries. In pharmaceuticals, they are used for the delivery of poorly water-soluble drugs, enhancing their bioavailability and therapeutic efficacy. In cosmetics, low-energy nanoemulsions are used to formulate skincare and haircare products, providing improved penetration and stability of active ingredients. In the food industry, these nanoemulsions are used to encapsulate flavors, vitamins, and essential oils, improving the sensory attributes and nutritional value of food products.

Low-energy methods are effective techniques for producing nanoemulsions with desirable properties for various applications. Methods such as the Phase Inversion Temperature (PIT) method, spontaneous emulsification, solvent displacement, and Emulsion Phase Inversion (EPI) method utilize the intrinsic properties of the system to form nanosized droplets. These methods offer advantages such as lower energy consumption, simplicity, and suitability for sensitive compounds, making them valuable for pharmaceutical, cosmetic, and food applications.

## 5.5 Nanoemulsions

### *5.5.3 Stability and Applications*

Nanoemulsions are prized for their small droplet sizes, high surface area, and potential for various applications in pharmaceuticals, cosmetics, and food industries. However, ensuring the stability of these nanoemulsions is crucial for their effectiveness and shelf life. Stability in nanoemulsions refers to the resistance of the droplets to processes such as coalescence, flocculation, Ostwald ripening, and creaming. Achieving and maintaining stability involves careful selection of formulation components and optimization of processing conditions.

**Stability Factors:** The stability of nanoemulsions can be influenced by several factors, including the choice of surfactants, the oil phase, the aqueous phase, and the conditions under which the nanoemulsion is prepared and stored. Surfactants play a critical role in stabilizing the droplets by reducing interfacial tension and providing a steric or electrostatic barrier to prevent droplet aggregation. Common surfactants used in nanoemulsions include nonionic surfactants like Tween and Span, as well as phospholipids such as lecithin.

**Electrostatic Stabilization:** Electrostatic stabilization involves the use of charged surfactants or stabilizers that create a repulsive force between the droplets. This repulsive force prevents the droplets from coming close enough to coalesce. For example, ionic surfactants like sodium dodecyl sulfate (SDS) can impart a negative charge to the droplet surface, creating an electrostatic barrier that enhances stability.

**Steric Stabilization:** Steric stabilization is achieved by using nonionic surfactants or polymers that create a physical barrier around the droplets. These molecules adsorb onto the droplet surface, forming a protective layer that prevents coalescence. Surfactants with bulky hydrophilic groups, such as Pluronic F-68, are effective in providing steric stabilization. The thickness and density of the stabilizing layer are critical factors that determine the effectiveness of steric stabilization.

**Combination of Stabilization Mechanisms:** In many cases, a combination of electrostatic and steric stabilization mechanisms is employed to enhance the stability of nanoemulsions. This approach is particularly effective in preventing both coalescence and flocculation, leading to more robust and stable formulations. For example, combining anionic surfactants with nonionic polymers can provide a synergistic stabilization effect.

**Ostwald Ripening:** Ostwald ripening is a process where smaller droplets dissolve, and the dispersed molecules diffuse through the continuous phase to larger droplets, leading to an increase in average droplet size over time. This process is driven by the difference in solubility between smaller and larger droplets. To minimize Ostwald ripening, the oil phase can be chosen to have low solubility in the aqueous phase. Additionally, using a mixture of oils, including oils with low diffusivity, can help reduce the rate of Ostwald ripening.

**Applications of Nanoemulsions:** Nanoemulsions have a wide range of applications due to their unique properties, such as small droplet size, high surface area, and enhanced bioavailability of encapsulated compounds.

**Pharmaceuticals:** In the pharmaceutical industry, nanoemulsions are used to improve the solubility and bioavailability of poorly water-soluble drugs. They can enhance drug absorption, provide controlled release, and improve the stability of labile drugs. Nanoemulsions are also used for targeted drug delivery, allowing for the delivery of therapeutic agents to specific tissues or cells.

**Cosmetics:** In the cosmetic industry, nanoemulsions are employed to deliver active ingredients such as vitamins, antioxidants, and anti-aging compounds. Their small droplet size enhances skin penetration and provides a smooth, non-greasy texture. Nanoemulsions also improve the stability of cosmetic formulations, extending the shelf life of the products.

**Food Industry:** In the food industry, nanoemulsions are used to encapsulate flavors, colors, and nutraceuticals, enhancing the sensory properties and nutritional value of food products. They can improve the solubility of lipophilic compounds and provide a controlled release of flavors and nutrients. Nanoemulsions also contribute to the stability and shelf life of functional foods and beverages.

**Agriculture:** In agriculture, nanoemulsions are used for the delivery of pesticides, herbicides, and fertilizers. They can improve the solubility and stability of agrochemicals, enhance their bioavailability, and provide a controlled release. Nanoemulsions also reduce the environmental impact of agrochemicals by minimizing their runoff and volatilization.

**Biomedical Applications:** Nanoemulsions are used in various biomedical applications, including diagnostic imaging, gene delivery, and vaccine formulations. They can enhance the delivery and efficacy of imaging agents, provide a platform for gene therapy, and improve the immunogenicity of vaccines.

**Environmental Remediation:** Nanoemulsions are employed in environmental remediation to remove contaminants from soil and water. They can solubilize hydrophobic pollutants, enhancing their bioavailability and facilitating their degradation or removal.

Stability is a critical factor in the effectiveness of nanoemulsions, and achieving stability requires careful selection of surfactants, oils, and formulation conditions. Nanoemulsions have diverse applications across pharmaceuticals, cosmetics, food, agriculture, biomedical fields, and environmental remediation, making them a versatile and valuable technology.

# CHAPTER SIX

# NANOTECHNOLOGY PRODUCTS FOR IN VITRO DIAGNOSTICS

## 6.1 Nanosensors

### 6.1.1 Types and Mechanisms

### Introduction to Nanosensors:

Nanosensors are a class of sensors that leverage the unique properties of nanomaterials to detect and measure biological, chemical, or physical phenomena with high sensitivity and specificity. These sensors operate at the nanoscale and can detect minute quantities of analytes, making them invaluable tools for in vitro diagnostics. Nanosensors can be classified based on the type of nanomaterials used, the sensing mechanism, and the nature of the analyte being detected.

**Types of Nanosensors:**

### Optical Nanosensors:

**Fluorescent Nanosensors:** These sensors utilize fluorescent nanomaterials, such as quantum dots, gold nanoparticles, or upconversion nanoparticles, which emit light upon excitation. The intensity or wavelength shift of the fluorescence signal can be correlated with the concentration of the target analyte.

**Mechanism:** Quantum dots exhibit size-dependent emission spectra, allowing for multiplexed detection of multiple analytes simultaneously. When functionalized with specific recognition molecules (e.g., antibodies or aptamers), they can selectively bind to the target analyte, resulting in changes in the fluorescence signal.

**Applications:** Fluorescent nanosensors are widely used in bioimaging, detection of biomarkers, and monitoring of cellular processes.

**Surface Plasmon Resonance (SPR) Nanosensors:** These sensors rely on the SPR phenomenon observed in metallic nanoparticles, primarily gold and silver. SPR occurs when incident light induces collective oscillations of electrons at the nanoparticle surface, leading to a resonance condition that is sensitive to changes in the local refractive index.

**Mechanism:** The binding of target molecules to the nanoparticle surface alters the local refractive index, shifting the SPR wavelength. This shift can be measured to determine the presence and concentration of the analyte.

**Applications:** SPR nanosensors are used for real-time, label-free detection of biomolecular interactions, including protein-protein, protein-DNA, and antigen-antibody binding.

## *Electrochemical Nanosensors:*

**Nanowire and Nanotube-Based Sensors:** These sensors use conductive nanowires or carbon nanotubes as the sensing element. The high surface area and excellent electrical conductivity of these nanomaterials enhance their sensitivity to changes in electrical properties upon analyte binding.

**Mechanism:** The binding of target molecules to the functionalized surface of nanowires or nanotubes induces changes in resistance, current, or voltage. These electrical changes are measured and correlated with the analyte concentration.

**Applications:** Nanowire and nanotube-based sensors are used for the detection of glucose, neurotransmitters, and various biomolecules in medical diagnostics and environmental monitoring.

**Nanoparticle-Modified Electrodes:** Electrodes modified with metallic or semiconducting nanoparticles enhance the electrochemical response of sensors. These nanoparticles increase the electrode surface area and catalytic activity, improving sensitivity and detection limits.

**Mechanism:** The presence of target analytes on the nanoparticle-modified electrode surface results in changes in electrochemical signals, such as current or potential, which are measured using techniques like cyclic voltammetry or amperometry.

**Applications:** These sensors are used for detecting heavy metals, toxins, and pathogens in clinical diagnostics and environmental analysis.

## *Mechanical Nanosensors:*

**Cantilever-Based Sensors:** These sensors employ microcantilevers coated with a nanomaterial that responds to the binding of target molecules by changing its mechanical properties. The bending or vibration frequency of the cantilever changes upon analyte binding.

**Mechanism:** The interaction between the target analyte and the nanomaterial-coated cantilever induces a mechanical response, such as deflection or a shift in resonance frequency. These mechanical changes are detected and correlated with the analyte concentration.

**Applications:** Cantilever-based sensors are used for detecting biomarkers, pathogens, and environmental pollutants with high sensitivity and specificity.

**Graphene-Based Sensors:** Graphene, a two-dimensional nanomaterial with exceptional mechanical properties, is used in mechanical nanosensors. The high surface area and sensitivity of graphene enable the detection of minute forces and mass changes.

**Mechanism:** The binding of target molecules to graphene induces changes in its mechanical resonance or electrical conductivity, which are measured to determine the presence and concentration of the analyte.

**Applications:** Graphene-based sensors are employed in detecting DNA, proteins, and chemical vapors, with applications in healthcare, security, and environmental monitoring.

## *Mechanisms of Nanosensors:*

1. **Recognition Elements:**

   - Nanosensors are functionalized with specific recognition elements, such as antibodies, aptamers, or molecular imprinted polymers, that selectively bind to the target analyte. The high affinity and specificity of these recognition elements ensure accurate detection and minimize false positives.

2. **Signal Transduction:**

   - The interaction between the target analyte and the recognition element on the nanomaterial surface induces a measurable change in a physical property, such as optical, electrical, or mechanical signals. These changes are transduced into quantifiable signals that correlate with the analyte concentration.

3. **Amplification and Sensitivity:**

   - Nanosensors leverage the unique properties of nanomaterials, such as high surface area, quantum effects, and enhanced reactivity, to achieve signal amplification and high sensitivity. This allows for the detection of low concentrations of analytes, making nanosensors suitable for early diagnosis and monitoring of diseases.

## 6.1.2 Applications in Biomarker Detection

## *6.1 Quantum Dots*

## *6.1.2 Applications in Biomarker Detection*

Quantum dots (QDs) are semiconductor nanocrystals that exhibit unique optical properties, such as size-tunable light emission, high brightness, and excellent photostability. These properties make QDs particularly suitable for various applications in biomarker detection, enhancing the sensitivity and specificity of diagnostic assays.

**Fluorescence Imaging:** Quantum dots are widely used in fluorescence imaging for the detection of biomarkers. Due to their broad absorption spectra and narrow, size-tunable emission spectra, QDs can be excited by a single light source and emit light at multiple wavelengths. This allows for the simultaneous detection of multiple biomarkers in a single assay, a technique known as multiplexing. For instance, in cancer diagnostics, QDs can be conjugated with antibodies or ligands that specifically bind to cancer-associated biomarkers, enabling the visualization of cancer cells in tissue samples with high sensitivity and specificity.

**Quantum Dot-Linked Immunosorbent Assay (QLISA):** Quantum dots have been integrated into traditional immunoassay formats to improve their performance. The Quantum Dot-Linked Immunosorbent Assay (QLISA) is an adaptation of the enzyme-linked immunosorbent assay (ELISA), where QDs replace conventional enzyme labels. In QLISA, QDs conjugated with antibodies bind to the target biomarker, and the fluorescence intensity of the QDs is measured. This method offers enhanced sensitivity, lower detection limits, and the potential for multiplexing compared to conventional ELISA. QLISA has been successfully employed in detecting various biomarkers, including proteins, nucleic acids, and small molecules.

**FRET-Based Detection:** Fluorescence resonance energy transfer (FRET) is a powerful technique for detecting biomolecular interactions, where energy transfer occurs between two fluorescent molecules in close proximity. Quantum dots serve as excellent FRET donors due to their high quantum yield and broad absorption spectra. In FRET-based detection assays, QDs are paired with suitable acceptor molecules, such as organic dyes or other QDs. When the target biomarker brings the donor and acceptor into close proximity, FRET occurs, resulting in a measurable change in fluorescence. This method is particularly useful for studying protein-protein interactions, nucleic acid hybridization, and other biomolecular events.

**Lateral Flow Assays (LFAs):** Quantum dots have been incorporated into lateral flow assays (LFAs) to enhance their sensitivity and enable quantitative analysis. In QD-based LFAs, QDs are conjugated to antibodies or other binding molecules and applied to the test strip. When the sample containing the target biomarker flows through the strip, it binds to the QD conjugates, and the resulting complex is captured on the test line. The fluorescence of the QDs is then measured using a portable fluorescence reader, providing quantitative results. This approach has been applied to the detection of various infectious diseases, such as COVID-19, where rapid and sensitive diagnostic tests are crucial.

**Nanobiosensors:** Quantum dots are also used in the development of nanobiosensors for real-time biomarker detection. These sensors often involve QDs integrated into microfluidic devices or other platforms, allowing for continuous monitoring of biomarkers in biological samples. For example, QD-based nanosensors have been designed to detect glucose levels in diabetes management, where QDs conjugated with glucose-binding molecules produce a fluorescence signal proportional to glucose concentration. Such sensors offer the advantages of high sensitivity, rapid response, and the potential for miniaturization and portability.

**DNA and RNA Detection:** Quantum dots are employed in the detection of nucleic acids, such as DNA and RNA, by labeling oligonucleotide probes with QDs. These probes can hybridize with complementary target sequences, allowing for the detection of specific genetic markers. QD-labeled probes provide high sensitivity and the ability to perform multiplexed detection of multiple genetic targets simultaneously. This application is particularly valuable in genetic testing, infectious disease diagnostics, and personalized medicine, where precise detection of nucleic acid sequences is essential.

**Point-of-Care Testing (POCT):** The integration of quantum dots into point-of-care testing (POCT) devices has revolutionized diagnostic capabilities in resource-limited settings. QD-based POCT devices offer rapid, sensitive, and user-friendly detection of biomarkers at the patient's bedside or in the field. These devices typically involve simple sample collection, minimal processing steps, and easy-to-interpret results, making them ideal for use in remote or low-resource environments.

Quantum dots offer significant advantages in biomarker detection due to their unique optical properties, enabling high sensitivity, specificity, and the potential for multiplexing. Their applications span fluorescence imaging, QLISA, FRET-based detection, LFAs, nanobiosensors, nucleic acid detection, and POCT. These advanced diagnostic techniques hold promise for improving early detection, monitoring, and personalized treatment of various diseases.

## *6.2 Nanoarrays*

## *6.2.1 Fabrication and Types*

Nanoarrays are structured assemblies of nanomaterials arranged on a substrate in a precise and reproducible manner. They offer high surface area, enhanced sensitivity, and the ability to perform multiplexed analyses, making them invaluable tools in various fields such as diagnostics, environmental monitoring, and materials science.

**Fabrication of Nanoarrays:** The fabrication of nanoarrays involves several key steps, including the preparation of the substrate, patterning of the array, and deposition of nanomaterials. Various techniques are employed to achieve the desired arrangement and properties of the nanoarrays, ensuring precision and functionality.

**Substrate Preparation:** The choice of substrate is crucial for the stability and performance of nanoarrays. Common substrates include silicon wafers, glass slides, and polymer films. These substrates are often treated to enhance their surface properties, such as hydrophilicity or hydrophobicity, to facilitate the deposition and adherence of nanomaterials. Surface treatments can involve chemical modifications, such as silanization, or physical treatments, such as plasma cleaning.

**Patterning Techniques:** The patterning of nanoarrays involves creating specific regions on the substrate where nanomaterials will be deposited. Several advanced techniques are used for patterning, including photolithography, electron beam lithography, and nanoimprint lithography.

- **Photolithography:** Photolithography uses light to transfer a pattern from a photomask to a photosensitive resist on the substrate. The patterned resist serves as a template for subsequent deposition or etching steps.

This technique is widely used due to its high resolution and scalability.

- **Electron Beam Lithography:** Electron beam lithography (EBL) employs a focused beam of electrons to directly write patterns onto an electron-sensitive resist. EBL offers extremely high resolution, allowing for the creation of nanoscale features. However, it is a time-consuming and expensive process, limiting its use to applications requiring ultra-high precision.
- **Nanoimprint Lithography:** Nanoimprint lithography (NIL) involves pressing a patterned mold into a resist-coated substrate to transfer the pattern. This technique is cost-effective and capable of producing high-resolution patterns over large areas, making it suitable for mass production of nanoarrays.

**Deposition of Nanomaterials:** After patterning the substrate, nanomaterials are deposited onto the designated regions. Various deposition techniques are used, depending on the type of nanomaterial and the desired properties of the nanoarray.

- **Chemical Vapor Deposition (CVD):** CVD involves the chemical reaction of gaseous precursors to form a thin film or nanomaterial on the substrate. This technique is suitable for depositing a wide range of nanomaterials, including metals, oxides, and carbon-based materials.
- **Physical Vapor Deposition (PVD):** PVD techniques, such as sputtering and evaporation, involve the physical transfer of material from a source to the substrate. PVD is commonly used for depositing metallic nanomaterials and thin films.
- **Self-Assembly:** Self-assembly techniques leverage the inherent properties of nanomaterials to spontaneously organize into ordered structures on the substrate. This approach is often used for creating nanoarrays of nanoparticles, quantum dots, or block copolymers.

**Types of Nanoarrays:** Nanoarrays can be classified based on the type of nanomaterial used, the patterning technique, or the intended application. Some common types include:

- **Nanoparticle Arrays:** These arrays consist of nanoparticles, such as gold, silver, or magnetic nanoparticles, arranged in a specific pattern. They are used in applications like biosensing, catalysis, and drug delivery.

For example, gold nanoparticle arrays are employed in surface-enhanced Raman scattering (SERS) for sensitive detection of biomolecules.

- **Quantum Dot Arrays:** Quantum dot arrays are composed of semiconductor nanocrystals arranged on a substrate. They are used in applications such as light-emitting devices, photovoltaic cells, and biosensors. Quantum dot arrays offer tunable optical properties, making them suitable for multiplexed fluorescence assays.
- **Carbon Nanotube Arrays:** These arrays consist of vertically or horizontally aligned carbon nanotubes (CNTs). They are used in field emission displays, sensors, and transistors. The high aspect ratio and excellent electrical properties of CNTs make them ideal for these applications.
- **Nanowire Arrays:** Nanowire arrays are composed of metallic or semiconductor nanowires aligned on a substrate. They are used in electronic devices, sensors, and energy storage systems. Nanowire arrays offer high surface area and enhanced electrical conductivity, improving the performance of these devices.

**Fabrication of nanoarrays involves meticulous preparation of the substrate, precise patterning, and controlled deposition of nanomaterials. The various types of nanoarrays, such as nanoparticle arrays, quantum dot arrays, carbon nanotube arrays, and nanowire arrays, find applications across a broad spectrum of fields due to their unique properties and capabilities.**

## 6.3 Lab-on-a-Chip Technologies

## 6.3.1 Integration with Microfluidics

Lab-on-a-chip (LOC) technologies represent a transformative advancement in analytical and diagnostic fields, offering miniaturized platforms that integrate multiple laboratory functions on a single chip. These systems provide rapid, sensitive, and high-throughput analysis with reduced reagent consumption and waste. A critical component of LOC technologies is the integration with microfluidics, which allows for precise control and manipulation of small volumes of fluids within microscale channels and chambers.

**Microfluidics Fundamentals:** Microfluidics involves the study and application of fluid flow in channels with dimensions typically ranging from tens to hundreds of micrometers. The behavior of fluids at this scale is governed by laminar flow, where fluid layers move parallel to each other with minimal mixing, governed by low Reynolds numbers. This predictable flow behavior enables precise control over fluid handling, essential for LOC applications.

**Fabrication of Microfluidic Chips:** The integration of microfluidics with LOC devices begins with the fabrication of microfluidic chips. These chips are commonly made from materials such as polydimethylsiloxane (PDMS), glass, or thermoplastics. Fabrication techniques include soft lithography, photolithography, and injection molding.

- **Soft Lithography:** Soft lithography uses a master mold to create PDMS microfluidic channels. The PDMS is poured over the mold, cured, and then peeled off, leaving a negative replica of the channel design. This method is cost-effective and allows for rapid prototyping.
- **Photolithography:** Photolithography involves the use of light to transfer a pattern from a photomask onto a photosensitive material. This technique is highly precise and suitable for creating complex microfluidic networks on glass or silicon substrates.
- **Injection Molding:** Injection molding is used for mass production of microfluidic devices. Thermoplastic materials are injected into a mold to form the desired microfluidic channels. This method is scalable and suitable for commercial production.

**Integration Techniques:** The integration of microfluidics with LOC technologies requires the seamless incorporation of various components, such as pumps, valves, sensors, and detectors, onto the microfluidic chip. Several techniques are employed to achieve this integration:

- **Microfluidic Valves and Pumps:** Microfluidic valves and pumps control the flow of fluids within the chip. Pneumatic, hydraulic, and electrokinetic valves are commonly used to regulate fluid movement. Pumps, such as peristaltic and electroosmotic pumps, enable precise fluid handling and dispensing.
- **Detection and Sensing:** LOC devices integrate various detection methods, including optical, electrochemical, and fluorescence-based

sensors, to analyze the target analytes. For example, optical sensors can detect changes in light absorption or fluorescence, while electrochemical sensors measure changes in current or voltage due to chemical reactions.

- **Sample Preparation:** Integrated microfluidic systems automate sample preparation steps, such as mixing, dilution, and separation, enhancing the efficiency and reliability of the analysis. Techniques like dielectrophoresis and magnetic separation are used to manipulate and concentrate target biomolecules or cells within the microfluidic channels.

**Applications in Diagnostics:** The integration of microfluidics with LOC technologies has revolutionized diagnostic applications, providing rapid and accurate testing at the point of care.

- **Clinical Diagnostics:** LOC devices are used for the detection of various biomarkers associated with diseases, such as glucose, cholesterol, and infectious agents. For instance, LOC platforms for COVID-19 diagnostics integrate microfluidics with nucleic acid amplification techniques, enabling rapid and sensitive detection of viral RNA.
- **Molecular Diagnostics:** Microfluidic LOC systems facilitate molecular diagnostics by integrating processes like PCR (polymerase chain reaction) and qPCR (quantitative PCR) on a single chip. These devices allow for the rapid amplification and detection of genetic material, aiding in the diagnosis of genetic disorders and infectious diseases.
- **Immunoassays:** LOC platforms incorporate microfluidic channels with antibody-coated surfaces to perform immunoassays. These assays detect the presence of specific proteins or antigens, providing valuable information for disease diagnosis and monitoring. The integration of microfluidics enhances the sensitivity and speed of immunoassays.
- **Cell Analysis:** Microfluidic LOC devices are used for single-cell analysis, enabling the study of individual cell behavior and characteristics. Techniques like flow cytometry and cell sorting are integrated into microfluidic platforms, allowing for high-throughput and precise cell analysis.

**Environmental Monitoring:** The integration of microfluidics with LOC technologies extends beyond clinical diagnostics to environmental monitoring. LOC devices are used for the detection of contaminants, pathogens, and pollutants in water, air, and soil samples. These devices offer rapid, on-site analysis, crucial for environmental protection and public health.

- **Water Quality Testing:** Microfluidic LOC platforms are employed for real-time monitoring of water quality, detecting contaminants like heavy metals, pesticides, and microbial pathogens. The portability and speed of these devices enable prompt response to potential environmental hazards.
- **Air Quality Monitoring:** LOC devices integrated with microfluidics are used to detect airborne pollutants, such as particulate matter and volatile organic compounds (VOCs). These devices provide continuous monitoring of air quality, aiding in the assessment and management of air pollution.

**Research and Development:** The integration of microfluidics with LOC technologies accelerates research and development in various scientific fields.

- **Drug Discovery:** LOC platforms are used in drug discovery for high-throughput screening of potential drug candidates. Microfluidic systems enable precise control over reaction conditions and facilitate the parallel testing of multiple compounds, improving the efficiency of the drug discovery process.
- **Synthetic Biology:** Microfluidic LOC devices are used in synthetic biology to manipulate and analyze biological systems at the microscale. These devices facilitate the assembly of genetic circuits, the screening of engineered organisms, and the study of cellular processes.

The integration of microfluidics with lab-on-a-chip technologies represents a significant advancement in analytical and diagnostic capabilities. By enabling precise control and manipulation of fluids at the microscale, microfluidic LOC devices offer rapid, sensitive, and high-throughput analysis for various applications in diagnostics, environmental monitoring, and research.

## 6.4 Quantum Dots in Diagnostics

## 6.4.1 Optical Properties

Quantum dots (QDs) are semiconductor nanocrystals that exhibit unique optical properties due to quantum confinement effects, making them highly valuable in diagnostic applications. These properties include size-tunable emission wavelengths, high brightness, and excellent photostability, which enable their use in various bioimaging and biosensing technologies.

**Size-Tunable Emission Wavelengths:** One of the most distinctive optical properties of quantum dots is their size-tunable emission wavelengths. Quantum dots can be engineered to emit light at specific wavelengths by adjusting their size during synthesis. Smaller quantum dots emit light at shorter wavelengths (blue region), while larger quantum dots emit light at longer wavelengths (red region). This tunability allows for the creation of quantum dots with a wide range of emission colors, which can be precisely selected for specific diagnostic applications.

For instance, in a study involving cadmium selenide (CdSe) quantum dots, researchers demonstrated that altering the size of the quantum dots from 2 nm to 6 nm shifted the emission wavelength from approximately 450 nm (blue) to 650 nm (red). This property is particularly advantageous for multiplexed imaging, where multiple targets can be labeled with quantum dots of different sizes, each emitting at a distinct wavelength, allowing simultaneous detection and analysis.

**High Brightness and Quantum Yield:** Quantum dots exhibit high brightness due to their large molar extinction coefficients and high quantum yields. The molar extinction coefficient of quantum dots can be several orders of magnitude higher than that of traditional organic fluorophores, resulting in significantly brighter fluorescence. Additionally, the quantum yield, which is the ratio of emitted photons to absorbed photons, can be as high as 90% in well-synthesized quantum dots.

For example, core-shell quantum dots, such as CdSe/ZnS, are designed with a CdSe core to provide high brightness and a ZnS shell to passivate the surface and enhance quantum yield. These core-shell structures not only improve brightness but also protect the core from environmental degradation, further enhancing their stability and performance in diagnostic applications.

**Excellent Photostability:** Quantum dots are known for their excellent photostability compared to traditional organic dyes. Photostability refers to the resistance of fluorescent materials to photobleaching, which is the loss of fluorescence intensity upon prolonged exposure to light. Quantum dots can withstand intense and prolonged illumination without significant loss of fluorescence, making them ideal for long-term imaging and repeated excitation cycles.

In practical applications, this means that quantum dots can be used in diagnostic assays that require continuous monitoring or extended observation periods. For example, in live-cell imaging, quantum dots can be excited multiple times without significant photobleaching, allowing for real-time tracking of cellular processes over extended periods.

**Narrow Emission Spectra and Broad Absorption Spectra:** Quantum dots have narrow emission spectra with full-width at half-maximum (FWHM) values typically ranging from 20 to 40 nm. This narrow emission allows for precise spectral separation and minimizes overlap between the emission signals of different quantum dots, which is crucial for multiplexed diagnostics.

At the same time, quantum dots exhibit broad absorption spectra, meaning they can absorb light over a wide range of wavelengths. This broad absorption, combined with their narrow emission, enables the simultaneous excitation of multiple quantum dots using a single light source, simplifying the optical setup and reducing potential interference in multiplexed assays.

**Stokes Shift:** The Stokes shift, which is the difference between the peak absorption and emission wavelengths, is typically large in quantum dots. This large Stokes shift reduces the overlap between excitation and emission spectra, minimizing background fluorescence and enhancing the signal-to-noise ratio in diagnostic assays.

For example, quantum dots with a large Stokes shift can be excited at wavelengths far from their emission peak, reducing the interference from scattered excitation light and improving the clarity of the fluorescence signal. This property is particularly beneficial in applications such as flow cytometry and fluorescence resonance energy transfer (FRET)-based assays, where high sensitivity and low background are essential.

**Surface Functionalization and Bioconjugation:** The optical properties of quantum dots can be further enhanced and tailored for specific diagnostic applications through surface functionalization and bioconjugation. Quantum dots can be coated with various ligands, such as peptides, antibodies, or nucleic acids, to target specific biomolecules or cells. This functionalization not only improves their biocompatibility but also enables specific binding and detection in complex biological environments.

For instance, quantum dots functionalized with streptavidin can bind to biotinylated antibodies, enabling the specific labeling and detection of target proteins in immunoassays. Similarly, quantum dots conjugated with oligonucleotides can be used in nucleic acid detection assays, offering high sensitivity and specificity.

The unique optical properties of quantum dots, including size-tunable emission wavelengths, high brightness, excellent photostability, narrow emission spectra, broad absorption spectra, large Stokes shift, and the ability for surface functionalization, make them highly advantageous for a wide range of diagnostic applications. These properties enable precise, sensitive, and multiplexed detection of biological targets, contributing to advancements in bioimaging, biosensing, and molecular diagnostics.

## 6.4.2 Multiplexed Imaging

Multiplexed imaging is a powerful technique that allows for the simultaneous detection and analysis of multiple targets within a single sample. Quantum dots (QDs) are ideally suited for multiplexed imaging due to their unique optical properties, including size-tunable emission wavelengths, high brightness, and excellent photostability. These properties enable the precise discrimination of multiple signals, leading to enhanced diagnostic capabilities.

**Principles of Multiplexed Imaging with Quantum Dots:** The fundamental principle of multiplexed imaging involves labeling different targets with quantum dots of distinct emission wavelengths. Quantum dots can be synthesized in various sizes, each corresponding to a specific emission color. This size-dependent emission is a result of quantum confinement effects, where the energy bandgap of the quantum dots changes with size, leading to different fluorescence wavelengths. For instance, smaller quantum dots emit light in the blue region of the spectrum, while larger quantum dots emit in the red region. This tunability allows for the creation of a palette of quantum dots, each emitting at a different wavelength, which can be used to label different biological targets.

**High Brightness and Photostability:** Quantum dots exhibit high brightness due to their large molar extinction coefficients and high quantum yields, often exceeding 90%. This high brightness ensures strong fluorescence signals, which are crucial for detecting low-abundance targets.

Additionally, quantum dots possess exceptional photostability, resisting photobleaching even under prolonged illumination. This stability is essential for long-term imaging studies, as it allows for continuous observation without significant loss of signal intensity.

**Narrow Emission Spectra and Broad Absorption Spectra:** The narrow emission spectra of quantum dots, typically with full-width at half-maximum (FWHM) values of 20-40 nm, enable clear separation of fluorescence signals from different quantum dots. This spectral purity is critical for multiplexed imaging, as it reduces spectral overlap and enhances the resolution of individual signals. Moreover, the broad absorption spectra of quantum dots allow for their simultaneous excitation using a single light source, simplifying the optical setup and minimizing cross-excitation issues.

**Applications in Biological Imaging:** Quantum dots are extensively used in various biological imaging applications, providing multiplexed imaging capabilities for cells, tissues, and whole organisms. In cell biology, quantum dots can be conjugated with specific antibodies or ligands to label different cellular components, such as proteins, nucleic acids, and organelles. For example, in a study investigating cellular signaling pathways, quantum dots of different colors were conjugated with antibodies targeting distinct signaling proteins. This approach enabled the simultaneous visualization and quantification of multiple proteins within the same cell, providing insights into their spatial and temporal dynamics.

**Flow Cytometry:** Flow cytometry is another area where quantum dots are utilized for multiplexed imaging. In flow cytometry, cells are labeled with quantum dots conjugated to specific antibodies, allowing for the simultaneous detection of multiple surface markers. The narrow emission spectra and high brightness of quantum dots enable the resolution of up to ten different colors, significantly enhancing the multiplexing capability compared to traditional fluorophores. For instance, in immunophenotyping of immune cells, quantum dots of different colors can be used to label various cell surface markers, facilitating the identification and analysis of distinct cell populations.

**In Vivo Imaging:** In vivo imaging applications also benefit from the unique properties of quantum dots. Quantum dots can be used for multiplexed imaging of different tissues and organs in living organisms. For example, in a study on tumor targeting, quantum dots conjugated with tumor-specific ligands were injected into mice. The distinct emission wavelengths of the quantum dots allowed for the simultaneous imaging of multiple tumor sites, providing valuable information on tumor distribution and metastasis.

**Challenges and Solutions:** Despite their advantages, the use of quantum dots in multiplexed imaging faces certain challenges. One challenge is the potential toxicity of quantum dots, especially those containing heavy metals like cadmium. To address this issue, researchers are developing biocompatible coatings and using alternative materials, such as silicon and carbon-based quantum dots, which exhibit lower toxicity profiles.

Another challenge is the potential for non-specific binding and background fluorescence. To minimize these issues, surface modifications are employed to enhance the specificity and biocompatibility of quantum dots. For instance, polyethylene glycol (PEG) coatings can be used to reduce non-specific interactions and improve circulation time in vivo.

**Future Directions:** The future of multiplexed imaging with quantum dots holds great promise, with ongoing advancements in quantum dot synthesis, surface functionalization, and imaging technologies. The development of new quantum dot materials with improved biocompatibility and reduced toxicity will further expand their applications in clinical diagnostics and biomedical research. Additionally, the integration of quantum dots with advanced imaging modalities, such as super-resolution microscopy and single-molecule imaging, will provide unprecedented insights into complex biological systems.

# CHAPTER SEVEN

# APPLICATIONS IN IMAGING AND TARGETING

## 7.1 Nanoparticles in Imaging

### 7.1.1 Gold Nanoparticles

Gold nanoparticles (AuNPs) have emerged as highly versatile agents in imaging applications due to their unique optical and electronic properties. These nanoparticles exhibit strong surface plasmon resonance (SPR), which results in enhanced light absorption and scattering. This property is particularly beneficial for imaging applications, enabling the detection and visualization of biological structures and processes with high sensitivity and resolution.

**Surface Plasmon Resonance (SPR):** The surface plasmon resonance of gold nanoparticles occurs when incident light induces collective oscillations of electrons at the nanoparticle surface. This resonance leads to a pronounced peak in the absorption spectrum, which is dependent on the size, shape, and aggregation state of the nanoparticles. For example, spherical gold nanoparticles typically exhibit an SPR peak around 520 nm, while anisotropic shapes, such as nanorods, show two SPR peaks due to their longitudinal and transverse modes. This tunability allows for the optimization of gold nanoparticles for specific imaging applications by adjusting their physical characteristics.

**Enhanced Optical Properties:** The SPR effect of gold nanoparticles not only enhances light absorption but also significantly increases scattering efficiency. This makes AuNPs excellent contrast agents for various optical imaging techniques, including dark-field microscopy and optical coherence tomography (OCT). In dark-field microscopy, gold nanoparticles scatter light efficiently, providing bright, high-contrast images of labeled structures against a dark background. For instance, in cellular imaging, gold nanoparticles conjugated with antibodies can specifically bind to target molecules, allowing for the precise localization and visualization of cellular components.

**Photoacoustic Imaging:** Gold nanoparticles are also utilized in photoacoustic imaging, a hybrid technique that combines optical and ultrasound imaging. In this method, the absorption of pulsed laser light by gold nanoparticles generates localized heat, causing thermal expansion and the subsequent emission of ultrasonic waves. These waves are detected and used to construct high-resolution images of the nanoparticle distribution within tissues. The strong absorption of gold nanoparticles at specific wavelengths enhances the photoacoustic signal, making them ideal for deep tissue imaging and the detection of tumors, blood vessels, and other structures.

**Multiplexed Imaging:** The tunable optical properties of gold nanoparticles facilitate their use in multiplexed imaging, where multiple targets can be detected simultaneously using nanoparticles with different SPR peaks. By functionalizing gold nanoparticles with different targeting ligands, such as antibodies or peptides, and selecting nanoparticles with distinct SPR peaks, researchers can achieve simultaneous imaging of multiple biomarkers within a single sample. For example, gold nanorods and gold nanospheres with different SPR peaks can be used to label and visualize different cell surface receptors in cancer diagnostics.

**Raman Imaging:** Gold nanoparticles also play a crucial role in surface-enhanced Raman scattering (SERS) imaging. SERS is a powerful technique that provides molecular-level information with high sensitivity. Gold nanoparticles, when used as SERS substrates, significantly enhance the Raman signals of molecules adsorbed on their surface due to the electromagnetic field enhancement at the nanoparticle surface. This enhancement allows for the detection of low-abundance molecules and provides detailed molecular fingerprints. In biomedical imaging, SERS-active gold nanoparticles conjugated with specific probes can be used to detect and image biomolecules, pathogens, and cellular components with high specificity and sensitivity.

**Clinical Applications and In Vivo Imaging:** Gold nanoparticles have shown great promise in clinical imaging applications, particularly in cancer diagnostics. Due to their biocompatibility and ease of functionalization, gold nanoparticles can be engineered to target specific cancer cells. For example, gold nanoparticles conjugated with tumor-specific antibodies can selectively bind to cancer cells, allowing for their detection and imaging using techniques such as computed tomography (CT), magnetic resonance imaging (MRI), and positron emission tomography (PET). In a study on breast cancer, gold nanoparticles functionalized with anti-HER2 antibodies demonstrated high specificity for HER2-positive cancer cells, enabling their detection and imaging in vivo.

**Challenges and Future Directions:** Despite their advantages, the clinical translation of gold nanoparticles faces challenges, including potential toxicity, biodistribution, and clearance from the body. Ongoing research is focused on improving the biocompatibility and safety of gold nanoparticles through surface modifications and the development of biodegradable coatings. Additionally, the combination of gold nanoparticles with other imaging modalities and therapeutic agents holds promise for the development of multifunctional theranostic platforms, integrating diagnosis and treatment in a single system.

## 7.1.3 Quantum Dots

Quantum dots (QDs) are nanoscale semiconductor particles that have unique optical and electronic properties, making them highly suitable for various imaging applications. These properties arise from the quantum confinement effect, which occurs when the size of the semiconductor particle is smaller than the exciton Bohr radius. This results in discrete energy levels and size-dependent emission wavelengths, giving quantum dots their distinct characteristics.

**Optical Properties of Quantum Dots:** The most notable optical property of quantum dots is their size-tunable emission. Quantum dots can emit light in a broad spectrum of colors, from ultraviolet to infrared, simply by changing their size. Smaller quantum dots emit blue light, while larger ones emit red light. This tunability allows for the creation of quantum dots with specific emission wavelengths tailored to different imaging needs. Additionally, quantum dots exhibit narrow and symmetric emission spectra, which is crucial for multiplexed imaging applications where multiple signals need to be distinguished clearly.

**High Brightness and Photostability:** Quantum dots have high quantum yields, often exceeding 90%, meaning they can efficiently convert absorbed light into emitted light. This high brightness makes them excellent fluorescent markers for imaging. Moreover, quantum dots are highly photostable, meaning they do not photobleach easily, even under prolonged illumination. This stability is particularly advantageous for long-term imaging studies, such as tracking the movement of molecules or cells over time.

**Surface Functionalization:** Quantum dots can be functionalized with a variety of biomolecules, such as antibodies, peptides, and nucleic acids, enabling their specific targeting to biological structures. This functionalization is typically achieved through surface modification techniques, which involve attaching these biomolecules to the quantum dot surface via covalent or non-covalent interactions. For example, quantum dots conjugated with antibodies can specifically bind to antigens on the surface of cancer cells, allowing for targeted imaging and diagnosis.

**Multiplexed Imaging:** Due to their narrow emission spectra and size-tunable properties, quantum dots are ideal for multiplexed imaging, where multiple biological targets are simultaneously imaged. In multiplexed imaging, different quantum dots with distinct emission wavelengths are used to label different targets. For instance, in a study involving the simultaneous imaging of multiple cellular proteins, quantum dots of various sizes were conjugated with antibodies specific to each protein. This approach allowed for the visualization of multiple proteins within a single cell, providing comprehensive insights into cellular functions and interactions.

**In Vivo Imaging:** Quantum dots have shown great potential for in vivo imaging applications due to their high brightness, photostability, and ability to be functionalized with targeting ligands. In in vivo studies, quantum dots are used to track the distribution and movement of cells, tissues, and organs. For example, quantum dots conjugated with tumor-specific ligands have been used to image and track the growth of tumors in animal models. Their strong and stable fluorescence signals enable the detection of tumors even at early stages, facilitating early diagnosis and treatment.

**Challenges and Solutions:** Despite their advantages, the use of quantum dots in biological imaging faces several challenges. One major challenge is their potential toxicity, particularly for quantum dots containing heavy metals like cadmium. To mitigate this issue, researchers are developing non-toxic alternatives, such as carbon-based quantum dots and silicon quantum dots. Additionally, surface coatings with biocompatible materials, such as polyethylene glycol (PEG), are employed to reduce toxicity and improve biocompatibility.

Another challenge is the potential for non-specific binding and background fluorescence. To address this, surface modifications are used to enhance the specificity of quantum dots for their target molecules. For instance, coating quantum dots with specific peptides or antibodies can improve their targeting accuracy, while minimizing non-specific interactions.

**Future Directions:** The future of quantum dots in imaging is promising, with ongoing research focused on improving their biocompatibility, targeting efficiency, and imaging capabilities. Advances in quantum dot synthesis and surface functionalization are expected to lead to new applications in both research and clinical settings. For example, the development of multifunctional quantum dots that combine imaging and therapeutic functions (theranostics) holds potential for integrated diagnosis and treatment of diseases.

## 7.2 Targeted Imaging Techniques

### 7.2.1 Ligand-Functionalized Nanoparticles

Ligand-functionalized nanoparticles represent a sophisticated approach in targeted imaging, designed to enhance the specificity and efficacy of diagnostic techniques. These nanoparticles are engineered by attaching one or more types of ligands to their surface, which can specifically bind to targeted molecules or receptors associated with particular diseases, most notably cancer. This targeted binding increases the accumulation of imaging agents at specific sites within the body, thereby enhancing the contrast and resolution of the images obtained.

**Types of Ligands and Their Functions:**

1. **Antibodies and Antibody Fragments:** These are among the most commonly used ligands for functionalizing nanoparticles due to their high specificity towards antigens. Antibody-functionalized nanoparticles can target specific cells or proteins, making them highly effective in identifying and imaging cancer cells or other pathogenic entities.

2. **Peptides:** Short chains of amino acids can be used as targeting ligands due to their ease of synthesis and modification. Peptides can mimic the recognition sequences of proteins, targeting specific receptors or cellular components with high affinity and selectivity.

3. **Aptamers:** These are short strands of DNA or RNA that can fold into unique three-dimensional structures capable of selectively binding to specific targets, including proteins and small molecules. Aptamers are highly stable, easy to synthesize, and can be engineered to have high specificity and affinity for their targets.

4. **Small Molecules:** These include vitamins, hormones, and other organic compounds that can target specific enzymes, receptors, or other cellular structures. For example, folic acid is a commonly used ligand for targeting cancer cells that overexpress the folate receptor.

**Fabrication and Functionalization:**

- **Synthesis of Nanoparticles:** The core of the nanoparticles can be made from a variety of materials, including metals (like gold and silver), semiconductors (quantum dots), or polymers. The choice of material depends on the desired imaging modality and the biological application.

- **Surface Modification:** Once synthesized, the nanoparticles are modified to enable ligand attachment. This often involves coating the surface with a biocompatible layer, such as polyethylene glycol (PEG), which provides stability in biological environments and functional groups for ligand conjugation.

- **Ligand Attachment:** Ligands are typically attached to the nanoparticle surface through covalent bonds or adsorption. Covalent attachment provides a strong, stable linkage and is achieved through chemical reactions between functional groups on the ligand and the nanoparticle surface. Adsorption, though less stable, can be utilized for rapid and simple ligand attachment.

**Imaging Modalities:**

- **MRI (Magnetic Resonance Imaging):** Iron oxide nanoparticles functionalized with ligands are used to enhance the contrast in MRI scans. These nanoparticles accumulate at the target site, improving the magnetic response and enhancing the visibility of tumors or other pathological tissues.

- **PET (Positron Emission Tomography) and SPECT (Single Photon Emission Computed Tomography):** Radioactive isotopes can be attached to ligand-functionalized nanoparticles for use in PET and SPECT imaging. These nanoparticles deliver the radioactive tracer to specific biological targets, allowing for detailed imaging of metabolic processes and molecular interactions.
- **Optical Imaging:** Quantum dots and gold nanoparticles are used in optical imaging. These nanoparticles can be functionalized with ligands to target specific cellular components, providing bright and stable signals that are useful for both in vitro and in vivo imaging applications.

**Applications in Disease Diagnosis and Research:**

- **Cancer Detection:** Ligand-functionalized nanoparticles can specifically target tumor cells or the tumor microenvironment, providing detailed images that help in the diagnosis, staging, and monitoring of cancer treatment.
- **Inflammatory Diseases:** Nanoparticles targeting markers of inflammation can be used to image inflammatory diseases, providing insights into disease progression and response to therapy.
- **Cardiovascular Diseases:** Targeted nanoparticles can be used to image plaques in blood vessels, helping to assess the risk of heart attacks or strokes.

Ligand-functionalized nanoparticles enhance the specificity and effectiveness of imaging techniques, making them invaluable tools in the diagnosis and study of diseases. Their ability to target specific molecular markers allows for precise imaging, leading to better diagnosis, improved treatment monitoring, and enhanced understanding of various biological processes.

## 7.2.2 Enhanced Permeability and Retention Effect

The Enhanced Permeability and Retention (EPR) effect is a fundamental concept in targeted imaging and drug delivery, particularly in the context of cancer treatment. The EPR effect exploits the unique pathophysiological characteristics of tumor tissues, which allow nanoparticles and macromolecular drugs to preferentially accumulate in tumor sites. Understanding the mechanisms behind the EPR effect is crucial for the development of effective nanoparticle-based imaging and therapeutic strategies.

**Pathophysiology of the EPR Effect:**

**Tumor Vasculature Characteristics:** Tumors require a blood supply to grow, leading to the formation of new blood vessels through a process called angiogenesis. However, the vasculature in tumors is typically abnormal, characterized by an irregular structure, large gaps between endothelial cells, and a lack of smooth muscle coverage. These abnormalities result in increased permeability of the blood vessels within the tumor, allowing nanoparticles to pass through the vessel walls more easily compared to normal tissues.

**Reduced Lymphatic Drainage:** Tumor tissues often have impaired lymphatic drainage. This dysfunction in the lymphatic system means that once nanoparticles enter the tumor interstitium, they are less likely to be removed efficiently. As a result, nanoparticles tend to accumulate and remain in the tumor site for extended periods, enhancing the retention aspect of the EPR effect.

**Mechanism of the EPR Effect in Nanoparticles:**

1. **Increased Permeability:** The leaky vasculature in tumors allows nanoparticles to extravasate from the blood vessels into the tumor interstitium. The size of the gaps between endothelial cells in tumor blood vessels is often between 100 and 800 nanometers, which is large enough for nanoparticles to pass through but small enough to retain larger macromolecules and complexes.

2. **Enhanced Retention:** Due to the poor lymphatic drainage in tumors, nanoparticles that enter the tumor interstitium are retained for longer periods. This prolonged retention improves the concentration of nanoparticles in the tumor site, which is beneficial for both imaging and therapeutic purposes.


## *Applications in Targeted Imaging:*

**Nanoparticle Design for EPR Effect:**

- **Size Optimization:** The size of nanoparticles is critical for maximizing the EPR effect. Typically, nanoparticles ranging from 10 to 200 nanometers in diameter are most effective. Smaller nanoparticles may be cleared rapidly by the kidneys, while larger ones may not penetrate the tumor vasculature efficiently.
- **Surface Modification:** Surface properties of nanoparticles, such as charge and hydrophilicity, influence their circulation time and ability to exploit the EPR effect. Polyethylene glycol (PEG) is commonly used to coat nanoparticles, providing a hydrophilic layer that reduces recognition and clearance by the immune system, thereby prolonging circulation time.

**Imaging Techniques Leveraging EPR:**

- **MRI (Magnetic Resonance Imaging):** Iron oxide nanoparticles and other contrast agents are designed to accumulate in tumor tissues through the EPR effect, enhancing the contrast of MRI images and allowing for more precise tumor localization and characterization.
- **CT (Computed Tomography):** Gold nanoparticles are often used as contrast agents in CT imaging. Their high atomic number provides strong contrast, and their ability to exploit the EPR effect enables clear visualization of tumor sites.
- **Optical Imaging:** Quantum dots and other fluorescent nanoparticles are designed to accumulate in tumors via the EPR effect, providing bright and specific signals for optical imaging techniques. This is particularly useful in preclinical research for tracking tumor growth and response to treatment.

## *Challenges and Enhancements:*

**Heterogeneity in EPR Effect:** One of the significant challenges in utilizing the EPR effect is the heterogeneity of tumor vasculature. Not all tumors exhibit the EPR effect to the same extent, and within a single tumor, the distribution of nanoparticles can be uneven. Researchers are exploring strategies to enhance the EPR effect, such as using vascular normalization agents, applying external stimuli (e.g., heat or ultrasound), and developing smarter nanoparticles that respond to the tumor microenvironment.

**Improving Specificity and Retention:** While the EPR effect enhances passive targeting, active targeting through ligand-functionalization can further improve specificity. By attaching targeting ligands (e.g., antibodies, peptides) to the surface of nanoparticles, it is possible to achieve a dual-targeting approach that leverages both passive and active mechanisms.

The Enhanced Permeability and Retention effect is a pivotal mechanism in the field of targeted imaging and drug delivery. By exploiting the unique characteristics of tumor vasculature and lymphatic drainage, nanoparticles can accumulate preferentially in tumor tissues, enhancing the effectiveness of imaging and therapeutic interventions. Ongoing research aims to overcome the challenges associated with the EPR effect and optimize nanoparticle design for improved clinical outcomes.

## 7.3 Therapeutic Targeting

## 7.3.1 Cellular Uptake Mechanisms

The successful application of nanoparticles in therapeutic targeting heavily relies on their efficient uptake by target cells. Understanding the various cellular uptake mechanisms is crucial for designing nanoparticles that can effectively deliver therapeutic agents to specific cells or tissues. These mechanisms are complex and depend on multiple factors, including the size, shape, surface charge, and functionalization of the nanoparticles. Here, we explore the primary cellular uptake mechanisms that facilitate the entry of nanoparticles into cells.

### Endocytosis:

Endocytosis is the predominant mechanism by which cells internalize nanoparticles. It involves the engulfing of nanoparticles by the cell membrane to form vesicles that are transported into the cell. Endocytosis can be classified into several subtypes based on the size of the vesicles and the involvement of specific cellular components:

- **Phagocytosis:** This is a form of endocytosis typically associated with the uptake of large particles (>500 nm) by specialized cells such as macrophages, neutrophils, and dendritic cells. During phagocytosis, the cell membrane extends around the nanoparticle, eventually engulfing it to form a phagosome. This process is critical for the immune system's ability to clear pathogens and debris but can also be exploited for the delivery of therapeutic nanoparticles.

- **Macropinocytosis:** In macropinocytosis, the cell membrane forms large, ruffle-like projections that engulf extracellular fluid and nanoparticles, resulting in the formation of large vesicles called macropinosomes. This pathway is non-specific and can internalize a variety of nanoparticles, typically ranging from 200 nm to 5 μm in size. Macropinocytosis is often upregulated in cancer cells, providing a potential target for therapeutic nanoparticle delivery.

- **Clathrin-Mediated Endocytosis:** This is a highly specific and well-characterized endocytic pathway where nanoparticles are internalized through clathrin-coated pits on the cell membrane. These pits invaginate and pinch off to form clathrin-coated vesicles, which then transport the nanoparticles into the cell. Clathrin-mediated endocytosis is generally involved in the uptake of smaller nanoparticles (10-200 nm) and is regulated by receptor-ligand interactions, making it a precise mechanism for targeting specific cell types.

- **Caveolae-Mediated Endocytosis:** This pathway involves flask-shaped invaginations on the cell membrane known as caveolae, which are rich in cholesterol and sphingolipids. Caveolae-mediated endocytosis is less common than clathrin-mediated endocytosis but is crucial for the uptake of certain nanoparticles. This pathway is often associated with the transport of nanoparticles to specific cellular compartments, such as the endoplasmic reticulum and Golgi apparatus.

## *Direct Penetration:*

In addition to endocytosis, some nanoparticles can penetrate the cell membrane directly, particularly when they are small enough or have specific surface modifications. Direct penetration does not involve vesicle formation and can occur through different mechanisms:

- **Passive Diffusion:** This mechanism is primarily relevant for very small nanoparticles (<10 nm) or those with amphiphilic properties. These nanoparticles can diffuse through the lipid bilayer of the cell membrane without the need for energy-dependent processes.

- **Membrane Fusion:** Certain nanoparticles are designed to fuse directly with the cell membrane, allowing their contents to be delivered into the cytoplasm. This is often facilitated by surface modifications that mimic viral fusion proteins or by using fusogenic lipids.
- **Transient Nanopores:** Some nanoparticles can induce the formation of temporary pores in the cell membrane, through which they can pass. This process often involves localized disruption of the membrane integrity and is typically observed with nanoparticles that possess high surface energy or specific chemical functionalities.

## *Factors Influencing Cellular Uptake:*

- **Size and Shape:** The size and shape of nanoparticles significantly influence their cellular uptake. Smaller nanoparticles are generally internalized more efficiently through endocytosis, while larger particles may be taken up through phagocytosis or macropinocytosis. Spherical nanoparticles are typically internalized more readily than rod-shaped or irregularly shaped particles.
- **Surface Charge:** The surface charge of nanoparticles affects their interaction with the negatively charged cell membrane. Positively charged nanoparticles are often internalized more efficiently due to electrostatic interactions with the cell membrane, but excessively high positive charges can lead to cytotoxicity.
- **Surface Functionalization:** Functionalizing the surface of nanoparticles with specific ligands (e.g., antibodies, peptides, or aptamers) enhances their targeting capability and uptake by specific cells through receptor-mediated endocytosis. The presence of PEG or other hydrophilic coatings can improve nanoparticle stability and circulation time in the bloodstream, further influencing uptake.
- **Environmental Factors:** The local environment, including pH, temperature, and the presence of specific ions or proteins, can modulate the uptake of nanoparticles. For instance, the acidic microenvironment of tumors can enhance the uptake of certain pH-sensitive nanoparticles.

Understanding these cellular uptake mechanisms and the factors influencing them is essential for the rational design of nanoparticles for therapeutic targeting. By optimizing nanoparticle properties and leveraging specific uptake pathways, it is possible to enhance the delivery and efficacy of therapeutic agents, thereby improving clinical outcomes in various diseases, including cancer and other pathological conditions.

## 7.4 Theranostics

### 7.4.1 Combination of Therapeutic and Diagnostic Functions

Theranostics represents a paradigm shift in the fields of nanomedicine and personalized medicine by combining therapeutic and diagnostic functions into a single platform. This dual functionality aims to improve disease management by enabling simultaneous diagnosis, treatment, and monitoring of therapeutic efficacy. The integration of these capabilities within a single nanoparticle system offers numerous advantages, including targeted delivery, real-time tracking of therapeutic response, and reduced side effects.

### *Principles of Theranostics:*

**Multifunctional Nanoparticles:** Theranostic platforms typically utilize multifunctional nanoparticles engineered to carry both therapeutic agents and imaging moieties. These nanoparticles are designed to target specific tissues or cells, allowing for precise delivery of therapeutics while providing diagnostic information through imaging techniques such as MRI, CT, PET, or fluorescence imaging. The choice of materials and functionalization strategies for these nanoparticles is critical to ensure their effectiveness in both roles.

**Targeted Delivery and Specificity:** One of the primary advantages of theranostic nanoparticles is their ability to target diseased cells specifically. This targeting is often achieved through surface modification with ligands such as antibodies, peptides, or small molecules that bind to receptors overexpressed on the surface of target cells. This specificity not only enhances the therapeutic efficacy by concentrating the drug at the disease site but also minimizes off-target effects, thereby reducing systemic toxicity.

**Diagnostic Imaging:** Theranostic nanoparticles are equipped with imaging agents that enable real-time visualization of the nanoparticles' distribution and accumulation in the body. Imaging modalities commonly used in theranostics include:

- **Magnetic Resonance Imaging (MRI):** Iron oxide nanoparticles or gadolinium-based agents are frequently used for MRI. These agents provide excellent contrast and allow for the detailed imaging of tissues, aiding in the diagnosis and monitoring of diseases.
- **Computed Tomography (CT):** Gold nanoparticles are often used in CT imaging due to their high atomic number, which provides strong contrast. This enables the clear visualization of nanoparticle distribution and accumulation.
- **Positron Emission Tomography (PET):** Radioactive isotopes can be attached to nanoparticles, allowing for PET imaging. This technique provides highly sensitive and quantitative imaging, useful for tracking the biodistribution of theranostic nanoparticles.
- **Fluorescence Imaging:** Quantum dots and other fluorescent nanoparticles can be used for optical imaging. This modality is particularly useful for preclinical studies and intraoperative imaging.

**Therapeutic Modalities:** Theranostic nanoparticles can deliver a wide range of therapeutic agents, including chemotherapeutics, gene therapies, and photothermal agents. The therapeutic component of theranostic platforms is designed to be released in a controlled manner, either through passive diffusion or in response to specific stimuli such as pH, temperature, or light. This controlled release ensures that the therapeutic agent is delivered precisely where and when it is needed.

**Mechanisms of Theranostic Action:**

**Controlled Drug Release:** The design of theranostic nanoparticles often incorporates mechanisms for controlled drug release. This can be achieved through various strategies, such as the use of stimuli-responsive materials that release the drug in response to environmental changes (e.g., pH-sensitive materials that release the drug in the acidic tumor microenvironment).

**Real-Time Monitoring:** The diagnostic component of theranostic nanoparticles allows for real-time monitoring of the therapeutic response. This capability enables clinicians to track the distribution and accumulation of nanoparticles, assess the effectiveness of the treatment, and make informed decisions about adjusting the therapeutic regimen.

**Combination Therapies:** Theranostic platforms can be designed to deliver multiple therapeutic agents simultaneously, providing a combination therapy approach. For example, nanoparticles can be loaded with both a chemotherapeutic drug and a gene-silencing agent, allowing for synergistic effects that enhance the overall therapeutic outcome.

## *Clinical Applications of Theranostics:*

**Cancer Treatment:** Theranostics has shown significant promise in oncology, where it can be used to diagnose tumors, deliver targeted therapy, and monitor treatment response. By integrating imaging and therapy, theranostic nanoparticles can help to identify the precise location of tumors, deliver drugs directly to cancer cells, and monitor the reduction in tumor size or changes in tumor biology.

**Cardiovascular Diseases:** In cardiology, theranostic nanoparticles can be used to diagnose and treat conditions such as atherosclerosis. For instance, nanoparticles can be engineered to target plaques within arteries, providing both diagnostic imaging and localized drug delivery to reduce plaque formation or inflammation.

**Infectious Diseases:** Theranostic platforms can be utilized to diagnose and treat infectious diseases by targeting specific pathogens or infected cells. This approach can enhance the accuracy of diagnosis and improve the effectiveness of antimicrobial therapies.

**Neurological Disorders:** Theranostics can also be applied to neurological disorders, where nanoparticles can cross the blood-brain barrier to diagnose and treat conditions such as Alzheimer's disease, Parkinson's disease, and brain tumors. Imaging agents can help visualize brain pathology, while therapeutic agents can target specific neural cells or pathways.

Theranostics represents a cutting-edge approach that integrates diagnosis and therapy into a single, multifunctional platform. By enabling targeted delivery, real-time monitoring, and combination therapies, theranostic nanoparticles hold the potential to revolutionize personalized medicine and improve patient outcomes across a range of diseases.

## 7.4.2 Examples and Clinical Applications

The field of theranostics has rapidly evolved, with numerous examples showcasing the practical applications of this innovative approach in clinical settings. These applications span a variety of diseases, most notably cancer, cardiovascular diseases, infectious diseases, and neurological disorders. Below are detailed examples and clinical applications demonstrating the potential and effectiveness of theranostic platforms.

### Cancer Theranostics:

**Gold Nanoparticles for Photothermal Therapy and Imaging**: Gold nanoparticles (AuNPs) have been extensively studied for their theranostic capabilities in cancer treatment. AuNPs can be functionalized with targeting ligands such as antibodies or peptides that bind specifically to cancer cell surface markers, such as HER2 in breast cancer or EGFR in various solid tumors. When these targeted AuNPs accumulate at the tumor site, they can be visualized using imaging techniques such as computed tomography (CT) due to the high contrast provided by gold. For therapeutic purposes, AuNPs can be irradiated with near-infrared (NIR) light, leading to localized heating (photothermal effect) that destroys cancer cells while sparing surrounding healthy tissues. This dual functionality allows for precise tumor targeting, real-time imaging, and effective treatment.

**Iron Oxide Nanoparticles for MRI and Drug Delivery**: Iron oxide nanoparticles (IONPs) are widely used in magnetic resonance imaging (MRI) due to their superparamagnetic properties, which enhance contrast in MRI scans. Clinically, IONPs can be conjugated with chemotherapeutic drugs like doxorubicin and coated with biocompatible polymers to improve their stability and circulation time. Targeting ligands such as folic acid can be attached to IONPs to direct them specifically to cancer cells overexpressing folate receptors. This approach allows for the simultaneous imaging of tumors and the targeted delivery of chemotherapeutic agents, minimizing systemic side effects and improving therapeutic efficacy.

**Quantum Dots for Multiplexed Imaging and Therapy**: Quantum dots (QDs) are semiconductor nanoparticles that exhibit unique optical properties, including size-tunable fluorescence and high photostability. In cancer theranostics, QDs can be engineered to target multiple biomarkers simultaneously, allowing for multiplexed imaging. For example, QDs conjugated with different antibodies can be used to visualize various cancer cell markers in a single imaging session. Additionally, QDs can be loaded with therapeutic agents such as siRNA or small-molecule drugs, enabling targeted therapy alongside diagnostic imaging. This capability is particularly valuable in monitoring the response to treatment and adjusting therapeutic strategies in real-time.

## *Cardiovascular Theranostics:*

**Nanoparticles for Atherosclerosis Imaging and Therapy:** Theranostic nanoparticles have been developed to diagnose and treat atherosclerosis, a condition characterized by the buildup of plaques within arterial walls. Lipid-based nanoparticles can be functionalized with targeting molecules that bind to inflamed endothelial cells or plaque components such as oxidized low-density lipoprotein (oxLDL). These nanoparticles can carry imaging agents like gadolinium for MRI or radioactive isotopes for PET imaging, allowing for the precise localization and characterization of atherosclerotic plaques. Therapeutic agents such as statins or anti-inflammatory drugs can be co-encapsulated in the nanoparticles to reduce plaque size and inflammation. This dual functionality aids in the early detection and effective management of cardiovascular disease.

## *Infectious Disease Theranostics:*

**Nanoparticles for Bacterial Infections:** Theranostic nanoparticles can be designed to diagnose and treat bacterial infections. For instance, silver nanoparticles (AgNPs) have inherent antimicrobial properties and can be used to treat infections caused by antibiotic-resistant bacteria. AgNPs can be conjugated with fluorescent dyes or radiolabels for imaging purposes, enabling the visualization of infection sites. Additionally, these nanoparticles can be functionalized with targeting ligands that bind to bacterial surface proteins, enhancing their specificity and efficacy. This approach allows for the simultaneous diagnosis and targeted treatment of bacterial infections, reducing the need for broad-spectrum antibiotics and minimizing the risk of resistance development.

## *Neurological Disorder Theranostics:*

**Nanoparticles for Alzheimer's Disease:** Theranostic nanoparticles have shown promise in the diagnosis and treatment of Alzheimer's disease (AD). Functionalized nanoparticles can be designed to cross the blood-brain barrier and target amyloid-beta plaques, a hallmark of AD. For diagnostic purposes, nanoparticles can be loaded with imaging

## *7.5 Regulatory and Safety Considerations*

## *7.5.1 Regulatory Guidelines*

Regulatory guidelines for theranostic nanoparticles are crucial for ensuring their safety, efficacy, and quality before they can be used in clinical applications. These guidelines are established by regulatory agencies such as the U.S. Food and Drug Administration (FDA), the European Medicines Agency (EMA), and other national health authorities. The development of theranostic nanoparticles involves adhering to a rigorous framework that encompasses preclinical studies, clinical trials, and post-market surveillance.

**Preclinical Studies:** Before theranostic nanoparticles can be tested in humans, extensive preclinical studies are required to assess their safety and efficacy. These studies involve in vitro and in vivo testing to evaluate the nanoparticles' pharmacokinetics, biodistribution, toxicity, and therapeutic potential.

- **Pharmacokinetics and Biodistribution:** Understanding how theranostic nanoparticles are absorbed, distributed, metabolized, and excreted is essential. Studies typically involve tracking the nanoparticles in animal models to determine their distribution in different tissues, their half-life, and their elimination pathways.
- **Toxicity Studies:** Assessing the toxicity of theranostic nanoparticles is critical. This includes evaluating acute and chronic toxicity, potential immunogenicity, and the effects on vital organs such as the liver, kidneys, and spleen. Standard tests such as the Maximum Tolerated Dose (MTD) and No Observed Adverse Effect Level (NOAEL) are conducted.

**Clinical Trials:** Clinical trials are conducted in phases to ensure the safety and efficacy of theranostic nanoparticles in humans. Each phase has specific objectives and regulatory requirements.

- **Phase I Trials:** These initial trials involve a small number of healthy volunteers or patients and focus on assessing the safety, tolerability, and pharmacokinetics of the theranostic nanoparticles. Dose-escalation studies are performed to identify the appropriate dosage range.
- **Phase II Trials:** This phase involves a larger group of patients and aims to evaluate the efficacy of the theranostic nanoparticles for a specific condition, as well as to further assess their safety. This phase helps to determine the optimal dose and to identify any potential side effects.
- **Phase III Trials:** These are large-scale studies that compare the theranostic nanoparticles to the current standard of care. They involve hundreds to thousands of patients to confirm the nanoparticles' efficacy, monitor side effects, and collect data that will allow for a comprehensive risk-benefit assessment.

**Post-Market Surveillance:** Once theranostic nanoparticles are approved for clinical use, they are subject to ongoing monitoring to ensure their continued safety and efficacy. This involves collecting and analyzing data on adverse events, long-term effects, and real-world effectiveness.

- **Pharmacovigilance:** Regulatory agencies require manufacturers to establish a pharmacovigilance system to detect, assess, and report adverse events associated with theranostic nanoparticles. This system helps in identifying any rare or long-term side effects that may not have been evident in clinical trials.
- **Post-Market Studies:** Additional studies may be required to further evaluate the safety and efficacy of theranostic nanoparticles in broader populations or in specific subgroups such as pediatric or geriatric patients. These studies help to refine the understanding of the nanoparticles' clinical performance and to make any necessary adjustments to their use guidelines.

**Quality Assurance and Manufacturing Standards:** Ensuring the quality of theranostic nanoparticles involves strict adherence to Good Manufacturing Practices (GMP) and other quality assurance protocols.

- **GMP Compliance:** Manufacturers must comply with GMP regulations to ensure that theranostic nanoparticles are consistently produced and controlled according to quality standards. This includes stringent controls over the production process, raw materials, and final product testing.
- **Characterization and Standardization:** Comprehensive characterization of theranostic nanoparticles is essential for ensuring their reproducibility and consistency. This includes detailed analysis of their size, shape, surface properties, and functionalization. Standardization of manufacturing processes and quality control measures is crucial to achieve batch-to-batch consistency.

**Ethical Considerations:** The development and use of theranostic nanoparticles must also address ethical considerations, particularly regarding informed consent, patient privacy, and equitable access to new technologies.

- **Informed Consent:** Patients must be fully informed about the potential risks and benefits of participating in clinical trials involving theranostic nanoparticles. Clear and transparent communication is essential to obtain valid informed consent.
- **Patient Privacy:** Ensuring the confidentiality and security of patient data is a key ethical requirement. This includes safeguarding personal health information collected during clinical trials and post-market surveillance.
- **Equitable Access:** Efforts should be made to ensure that advancements in theranostic technology are accessible to diverse populations and do not exacerbate existing health disparities. This includes considering the affordability and availability of theranostic treatments in different healthcare settings.

Adhering to regulatory guidelines and addressing safety and ethical considerations are critical for the successful development and clinical application of theranostic nanoparticles. These measures help to ensure that these advanced technologies can provide significant benefits to patients while minimizing risks and maintaining public trust.

## 7.5 Regulatory and Safety Considerations

## 7.5.2 Safety and Toxicity Assessments

Safety and toxicity assessments are crucial components in the development and clinical application of theranostic nanoparticles. These assessments ensure that the nanoparticles do not pose undue risks to patients and that their benefits outweigh any potential hazards. Comprehensive safety evaluations encompass various types of toxicity studies, each designed to address specific aspects of the nanoparticles' interactions with biological systems.

**Acute Toxicity Studies:** Acute toxicity studies are conducted to determine the immediate toxic effects of a single or short-term exposure to theranostic nanoparticles. These studies typically involve administering a single high dose of the nanoparticles to animal models and monitoring them for signs of toxicity over a period of 24 to 72 hours.

- **Assessment Parameters:** Key parameters assessed include clinical signs of toxicity, changes in body weight, food and water consumption, and mortality rates. Biochemical analyses of blood samples are performed to evaluate the function of vital organs such as the liver and kidneys. Histopathological examinations of tissues are conducted to identify any morphological changes indicative of toxicity.

**Chronic Toxicity Studies:** Chronic toxicity studies involve the administration of theranostic nanoparticles over an extended period, typically weeks to months, to assess the long-term toxic effects of repeated exposure. These studies are essential for understanding the potential cumulative effects of the nanoparticles.

- **Assessment Parameters:** Chronic toxicity studies monitor a wide range of parameters, including body weight, hematological and biochemical markers, organ weights, and detailed histopathological examinations. Special attention is given to organs involved in nanoparticle clearance, such as the liver, spleen, and kidneys, as well as potential target organs for toxicity.

**Genotoxicity and Carcinogenicity Studies:** Genotoxicity studies are conducted to evaluate the potential of theranostic nanoparticles to cause genetic mutations or chromosomal damage, which could lead to cancer. These studies are essential for identifying any carcinogenic risks associated with the nanoparticles.

- **Assessment Methods:** Common tests for genotoxicity include the Ames test, which detects mutations in bacterial cells; the micronucleus test, which identifies chromosomal damage in mammalian cells; and the comet assay, which measures DNA strand breaks. Carcinogenicity studies, often involving long-term exposure in animal models, assess the potential for tumor formation.

**Immunotoxicity Studies:** Immunotoxicity studies evaluate the impact of theranostic nanoparticles on the immune system. These studies are crucial because nanoparticles can interact with immune cells, potentially leading to immunosuppression or overstimulation.

- **Assessment Parameters:** Parameters assessed in immunotoxicity studies include changes in immune cell populations, cytokine production, and antibody responses. Functional assays, such as the evaluation of phagocytic activity and natural killer cell activity, are also conducted to assess immune competence.

**Reproductive and Developmental Toxicity Studies:** Reproductive and developmental toxicity studies assess the potential effects of theranostic nanoparticles on fertility, embryonic development, and offspring health. These studies are particularly important for ensuring the safety of nanoparticles in pregnant patients.

- **Assessment Parameters:** These studies involve administering nanoparticles to male and female animals before and during mating, as well as to pregnant females. Parameters assessed include mating success, fertility rates, embryonic development, and postnatal growth and development of offspring. Detailed examinations of reproductive organs and histopathological analysis of fetal tissues are performed to identify any adverse effects.

**Biodistribution and Clearance Studies:** Understanding the biodistribution and clearance of theranostic nanoparticles is essential for evaluating their safety profile. These studies investigate how nanoparticles are distributed throughout the body, their accumulation in specific organs, and their elimination routes.

- **Assessment Methods:** Biodistribution studies typically involve labeling nanoparticles with radioactive or fluorescent markers and tracking their distribution using imaging techniques such as positron emission tomography (PET) or fluorescence microscopy. Clearance studies measure the rate at which nanoparticles are eliminated from the body through excretion in urine and feces.

**Biocompatibility and Cytotoxicity Studies:** Biocompatibility studies assess the compatibility of theranostic nanoparticles with biological tissues, while cytotoxicity studies evaluate their effects on cell viability and function.

- **Assessment Methods:** Biocompatibility tests include in vitro assays using cell cultures and in vivo implantation studies. Cytotoxicity assays, such as the MTT assay, lactate dehydrogenase (LDH) release assay, and live/dead staining, measure cell viability, membrane integrity, and apoptosis. These studies help determine the safe concentration range of nanoparticles for therapeutic applications.

**In Vivo Imaging and Functional Studies:** Functional studies using in vivo imaging techniques provide real-time insights into the behavior of theranostic nanoparticles in living organisms. These studies are critical for understanding how nanoparticles interact with target tissues and how effectively they deliver therapeutic agents.

- **Assessment Methods:** Imaging modalities such as magnetic resonance imaging (MRI), computed tomography (CT), and optical imaging are used to monitor the localization, accumulation, and clearance of nanoparticles. Functional studies assess the therapeutic efficacy of nanoparticles in disease models, such as tumor regression in cancer models or plaque reduction in atherosclerosis models.

Conducting thorough safety and toxicity assessments is imperative for the successful translation of theranostic nanoparticles from the laboratory to clinical practice. These evaluations ensure that nanoparticles are safe for human use, providing a strong foundation for regulatory approval and widespread adoption in medical applications.

# CHAPTER EIGHT

# PULMONARY AND NASAL DRUG DELIVERY

## 8.1. Introduction to Pulmonary Drug Delivery

Pulmonary drug delivery represents a promising route for administering medications directly to the lungs, offering advantages such as rapid onset of action, high bioavailability, and localized therapeutic effects. This method bypasses the gastrointestinal tract, avoiding issues such as enzymatic degradation and first-pass metabolism. Understanding the anatomy and physiology of the respiratory system is crucial for optimizing drug delivery to this region.

### 8.1.1. Respiratory System Anatomy

The respiratory system comprises a complex network of organs and tissues responsible for gas exchange and maintaining physiological homeostasis. The primary structures involved in pulmonary drug delivery include the nasal passages, pharynx, larynx, trachea, bronchi, bronchioles, and alveoli. Each component of this system serves a distinct function in the process of respiration, from air filtration and humidification to gas exchange within the alveoli. Knowledge of these anatomical structures is essential for designing drug delivery systems that target specific regions of the respiratory tract.

### 8.1.1.1 Nasal Cavity

The nasal cavity serves as the initial entry point for inhaled substances, playing a crucial role in filtering, warming, and humidifying inspired air before it reaches the lower respiratory tract. The nasal passages are lined with a mucous membrane rich in blood vessels and mucous-secreting glands, which help trap and remove foreign particles and microorganisms. Additionally, the nasal epithelium contains cilia that facilitate the movement of mucous and trapped particles toward the pharynx for eventual clearance.

## 8.1.1.2. Pharynx and Larynx

Located behind the nasal cavity, the pharynx serves as a common pathway for both air and food. It plays a vital role in swallowing, preventing aspiration of food or liquids into the lower respiratory tract. The larynx, or voice box, sits below the pharynx and houses the vocal cords, which are essential for speech production. Additionally, the larynx contains the epiglottis, a flap of tissue that closes during swallowing to prevent aspiration into the trachea.

## 8.1.1.3. Trachea and Bronchial Tree

The trachea, commonly known as the windpipe, is a tubular structure composed of cartilage rings that provide support and prevent collapse during respiration. It bifurcates into the left and right main bronchi, which further divide into smaller bronchi and bronchioles as they extend into the lungs. These branching airways are lined with smooth muscle and mucous-secreting glands, contributing to airway resistance and secretion clearance mechanisms.

## 8.1.1.4 Alveolar Region

The alveoli are microscopic air sacs located at the distal ends of the bronchioles, where gas exchange occurs between the air and the bloodstream. Surfactant-producing type II alveolar cells line the alveolar walls, reducing surface tension and preventing alveolar collapse during expiration. The extensive network of capillaries surrounding the alveoli facilitates the diffusion of oxygen into the bloodstream and the removal of carbon dioxide from the body.

A comprehensive understanding of the anatomy and physiology of the respiratory system is essential for the development and optimization of pulmonary drug delivery systems. By leveraging the unique characteristics of the respiratory tract, such as its large surface area, thin epithelial barrier, and efficient blood supply, researchers can design innovative strategies to enhance drug absorption, distribution, and therapeutic efficacy within the lungs. Further exploration of pulmonary drug delivery holds promise for improving the treatment of respiratory diseases and systemic conditions through targeted and non-invasive interventions.

## 8.1.2 Particle Deposition and Uptake

Particle deposition and uptake mechanisms play a crucial role in determining the distribution and efficacy of drugs delivered to the pulmonary system. Understanding these processes is essential for designing efficient drug delivery systems that can target specific regions of the respiratory tract while minimizing systemic side effects.

### 8.1.2.1 Deposition Mechanisms

Particle deposition in the respiratory tract is influenced by various factors, including particle size, shape, density, and aerodynamic properties. Larger particles tend to deposit in the upper airways, such as the nasopharyngeal and tracheobronchial regions, through mechanisms such as inertial impaction and gravitational settling. In contrast, smaller particles (<5 μm) have a higher probability of reaching the alveolar region due to their ability to remain suspended in the air and follow the airstream as it branches into smaller airways. Additionally, particle deposition may be influenced by airflow patterns, breathing maneuvers, and anatomical features such as airway geometry and surface properties.

### 8.1.2.2 Uptake Mechanisms

Once deposited in the respiratory tract, particles interact with the mucosal lining and undergo various uptake mechanisms to enter the systemic circulation or exert local therapeutic effects. These mechanisms include passive diffusion, endocytosis, phagocytosis, and mucociliary clearance. Passive diffusion relies on concentration gradients to drive the movement of drugs across the epithelial barrier into the bloodstream or surrounding tissues. Endocytosis involves the internalization of particles by epithelial cells through the formation of vesicles, allowing for controlled release of drugs into the systemic circulation. Phagocytosis, primarily mediated by alveolar macrophages, plays a crucial role in removing foreign particles and pathogens from the lungs but can also impact drug delivery by sequestering particles before they reach their intended target. Mucociliary clearance, facilitated by the coordinated movement of cilia and mucus, helps remove deposited particles from the respiratory tract through coughing and swallowing, limiting their residence time and potential therapeutic effects.

## 8.1.2.3 Optimization Strategies

To enhance particle deposition and uptake in the pulmonary system, researchers employ various optimization strategies targeting particle properties, formulation characteristics, and delivery devices. These include engineering particles with specific size distributions and surface properties to maximize deposition efficiency and minimize clearance mechanisms. Formulation approaches such as encapsulation, particle surface modification, and inclusion of mucoadhesive agents can improve drug retention and prolong residence time in the respiratory tract, enhancing local drug concentrations and therapeutic outcomes. Furthermore, advances in inhaler technology, such as dry powder inhalers and nebulizers, enable precise control over particle dispersion and delivery kinetics, optimizing drug delivery to targeted regions of the lung while minimizing systemic exposure and adverse effects.

## 8.1.2.4 Clinical Implications

A deeper understanding of particle deposition and uptake mechanisms in the pulmonary system has significant clinical implications for the treatment of respiratory diseases and systemic conditions. By elucidating the factors governing drug distribution and efficacy within the lungs, researchers can develop tailored therapeutic interventions that maximize therapeutic outcomes while minimizing off-target effects and patient discomfort. Furthermore, insights gained from studying particle transport and clearance mechanisms contribute to the refinement of drug delivery technologies and inhalation devices, paving the way for the development of novel therapies with improved safety, efficacy, and patient adherence.

## 8.1.3 Nanocarriers for Pulmonary Delivery

Nanocarriers have emerged as promising vehicles for pulmonary drug delivery, offering unique advantages such as enhanced drug solubility, prolonged circulation time, and targeted delivery to specific sites within the respiratory tract. This section explores the various types of nanocarriers utilized for pulmonary delivery and their potential applications in the treatment of respiratory diseases and systemic conditions.

## 8.1.3.1 Types of Nanocarriers

Nanocarriers encompass a diverse range of nano-sized structures designed to encapsulate and deliver therapeutic agents to target tissues. Common types of nanocarriers employed for pulmonary delivery include liposomes, polymeric nanoparticles, solid lipid nanoparticles, dendrimers, and nanoemulsions. Liposomes are lipid-based vesicles with a phospholipid bilayer structure, capable of encapsulating both hydrophilic and hydrophobic drugs and facilitating their transport across biological barriers. Polymeric nanoparticles are composed of biocompatible polymers such as poly(lactic-co-glycolic acid) (PLGA) or chitosan, offering tunable drug release kinetics and sustained therapeutic effects. Solid lipid nanoparticles consist of lipids stabilized by surfactants, providing improved drug stability and bioavailability. Dendrimers are highly branched macromolecules with precise molecular structures, offering high drug loading capacity and controlled release properties. Nanoemulsions are colloidal dispersions of oil and water stabilized by surfactants, enabling the encapsulation of lipophilic drugs and efficient drug delivery to target tissues.

## 8.1.3.2 Mechanisms of Pulmonary Delivery

Nanocarriers employ various mechanisms to facilitate drug delivery to the lungs, including passive diffusion, endocytosis, and receptor-mediated uptake. Upon inhalation, nanocarriers deposit in the respiratory tract and interact with the epithelial lining, where they may undergo mucosal penetration or uptake by resident immune cells such as alveolar macrophages. Passive diffusion allows for the transport of drugs across the epithelial barrier into the bloodstream or surrounding tissues, depending on factors such as particle size, surface charge, and drug release kinetics. Endocytosis involves the internalization of nanocarriers by epithelial cells through the formation of vesicles, enabling controlled release of drugs into the systemic circulation. Receptor-mediated uptake exploits specific ligand-receptor interactions to enhance nanocarrier uptake and targeting to specific cell types or tissues within the lungs, offering potential for personalized therapeutic interventions.

## 8.1.3.3 Applications in Respiratory Diseases

Nanocarriers hold promise for the treatment of various respiratory diseases, including asthma, chronic obstructive pulmonary disease (COPD), cystic fibrosis, and lung cancer. By encapsulating bronchodilators, anti-inflammatory agents, antibiotics, or anticancer drugs, nanocarrier-based formulations can improve drug efficacy, reduce dosing frequency, and minimize systemic side effects compared to conventional dosage forms. Furthermore, targeted delivery to inflamed or diseased lung tissues enables enhanced therapeutic outcomes and improved patient compliance. Additionally, nanocarriers can serve as versatile platforms for co-delivery of multiple drugs or combination therapies, addressing the complex pathophysiology of respiratory diseases and overcoming drug resistance mechanisms.

## 8.1.3.4 Future Directions and Challenges

Despite the significant advancements in nanocarrier-based pulmonary drug delivery, several challenges remain to be addressed, including scale-up production, regulatory considerations, and safety concerns. Further research is needed to optimize nanocarrier formulations for clinical translation, ensuring stability, biocompatibility, and reproducibility across different manufacturing processes. Additionally, studies elucidating the pharmacokinetics, biodistribution, and biodegradation of nanocarriers in the lungs are essential for assessing their long-term safety and efficacy. Future directions in this field include the development of personalized nanomedicines tailored to individual patient profiles, integration of advanced imaging and targeting strategies, and exploration of synergistic interactions between nanocarriers and biological systems to maximize therapeutic outcomes while minimizing adverse effects.

## 8.1.4 Clinical Applications

The clinical applications of pulmonary drug delivery encompass a wide range of therapeutic interventions for respiratory diseases, systemic conditions, and infectious disorders. Leveraging the unique advantages of the pulmonary route, clinicians can administer medications directly to the lungs, achieving rapid onset of action, enhanced bioavailability, and localized therapeutic effects while minimizing systemic side effects and improving patient adherence.

### 8.1.4.1 Respiratory Diseases

Pulmonary drug delivery holds significant promise for the treatment of respiratory diseases such as asthma, chronic obstructive pulmonary disease (COPD), cystic fibrosis, and pulmonary hypertension. Inhaled bronchodilators, corticosteroids, and anticholinergic agents serve as cornerstone therapies for managing airway inflammation, bronchoconstriction, and mucus hypersecretion in asthma and COPD patients. Nebulized antibiotics, mucolytics, and airway clearance techniques are essential components of treatment regimens for cystic fibrosis, aiming to reduce bacterial colonization, improve mucus clearance, and prevent exacerbations. Additionally, inhaled vasodilators and prostacyclin analogs play a crucial role in the management of pulmonary hypertension, improving pulmonary vascular tone and exercise tolerance in affected individuals.

### 8.1.4.2 Systemic Conditions

Beyond respiratory diseases, pulmonary drug delivery offers therapeutic opportunities for systemic conditions such as diabetes, cardiovascular disorders, and cancer. Inhaled insulin formulations provide an alternative route of insulin administration for diabetic patients, offering rapid absorption and improved glycemic control compared to subcutaneous injections. Pulmonary administration of vasodilators, anticoagulants, and antiarrhythmic agents holds potential for the management of cardiovascular conditions, delivering drugs directly to the pulmonary vasculature and minimizing systemic exposure and adverse effects. Furthermore, inhalation chemotherapy represents a promising approach for the treatment of lung cancer and metastatic disease, enabling targeted delivery of cytotoxic agents to tumor cells while reducing systemic toxicity and preserving quality of life.

## 8.1.4.3 Infectious Disorders

Pulmonary drug delivery plays a critical role in the management of infectious disorders affecting the respiratory tract, including pneumonia, tuberculosis, and respiratory viral infections. Nebulized antibiotics such as tobramycin and colistin are commonly used for the treatment of nosocomial pneumonia and cystic fibrosis-associated lung infections, achieving high drug concentrations at the site of infection while minimizing systemic exposure and renal toxicity. Inhalation therapy with antifungal agents such as amphotericin B and voriconazole is employed for the management of invasive fungal infections and allergic bronchopulmonary aspergillosis. Additionally, inhaled antiviral agents such as ribavirin and oseltamivir are utilized in the treatment of respiratory viral infections such as influenza and respiratory syncytial virus (RSV), reducing viral replication and improving clinical outcomes in high-risk patient populations.

## 8.1.4.4 Future Perspectives

The ongoing advancements in pulmonary drug delivery hold promise for expanding the therapeutic arsenal against respiratory diseases, systemic conditions, and infectious disorders. Future research efforts focus on developing innovative drug formulations, enhancing drug targeting and delivery strategies, and improving patient outcomes through personalized medicine approaches. By harnessing the full potential of pulmonary drug delivery, clinicians can address unmet medical needs, optimize therapeutic efficacy, and improve the overall quality of life for patients with respiratory and systemic disorders.

## 8.2 Nasal Drug Delivery

Nasal drug delivery represents a non-invasive and effective route for administering medications, offering advantages such as rapid onset of action, avoidance of first-pass metabolism, and potential for targeted delivery to the central nervous system. This section explores the advantages and underlying mechanisms of nasal drug delivery, highlighting its applications in the treatment of various medical conditions.

## 8.2.1 Advantages and Mechanisms

Nasal drug delivery offers several advantages over conventional routes of administration, making it an attractive option for both local and systemic drug delivery. The nasal mucosa is highly vascularized and permeable, allowing for rapid absorption of drugs into the bloodstream and bypassing the gastrointestinal tract, thereby avoiding degradation by gastric acid and hepatic metabolism. Additionally, the large surface area and rich blood supply of the nasal cavity facilitate efficient drug absorption, leading to faster onset of action and reduced dosing frequency compared to oral or parenteral routes. Furthermore, the nasal route provides access to the olfactory region and the blood-brain barrier, enabling targeted delivery of therapeutics to the central nervous system for the treatment of neurological disorders such as migraine, epilepsy, and Parkinson's disease.

The mechanisms underlying nasal drug absorption involve passive diffusion, paracellular transport, and transcellular transport across the nasal epithelium. Passive diffusion occurs when drugs move down concentration gradients through the aqueous pores and lipid bilayers of nasal epithelial cells, driven by factors such as molecular size, lipophilicity, and pH-dependent ionization. Paracellular transport involves the movement of drugs between adjacent epithelial cells via tight junctions, allowing for the passage of small hydrophilic molecules. Transcellular transport, on the other hand, entails drug permeation through epithelial cells via various transport mechanisms such as carrier-mediated transport, receptor-mediated endocytosis, and pinocytosis. These mechanisms collectively contribute to the efficient absorption and systemic distribution of drugs following nasal administration, offering a versatile platform for drug delivery across a wide range of therapeutic indications.

In addition to its systemic benefits, nasal drug delivery holds promise for the treatment of local conditions affecting the nasal cavity and paranasal sinuses, including allergic rhinitis, sinusitis, and nasal congestion. Nasal sprays, drops, gels, and powders are commonly used dosage forms for delivering antihistamines, decongestants, corticosteroids, and anticholinergic agents to alleviate nasal symptoms and improve respiratory function. Furthermore, nasal vaccines represent an emerging area of research for the prevention of respiratory infections such as influenza, COVID-19, and rhinovirus, harnessing the immune-rich environment of the nasal mucosa to induce mucosal and systemic immune responses against pathogens. Overall, nasal drug delivery offers a versatile and patient-friendly approach for achieving therapeutic outcomes across a broad spectrum of medical conditions, capitalizing on the unique anatomical and physiological characteristics of the nasal cavity for efficient drug absorption and targeted delivery.

## 8.2.2 Nanocarriers for Nasal Delivery

Nanocarriers have emerged as promising platforms for nasal drug delivery, offering advantages such as enhanced drug solubility, prolonged residence time, and targeted delivery to specific sites within the nasal cavity. This section explores the various types of nanocarriers utilized for nasal delivery and their potential applications in the treatment of nasal disorders and systemic conditions.

## 8.2.2.1 Types of Nanocarriers

Nanocarriers for nasal delivery encompass a diverse array of nano-sized structures designed to encapsulate and transport therapeutic agents across the nasal epithelium. Common types of nanocarriers employed for nasal delivery include liposomes, polymeric nanoparticles, solid lipid nanoparticles, dendrimers, and nanoemulsions. Liposomes are lipid-based vesicles composed of phospholipid bilayers, capable of encapsulating both hydrophilic and hydrophobic drugs and facilitating their transport across biological barriers. Polymeric nanoparticles are composed of biocompatible polymers such as poly(lactic-co-glycolic acid) (PLGA) or chitosan, offering tunable drug release kinetics and sustained therapeutic effects. Solid lipid nanoparticles consist of lipids stabilized by surfactants, providing improved drug stability and bioavailability. Dendrimers are highly branched macromolecules with precise molecular structures, offering high drug loading capacity and controlled release properties. Nanoemulsions are colloidal dispersions of oil and water stabilized by surfactants, enabling the encapsulation of lipophilic drugs and efficient drug delivery to target tissues within the nasal cavity.

## 8.2.2.2 Mechanisms of Nasal Delivery

Nanocarriers employ various mechanisms to facilitate drug delivery across the nasal epithelium and achieve therapeutic effects. Upon nasal administration, nanocarriers interact with the mucus layer and nasal epithelial cells, where they may undergo mucosal penetration or uptake by epithelial cells. Particle size, surface charge, and mucoadhesive properties play critical roles in determining the interaction of nanocarriers with the nasal mucosa and the subsequent drug release and absorption kinetics. Passive diffusion, paracellular transport, and transcellular transport mechanisms contribute to the efficient absorption of drugs from nanocarrier formulations, allowing for rapid onset of action and sustained therapeutic effects. Additionally, targeted delivery strategies involving ligand-receptor interactions or cell-specific targeting moieties enable selective accumulation of nanocarriers and drugs at desired sites within the nasal cavity, enhancing therapeutic outcomes and minimizing off-target effects.

## 8.2.2.3 Applications in Nasal Disorders

Nanocarriers hold promise for the treatment of various nasal disorders, including allergic rhinitis, sinusitis, nasal polyps, and nasal congestion. Nasal formulations containing antihistamines, corticosteroids, decongestants, and mast cell stabilizers offer symptomatic relief and improve quality of life for patients suffering from allergic rhinitis and related nasal symptoms. Moreover, nanocarrier-based formulations can target inflamed or infected nasal tissues, delivering antibiotics, antifungals, or anti-inflammatory agents to alleviate symptoms and prevent disease progression in sinusitis and rhinosinusitis patients. Nasal delivery of vaccines and immunomodulators represents an emerging area of research for the prevention and treatment of respiratory infections such as influenza, COVID-19, and rhinovirus, harnessing the immune-modulating properties of nanocarriers to enhance mucosal and systemic immune responses.

## 8.2.2.4 Systemic Delivery and Beyond

In addition to local applications, nasal nanocarriers offer potential for systemic drug delivery and targeting of distant organs and tissues. Nasal formulations containing peptides, proteins, hormones, or small molecules can bypass the gastrointestinal tract and first-pass metabolism, achieving rapid and predictable systemic absorption and bioavailability. Furthermore, nasal delivery of central nervous system (CNS) drugs represents a promising strategy for targeting the brain and treating neurological disorders such as migraine, epilepsy, Alzheimer's disease, and Parkinson's disease. By exploiting the unique anatomical and physiological characteristics of the nasal cavity, nanocarriers for nasal delivery offer a versatile and patient-friendly approach for achieving therapeutic outcomes across a wide range of medical conditions, paving the way for personalized and targeted drug delivery strategies in the future.

## 8.2.3 Clinical Applications

Nasal drug delivery holds significant clinical relevance across a spectrum of medical conditions, offering a non-invasive and effective route for administering medications with rapid onset of action and targeted delivery to the nasal mucosa and systemic circulation. This section explores the diverse clinical applications of nasal drug delivery, encompassing the treatment of nasal disorders, systemic conditions, and neurological diseases.

## 8.2.3.1 Nasal Disorders

Nasal drug delivery plays a crucial role in the management of various nasal disorders, including allergic rhinitis, sinusitis, nasal polyps, and nasal congestion. Nasal formulations containing antihistamines, corticosteroids, decongestants, and mast cell stabilizers provide symptomatic relief from nasal congestion, itching, sneezing, and rhinorrhea associated with allergic rhinitis. Additionally, nasal sprays and irrigation solutions containing saline or corticosteroids help alleviate sinus inflammation, reduce nasal polyp size, and improve sinus drainage in patients with chronic rhinosinusitis. Furthermore, nasal decongestants and vasoconstrictors provide rapid relief from nasal congestion due to colds, allergies, or sinusitis, promoting nasal airflow and improving respiratory function.

## 8.2.3.2 Systemic Conditions

Beyond nasal disorders, nasal drug delivery offers therapeutic opportunities for systemic conditions such as diabetes, cardiovascular diseases, and hormonal imbalances. Nasal insulin formulations provide an alternative route of insulin administration for diabetic patients, achieving rapid absorption into the systemic circulation and mimicking physiological insulin secretion patterns. Nasal delivery of vasopressin analogs such as desmopressin is employed for the treatment of diabetes insipidus and nocturnal enuresis, offering convenient dosing and improved patient compliance compared to oral or injectable formulations. Additionally, nasal formulations containing vasoactive agents, anticoagulants, or hormones can bypass first-pass metabolism and achieve rapid onset of action, making them suitable for emergency situations or acute conditions requiring immediate intervention.

## 8.2.3.3 Neurological Diseases

Nasal drug delivery holds promise for the treatment of neurological disorders affecting the central nervous system (CNS), including migraine, epilepsy, Alzheimer's disease, and Parkinson's disease. Intranasal formulations of migraine medications such as sumatriptan and dihydroergotamine provide rapid relief from headache pain and associated symptoms, bypassing the gastrointestinal tract and avoiding delayed onset of action or gastrointestinal side effects. Nasal delivery of antiepileptic drugs such as midazolam and diazepam offers a non-invasive and convenient route for controlling acute seizures and status epilepticus, particularly in pediatric or elderly patients unable to swallow oral medications. Furthermore, intranasal administration of CNS-targeted therapies such as insulin, nerve growth factors, and neuroprotective agents holds potential for slowing disease progression and improving cognitive function in neurodegenerative diseases such as Alzheimer's and Parkinson's.

## 8.2.3.4 Emerging Trends and Future Directions

The ongoing advancements in nasal drug delivery pave the way for personalized and targeted therapeutic interventions across a wide range of medical conditions. Future research efforts focus on optimizing nasal formulations for enhanced drug stability, absorption, and distribution, as well as exploring novel drug delivery strategies such as nanotechnology, mucoadhesive polymers, and nasal drug-device combinations. By harnessing the full potential of nasal drug delivery, clinicians can improve treatment outcomes, reduce healthcare costs, and enhance patient quality of life, ultimately advancing the field of drug delivery and personalized medicine.

# CHAPTER NINE

# CARDIOVASCULAR AND LOCALIZED DRUG DELIVERY

## 9.1 Cardiovascular Drug Delivery

Cardiovascular drug delivery encompasses the targeted administration of medications to the cardiovascular system, including the heart, blood vessels, and associated tissues, for the management of various cardiovascular diseases. This section delves into the challenges encountered in cardiovascular drug delivery, highlighting the complexities involved in achieving optimal therapeutic outcomes.

### 9.1.1 Challenges in Cardiovascular Delivery

Despite significant advancements in cardiovascular therapeutics, several challenges persist in the effective delivery of drugs to target sites within the cardiovascular system. One of the primary challenges is the dynamic and complex nature of cardiovascular physiology, characterized by intricate hemodynamic processes, vascular anatomy, and cellular interactions. The pulsatile nature of blood flow, variations in blood pressure, and changes in vascular tone pose challenges for achieving sustained drug delivery and uniform drug distribution to target tissues.

Moreover, the presence of physiological barriers such as the blood-brain barrier, endothelial barriers, and vascular endothelium further complicates drug delivery to cardiovascular tissues. These barriers limit the penetration of drugs into the target sites, necessitating the development of drug delivery systems capable of bypassing or overcoming these barriers to achieve therapeutic concentrations at the desired sites of action.

Another challenge in cardiovascular drug delivery is the need for precise targeting of drugs to specific regions within the cardiovascular system while minimizing off-target effects and systemic toxicity. Targeted delivery strategies aim to enhance drug localization to diseased tissues, such as atherosclerotic plaques, ischemic myocardium, or dysfunctional endothelium, thereby improving therapeutic efficacy and reducing side effects associated with systemic drug exposure.

Furthermore, the development of drug resistance, pharmacokinetic variability, and patient-specific factors such as genetic polymorphisms and comorbidities contribute to the complexity of cardiovascular drug delivery. Tailoring drug delivery strategies to individual patient profiles and disease characteristics is essential for optimizing treatment outcomes and minimizing adverse effects.

## 9.1.2 Nanocarriers for Cardiovascular Applications

Nanocarriers have emerged as versatile platforms for cardiovascular drug delivery, offering unique advantages such as enhanced drug solubility, prolonged circulation time, and targeted delivery to specific sites within the cardiovascular system. This section explores the diverse applications of nanocarriers in cardiovascular medicine and the potential impact on therapeutic interventions.

### 9.1.2.1 Types of Nanocarriers

Nanocarriers for cardiovascular applications encompass a wide range of nano-sized structures designed to encapsulate and transport therapeutic agents to target tissues. Common types of nanocarriers utilized in cardiovascular drug delivery include liposomes, polymeric nanoparticles, micelles, dendrimers, and nanoemulsions. Liposomes are lipid-based vesicles composed of phospholipid bilayers, capable of encapsulating hydrophilic and lipophilic drugs and facilitating their transport across biological barriers. Polymeric nanoparticles are composed of biocompatible polymers such as poly(lactic-co-glycolic acid) (PLGA) or polyethylene glycol (PEG), offering controlled drug release kinetics and prolonged circulation time. Micelles are self-assembled structures formed by amphiphilic molecules, enabling solubilization of hydrophobic drugs and targeted delivery to specific cell types or tissues. Dendrimers are highly branched macromolecules with precise molecular structures, offering high drug loading capacity and tunable drug release properties. Nanoemulsions are colloidal dispersions of oil and water stabilized by surfactants, facilitating the encapsulation of lipophilic drugs and efficient delivery to target tissues within the cardiovascular system.

## 9.1.2.2 Mechanisms of Action

Nanocarriers employ various mechanisms to facilitate drug delivery to target sites within the cardiovascular system, including passive targeting, active targeting, and triggered release. Passive targeting relies on the enhanced permeability and retention (EPR) effect, whereby nanocarriers accumulate preferentially in leaky or angiogenic blood vessels associated with diseased tissues such as tumors or atherosclerotic plaques. Active targeting strategies involve surface modification of nanocarriers with ligands or antibodies that bind to specific receptors or biomarkers expressed on target cells or tissues, enhancing cellular uptake and intracellular drug delivery. Triggered release mechanisms enable controlled drug release in response to external stimuli such as pH, temperature, or enzymatic activity, allowing for precise spatiotemporal control over drug release and therapeutic effects.

## 9.1.2.3 Applications in Cardiovascular Diseases

Nanocarriers hold promise for the treatment of various cardiovascular diseases, including atherosclerosis, myocardial infarction, heart failure, and thrombosis. Nanocarrier-based formulations of statins, antiplatelet agents, anticoagulants, and antioxidants offer potential for inhibiting plaque formation, reducing inflammation, and stabilizing vulnerable atherosclerotic plaques, thereby preventing acute cardiovascular events such as myocardial infarction or stroke. Additionally, nanocarriers can encapsulate cardioprotective agents such as growth factors, stem cells, or gene therapies for promoting cardiac repair and regeneration following myocardial infarction or ischemic injury. Furthermore, targeted delivery of vasodilators, angiogenesis promoters, or tissue-engineered constructs to ischemic myocardium holds promise for improving myocardial perfusion and functional recovery in patients with coronary artery disease or heart failure.

## 9.1.2.4 Future Perspectives

The ongoing advancements in nanocarrier-based cardiovascular drug delivery pave the way for personalized and targeted therapeutic interventions aimed at improving patient outcomes and reducing the burden of cardiovascular diseases. Future research efforts focus on optimizing nanocarrier formulations for enhanced stability, biocompatibility, and targeted delivery to specific cardiovascular tissues or cell types. Additionally, integrating advanced imaging and diagnostic techniques with nanocarrier-based drug delivery systems enables real-time monitoring of drug distribution, pharmacokinetics, and therapeutic response, facilitating personalized treatment strategies and precision medicine approaches in cardiovascular medicine. By harnessing the full potential of nanocarriers for cardiovascular applications, clinicians can address unmet medical needs, overcome drug resistance mechanisms, and revolutionize the management of cardiovascular diseases, ultimately improving patient quality of life and reducing morbidity and mortality associated with these conditions.

## 9.1.3 Clinical Applications

Clinical applications of cardiovascular drug delivery encompass a broad spectrum of therapeutic interventions aimed at managing cardiovascular diseases and improving patient outcomes. This section explores the diverse clinical applications of cardiovascular drug delivery, highlighting its role in the treatment and prevention of various cardiovascular conditions.

## 9.1.3.1 Atherosclerosis Management

Cardiovascular drug delivery plays a crucial role in the management of atherosclerosis, a chronic inflammatory condition characterized by the buildup of plaques within arterial walls. Nanocarrier-based formulations of statins, antiplatelet agents, and antioxidants offer potential for inhibiting plaque formation, reducing inflammation, and stabilizing vulnerable plaques, thereby preventing acute cardiovascular events such as myocardial infarction or stroke. Furthermore, targeted delivery of lipophilic drugs to atherosclerotic lesions via nanocarriers enables efficient drug accumulation at the site of pathology, enhancing therapeutic efficacy and minimizing systemic side effects.

## 9.1.3.2 Myocardial Infarction Treatment

In the acute management of myocardial infarction (MI), cardiovascular drug delivery plays a critical role in limiting myocardial injury, promoting tissue repair, and preventing adverse cardiac remodeling. Nanocarrier-based formulations of thrombolytic agents, cardioprotective agents, and tissue-engineered constructs offer potential for restoring myocardial perfusion, reducing infarct size, and improving cardiac function following MI. Targeted delivery of stem cells, growth factors, or gene therapies to the ischemic myocardium via nanocarriers facilitates regenerative processes and enhances tissue repair, ultimately improving long-term outcomes and reducing the risk of heart failure and complications.

## 9.1.3.3 Heart Failure Management

Heart failure represents a complex syndrome characterized by impaired cardiac function and inadequate tissue perfusion, necessitating multimodal therapeutic approaches for symptom management and disease progression. Cardiovascular drug delivery plays a pivotal role in heart failure management by delivering vasodilators, diuretics, inotropic agents, and neurohormonal modulators to improve cardiac output, reduce preload and afterload, and alleviate symptoms such as dyspnea and fluid retention. Nanocarrier-based formulations of angiotensin-converting enzyme (ACE) inhibitors, beta-blockers, and mineralocorticoid receptor antagonists offer potential for targeted drug delivery to dysfunctional myocardium, mitigating adverse cardiac remodeling and improving long-term prognosis in heart failure patients.

## 9.1.3.4 Future Directions and Challenges

Despite significant advancements in cardiovascular drug delivery, several challenges remain to be addressed, including optimizing nanocarrier formulations for enhanced stability, biocompatibility, and targeted delivery to specific cardiovascular tissues. Furthermore, translating preclinical findings into clinical practice requires rigorous evaluation of safety, efficacy, and pharmacokinetics in human subjects, as well as overcoming regulatory hurdles and commercialization barriers. Future research efforts focus on developing personalized treatment strategies tailored to individual patient profiles and disease characteristics, integrating advanced imaging and diagnostic techniques with nanocarrier-based drug delivery systems, and exploring innovative therapeutic modalities such as gene editing, cell therapy, and regenerative medicine in cardiovascular medicine. By addressing these challenges and harnessing the full potential of cardiovascular drug delivery, clinicians can improve treatment outcomes, reduce morbidity and mortality, and enhance the quality of life for patients with cardiovascular diseases, ultimately advancing the field of cardiovascular medicine and personalized patient care.

## 9.2 Localized Drug Delivery Systems

Localized drug delivery systems are designed to target specific anatomical sites or tissues within the body, allowing for precise control over drug release kinetics and therapeutic effects while minimizing systemic exposure and off-target effects. This section explores the principles and strategies underlying localized drug delivery systems, highlighting their potential applications in various medical fields.

## 9.2.1 Principles and Strategies

Localized drug delivery systems employ various principles and strategies to achieve targeted drug delivery to specific anatomical sites or tissues. One of the key principles is site-specific targeting, which involves the selective accumulation of drugs at desired locations within the body while minimizing exposure to healthy tissues. Site-specific targeting can be achieved through passive or active targeting mechanisms. Passive targeting relies on physiological characteristics such as tissue permeability, vascularization, and pH gradients to enhance drug accumulation at target sites, whereas active targeting involves the use of ligands, antibodies, or peptides that bind to specific receptors or biomarkers expressed on target cells or tissues, facilitating targeted drug delivery.

Another principle underlying localized drug delivery systems is controlled drug release, which allows for precise modulation of drug release kinetics and therapeutic effects over time. Controlled drug release can be achieved through various mechanisms, including diffusion, erosion, and stimuli-responsive drug delivery systems. Diffusion-based systems rely on the passive diffusion of drugs through polymeric matrices or membranes, enabling sustained drug release over an extended period. Erosion-based systems involve the gradual degradation or dissolution of drug carriers, leading to controlled release of encapsulated drugs. Stimuli-responsive drug delivery systems respond to external stimuli such as pH, temperature, light, or enzymatic activity, triggering drug release at specific time points or locations within the body.

Localized drug delivery systems also utilize various formulation strategies to optimize drug stability, solubility, and bioavailability while minimizing toxicity and adverse effects. Formulation strategies may include encapsulation of drugs within nanoparticles, liposomes, hydrogels, or implants, which offer protection against degradation, improved drug solubility, and sustained release profiles. Additionally, surface modification of drug carriers with targeting ligands, stealth coatings, or mucoadhesive polymers enhances drug delivery efficiency, prolongs circulation time, and improves tissue penetration and retention.

Furthermore, advances in nanotechnology, biomaterials, and biomedical engineering have enabled the development of innovative localized drug delivery systems with enhanced therapeutic efficacy and biocompatibility. Nanocarriers, such as liposomes, polymeric nanoparticles, and dendrimers, offer advantages such as high drug loading capacity, tunable drug release kinetics, and targeted delivery to specific tissues or cells. Biomaterial-based scaffolds, hydrogels, and microparticles provide three-dimensional matrices for cell encapsulation, tissue engineering, and regenerative medicine applications, facilitating localized drug delivery and tissue regeneration in damaged or diseased tissues.

## 9.2.2 Nanocarriers for Localized Delivery

Nanocarriers represent a promising approach for localized drug delivery, offering precise control over drug release kinetics and targeting capabilities to specific anatomical sites or tissues within the body. This section explores the role of nanocarriers in localized drug delivery systems, highlighting their unique properties and applications in various medical fields.

## 9.2.2.1 Properties of Nanocarriers

Nanocarriers for localized drug delivery are characterized by their nano-sized dimensions, typically ranging from 1 to 1000 nanometers, which enable efficient cellular uptake, tissue penetration, and targeted delivery to specific sites within the body. Common types of nanocarriers utilized for localized drug delivery include liposomes, polymeric nanoparticles, dendrimers, and nanoemulsions. These nanocarriers offer advantages such as high drug loading capacity, tunable drug release kinetics, and enhanced stability and biocompatibility.

Liposomes are lipid-based vesicles composed of phospholipid bilayers, capable of encapsulating hydrophilic and lipophilic drugs and facilitating their transport across biological barriers. Polymeric nanoparticles are composed of biocompatible polymers such as poly(lactic-co-glycolic acid) (PLGA), polyethylene glycol (PEG), or chitosan, offering controlled drug release profiles and targeted delivery to specific tissues or cells. Dendrimers are highly branched macromolecules with precise molecular structures, offering high drug loading capacity and surface functionalization for targeted drug delivery. Nanoemulsions are colloidal dispersions of oil and water stabilized by surfactants, enabling the encapsulation of lipophilic drugs and efficient drug delivery to target tissues.

## 9.2.2.2 Mechanisms of Action

Nanocarriers employ various mechanisms to facilitate localized drug delivery, including passive targeting, active targeting, and controlled drug release. Passive targeting relies on the enhanced permeability and retention (EPR) effect, whereby nanocarriers accumulate preferentially in leaky or angiogenic blood vessels associated with diseased tissues such as tumors or inflamed tissues. Active targeting strategies involve surface modification of nanocarriers with ligands, antibodies, or peptides that bind to specific receptors or biomarkers expressed on target cells or tissues, facilitating targeted drug delivery and cellular uptake. Controlled drug release mechanisms enable precise modulation of drug release kinetics and therapeutic effects over time, allowing for sustained drug release and improved therapeutic outcomes.

## 9.2.2.3 Applications in Localized Drug Delivery

Nanocarriers hold promise for localized drug delivery in various medical fields, including oncology, neurology, ophthalmology, and regenerative medicine. In oncology, nanocarrier-based formulations of chemotherapeutic agents offer targeted delivery to solid tumors while minimizing systemic toxicity and off-target effects. In neurology, nanocarriers can traverse the blood-brain barrier and deliver drugs to the central nervous system for the treatment of neurological disorders such as Alzheimer's disease, Parkinson's disease, and brain tumors. In ophthalmology, nanocarriers enable targeted delivery of drugs to the posterior segment of the eye for the treatment of retinal diseases such as age-related macular degeneration and diabetic retinopathy. In regenerative medicine, nanocarriers facilitate localized delivery of growth factors, stem cells, or gene therapies to promote tissue repair and regeneration in damaged or diseased tissues.

## 9.2.2.4 Future Directions and Challenges

Despite significant advancements in nanocarrier-based localized drug delivery, several challenges remain to be addressed, including optimizing nanocarrier formulations for enhanced stability, biocompatibility, and targeted delivery to specific tissues or cells. Furthermore, translating preclinical findings into clinical practice requires rigorous evaluation of safety, efficacy, and pharmacokinetics in human subjects, as well as overcoming regulatory hurdles and commercialization barriers. Future research efforts focus on developing personalized treatment strategies tailored to individual patient profiles and disease characteristics, integrating advanced imaging and diagnostic techniques with nanocarrier-based drug delivery systems, and exploring innovative therapeutic modalities such as gene editing, cell therapy, and regenerative medicine in various medical fields. By addressing these challenges and harnessing the full potential of nanocarriers for localized drug delivery, researchers and clinicians can improve treatment outcomes, reduce off-target effects, and advance the field of drug delivery and personalized medicine.

# CHAPTER TEN

# CHARACTERIZATION,DRUG RELEASE, AND STABILITY STUDIES

## *10.1 Characterization of Nanomaterials*

Characterization of nanomaterials is essential for understanding their physical, chemical, and structural properties, which influence their behavior and performance in drug delivery systems. This section focuses on the techniques used for the physical characterization of nanomaterials, providing insights into their size, shape, surface properties, and morphology.

## *10.1.1 Physical Characterization Techniques*

Physical characterization techniques play a crucial role in assessing the properties of nanomaterials, providing valuable information about their size distribution, morphology, surface charge, and structural integrity. Several techniques are commonly employed for the physical characterization of nanomaterials, including:

1. **Dynamic Light Scattering (DLS)**: DLS is a non-invasive technique used to measure the size distribution of nanoparticles in solution. By analyzing the fluctuations in scattered light intensity caused by Brownian motion, DLS provides information about the hydrodynamic diameter of nanoparticles and their aggregation state in solution.

2. **Transmission Electron Microscopy (TEM)**: TEM is a high-resolution imaging technique that allows for the visualization of nanomaterials at the nanoscale. By passing a beam of electrons through a thin specimen, TEM generates detailed images of nanoparticle morphology, size, and shape, providing insights into their structural characteristics.

3. **Scanning Electron Microscopy (SEM)**: SEM is another imaging technique used to visualize nanomaterials at high resolution. By scanning a focused beam of electrons across the surface of a specimen, SEM generates three-dimensional images of nanoparticle morphology, surface topography, and size distribution.

4. **Atomic Force Microscopy (AFM)**: AFM is a powerful imaging technique that provides information about the surface topography and mechanical properties of nanomaterials. By scanning a sharp probe tip over the surface of a sample, AFM generates high-resolution images and quantitative data on nanoparticle size, shape, and surface roughness.

5. **Zeta Potential Analysis**: Zeta potential analysis is used to measure the surface charge of nanoparticles in solution, providing insights into their stability and colloidal behavior. By applying an electric field to a dispersion of nanoparticles, zeta potential analysis determines the electrostatic potential at the nanoparticle surface, which influences their interactions with surrounding molecules and particles.

6. **X-ray Diffraction (XRD)**: XRD is a technique used to analyze the crystal structure and phase composition of nanomaterials. By measuring the diffraction pattern of X-rays scattered by a crystalline sample, XRD provides information about the lattice parameters, crystal size, and orientation of nanoparticles, enabling the identification of crystalline phases and polymorphs.

7. **Fourier Transform Infrared Spectroscopy (FTIR)**: FTIR is a spectroscopic technique used to analyze the chemical composition and functional groups present in nanomaterials. By measuring the absorption and transmission of infrared radiation by a sample, FTIR generates spectra that reveal characteristic vibrational modes of chemical bonds, allowing for the identification of molecular species and surface functionalization of nanoparticles.

## *10.1.1.1 Microscopy Techniques (TEM, SEM, AFM)*

Microscopy techniques, including Transmission Electron Microscopy (TEM), Scanning Electron Microscopy (SEM), and Atomic Force Microscopy (AFM), are powerful tools for visualizing and characterizing nanomaterials at the nanoscale level. Each technique offers unique advantages and insights into the morphology, size, and structural properties of nanomaterials, contributing to our understanding of their behavior and performance in drug delivery systems.

1. **Transmission Electron Microscopy (TEM)**: TEM is a high-resolution imaging technique that provides detailed visualization of nanomaterials at the atomic scale. By passing a beam of electrons through a thin specimen, TEM generates high-resolution images of nanoparticle morphology, size, and crystallinity. TEM is particularly useful for visualizing the internal structure of nanoparticles, including core-shell structures, lattice defects, and surface modifications. Additionally, TEM can be used to measure nanoparticle size distribution and aspect ratio, providing quantitative data on nanoparticle dimensions and shape. However, TEM requires specialized sample preparation techniques, including thin sectioning and staining with heavy metals, and it is limited to imaging solid specimens in vacuum conditions.

2. **Scanning Electron Microscopy (SEM)**: SEM is another imaging technique used to visualize nanomaterials at high resolution. Unlike TEM, which transmits electrons through a thin specimen, SEM scans a focused beam of electrons across the surface of a sample, generating three-dimensional images of nanoparticle morphology and surface topography. SEM provides insights into nanoparticle size, shape, and surface features, including surface roughness, porosity, and agglomeration. SEM is well-suited for imaging a wide range of sample types, including solid, porous, and fibrous materials, and it allows for versatile sample preparation techniques, such as coating with conductive materials for enhanced imaging resolution. However, SEM typically offers lower resolution compared to TEM and requires a conductive sample surface for electron beam interaction.

3. **Atomic Force Microscopy (AFM)**: AFM is a powerful imaging technique that provides information about the surface topography and mechanical properties of nanomaterials. By scanning a sharp probe tip over the surface of a sample, AFM generates high-resolution images and quantitative data on nanoparticle height, width, and surface roughness.

AFM can be operated in various modes, including contact mode, tapping mode, and force spectroscopy, allowing for imaging of soft and biological samples without damage or distortion. AFM is particularly useful for studying biomolecular interactions, self-assembled monolayers, and nanomechanical properties of materials. However, AFM typically offers slower imaging speeds compared to TEM and SEM, and it requires careful calibration and sample preparation to obtain accurate measurements.

## 10.1.1.2 Size and Surface Area Analysis (DLS, BET)

Size and surface area analysis are crucial aspects of characterizing nanomaterials, providing insights into their physical properties and behavior in drug delivery systems. Dynamic Light Scattering (DLS) and Brunauer-Emmett-Teller (BET) analysis are commonly used techniques for determining the size distribution and surface area of nanomaterials, respectively, offering valuable information for their optimization and application in biomedical research.

1. **Dynamic Light Scattering (DLS):** DLS is a non-invasive technique used to measure the hydrodynamic size distribution of nanoparticles in solution. By analyzing the intensity fluctuations of scattered light caused by Brownian motion, DLS provides information about the size distribution, polydispersity, and aggregation state of nanoparticles. DLS is particularly well-suited for measuring the size of nanoparticles in colloidal dispersions, liposomal formulations, and polymeric nanoparticles. It is a rapid and convenient technique for assessing nanoparticle size distribution in solution, providing valuable insights into their stability, colloidal behavior, and interactions with biological molecules. However, DLS may underestimate the size of aggregated or non-spherical nanoparticles, and it is sensitive to factors such as particle concentration, sample preparation, and optical properties of the nanoparticles.

2. **Brunauer-Emmett-Teller (BET) Analysis:** BET analysis is a gas adsorption technique used to measure the specific surface area of nanomaterials. By measuring the adsorption and desorption of gas molecules onto the surface of a solid sample, BET analysis calculates the

surface area based on the formation of a monolayer of gas molecules on the sample surface. BET analysis provides quantitative data on the surface area, pore volume, and pore size distribution of nanomaterials, offering insights into their surface reactivity, porosity, and adsorption capacity. BET analysis is particularly useful for characterizing porous materials such as mesoporous silica nanoparticles, carbon nanotubes, and metal-organic frameworks. It enables the optimization of nanomaterial synthesis and processing parameters to achieve desired surface properties and performance in drug delivery applications. However, BET analysis requires careful sample preparation and data interpretation to ensure accurate measurements, and it is sensitive to factors such as sample degassing, temperature, and pressure.

## 10.2 Drug Release Studies of Nanomaterials

## 10.2.1 Mechanisms of Drug Release

Understanding the mechanisms of drug release from nanomaterials is crucial for optimizing their therapeutic efficacy and ensuring controlled delivery of pharmaceutical agents. Drug release mechanisms from nanomaterials can be broadly categorized into three main types: diffusion-controlled release, degradation-controlled release, and stimulus-responsive release. Each mechanism operates based on different principles and environmental conditions, allowing for tailored drug delivery systems that meet specific therapeutic needs.

**Diffusion-Controlled Release:**

In diffusion-controlled release, the drug is physically encapsulated within or adsorbed onto the surface of the nanomaterial, and its release occurs primarily through diffusion. The rate of drug release is governed by Fick's laws of diffusion, which describe how the concentration gradient drives the movement of molecules.

- **Encapsulation and Matrix Systems:** In encapsulation systems, the drug is enclosed within a nanocarrier, such as liposomes, micelles, or polymeric nanoparticles. The drug diffuses through the carrier's matrix or shell, leading to a sustained release over time. For instance, liposomal formulations encapsulate hydrophilic drugs in their aqueous core and hydrophobic drugs within their lipid bilayer.

- **Surface Adsorption:** Drugs can also be adsorbed onto the surface of nanomaterials, such as gold nanoparticles or silica nanoparticles. The release in this case depends on the desorption kinetics from the surface, which can be modulated by altering the surface properties and interactions between the drug and the nanomaterial.

### Degradation-Controlled Release:

Degradation-controlled release involves the release of the drug as the nanomaterial carrier undergoes degradation or erosion. This mechanism is commonly seen in biodegradable polymeric nanoparticles, where the polymer matrix gradually breaks down, releasing the encapsulated drug.

- **Polymer Degradation:** Biodegradable polymers such as poly(lactic-co-glycolic acid) (PLGA) are widely used for drug delivery. The hydrolytic or enzymatic degradation of the polymer backbone leads to the release of the drug. The rate of polymer degradation can be tailored by adjusting the polymer composition, molecular weight, and copolymer ratio.
- **Erosion and Surface Erosion:** Erosion can occur throughout the bulk of the material (bulk erosion) or predominantly at the surface (surface erosion). Surface erosion provides a more predictable and linear release profile, which is advantageous for maintaining consistent drug levels over time.

### Stimulus-Responsive Release:

Stimulus-responsive release, also known as "smart" or "triggered" release, involves the release of the drug in response to specific environmental triggers. These triggers can be internal (e.g., pH, temperature, enzymes) or external (e.g., light, magnetic fields).

- **pH-Responsive Systems:** Many nanomaterials are designed to release drugs in response to pH changes. For example, in tumor microenvironments, which are often more acidic than normal tissues, pH-sensitive polymers can undergo conformational changes or degradation, leading to drug release. Polymeric micelles with pH-sensitive linkers or coatings are commonly used in such applications.

- **Temperature-Responsive Systems:** Temperature-sensitive nanomaterials release drugs in response to changes in temperature. Thermo-responsive polymers, such as poly(N-isopropylacrylamide) (PNIPAM), undergo phase transitions at specific temperatures, triggering drug release. These systems are useful for localized hyperthermia treatments where the local temperature is raised to induce drug release.

- **Enzyme-Responsive Systems:** Enzyme-responsive nanomaterials release drugs in the presence of specific enzymes that are overexpressed in certain pathological conditions. For example, matrix metalloproteinase (MMP)-sensitive nanoparticles release drugs in response to MMPs, which are abundant in tumor tissues and inflammatory sites.

- **Externally Triggered Systems:** External triggers such as light, ultrasound, and magnetic fields can also be used to control drug release. For instance, photo-responsive nanoparticles release drugs upon exposure to specific wavelengths of light, while magnetically responsive nanoparticles release drugs under the influence of an external magnetic field.

Each of these drug release mechanisms offers unique advantages and can be tailored to meet the specific requirements of different therapeutic applications. By understanding and optimizing these mechanisms, researchers can develop advanced nanomaterial-based drug delivery systems that provide controlled, sustained, and targeted release of therapeutic agents, enhancing their efficacy and reducing side effects.

## 10.2 Drug Release Studies of Nanomaterials

### 10.2.1 Mechanisms of Drug Release

#### 10.2.1.2 Erosion-Controlled Release

Erosion-controlled release is a pivotal mechanism in the realm of drug delivery systems, particularly those involving biodegradable nanomaterials. This release mechanism hinges on the gradual erosion or degradation of the nanocarrier matrix, facilitating the sustained and controlled release of the encapsulated drug over time. Erosion-controlled release is extensively employed in systems using biodegradable polymers, as these materials can degrade into biocompatible and non-toxic byproducts that are safely eliminated from the body.

**Polymer Matrix Degradation:** The core of erosion-controlled release lies in the degradation of the polymer matrix that constitutes the nanocarrier. Biodegradable polymers such as poly(lactic acid) (PLA), poly(glycolic acid) (PGA), and their copolymer poly(lactic-co-glycolic acid) (PLGA) are commonly used. These polymers degrade through hydrolytic or enzymatic cleavage of their ester bonds, breaking down into smaller fragments that are eventually metabolized or excreted.

- **Hydrolytic Degradation:** Hydrolytic degradation occurs when water molecules penetrate the polymer matrix, cleaving the ester bonds within the polymer chains. This process is influenced by the polymer's chemical composition, molecular weight, and crystallinity. For instance, PLGA copolymers with varying ratios of lactic acid to glycolic acid can be tailored to degrade at different rates, providing precise control over drug release profiles. The degradation rate can also be adjusted by modifying the polymer's end groups or incorporating additives that enhance hydrolysis.
- **Enzymatic Degradation:** Enzymatic degradation involves the breakdown of the polymer matrix by specific enzymes present in the physiological environment. Enzymes such as esterases and proteases catalyze the cleavage of polymer bonds, accelerating the degradation process. This mechanism is particularly relevant for natural polymers like chitosan and alginate, which are susceptible to enzymatic attack. Enzymatic degradation can be highly selective and occur at specific sites within the body, allowing for targeted drug release in response to local enzyme concentrations.

**Surface Erosion vs. Bulk Erosion:** Erosion-controlled release can be categorized into surface erosion and bulk erosion, each with distinct release characteristics.

- **Surface Erosion:** Surface erosion is characterized by the gradual removal of the polymer matrix from the outer surface inward. This type of erosion results in a more predictable and linear drug release profile, as the surface area exposed to the degrading medium remains relatively constant over time. Polymers such as polyanhydrides and poly(ortho esters) are known for their surface-eroding properties. Surface erosion is advantageous for applications requiring a constant drug release rate, such as chronic disease management and long-term therapies.

- **Bulk Erosion:** In bulk erosion, the polymer matrix degrades throughout its entire volume simultaneously. Water penetrates the matrix, causing it to swell and degrade internally. This can lead to a more complex release profile, often characterized by an initial burst release followed by a slower, sustained release. Bulk-eroding polymers like PLGA and PLA are widely used in drug delivery systems. The burst release phase can be beneficial for achieving immediate therapeutic levels, while the subsequent sustained release maintains drug concentration within the therapeutic window.

**Factors Influencing Erosion-Controlled Release:** Several factors influence the rate and extent of erosion-controlled drug release, allowing for fine-tuning of the delivery system.

- **Polymer Composition:** The chemical composition of the polymer significantly affects its degradation behavior. Copolymers like PLGA, with varying lactic to glycolic acid ratios, offer a range of degradation rates. Higher glycolic acid content generally accelerates degradation due to increased hydrophilicity and faster hydrolytic cleavage.
- **Molecular Weight:** The molecular weight of the polymer impacts its degradation rate and mechanical properties. Lower molecular weight polymers degrade more quickly due to shorter polymer chains and increased surface area. However, they may also exhibit reduced mechanical strength and stability.
- **Crystallinity:** The degree of crystallinity in the polymer matrix influences its degradation rate. Amorphous regions degrade faster than crystalline regions due to easier water penetration and polymer chain mobility. Semi-crystalline polymers exhibit a combination of rapid degradation in amorphous regions and slower degradation in crystalline regions.
- **Additives and Plasticizers:** The incorporation of additives and plasticizers can modify the degradation behavior of the polymer matrix. Plasticizers increase the flexibility and hydrophilicity of the polymer, accelerating degradation. Additives like porogens create pores within the matrix, enhancing water penetration and facilitating faster erosion.

**Applications and Advantages:** Erosion-controlled release systems are extensively used in various biomedical applications due to their versatility and tunable properties. They are employed in implantable devices, injectable depots, and oral drug delivery systems.

- **Implantable Devices:** Erosion-controlled release systems are ideal for implantable devices that provide long-term drug delivery. For example, PLGA-based implants are used for the sustained release of hormones, anti-inflammatory agents, and chemotherapeutic drugs, ensuring consistent therapeutic levels over extended periods.
- **Injectable Depots:** Injectable depots utilizing erosion-controlled polymers offer a minimally invasive option for delivering drugs over weeks to months. These systems are beneficial for treating chronic conditions like diabetes, where controlled release of insulin or other therapeutic agents is required.
- **Oral Drug Delivery:** Erosion-controlled polymer matrices are used in oral formulations to achieve sustained release and improve bioavailability. They protect the drug from the harsh gastrointestinal environment and provide prolonged drug release, enhancing patient compliance and therapeutic outcomes.

Erosion-controlled release mechanisms provide a robust and flexible platform for developing advanced drug delivery systems. By leveraging the principles of polymer degradation and erosion, researchers can design nanomaterials that deliver drugs in a controlled, sustained, and targeted manner, ultimately improving therapeutic efficacy and patient outcomes.

## *10.2.1 Mechanisms of Drug Release*

### 10.2.1.3 Stimuli-Responsive Release

Stimuli-responsive release is an advanced and innovative approach in the field of drug delivery systems, where the release of therapeutic agents from nanomaterials is controlled by specific external or internal stimuli. These stimuli can include changes in pH, temperature, light, magnetic fields, ultrasound, or the presence of specific enzymes. Stimuli-responsive nanomaterials are engineered to respond to these triggers, allowing for precise, on-demand drug release that can be spatially and temporally controlled, enhancing therapeutic efficacy and minimizing side effects.

**pH-Responsive Release:** pH-responsive nanomaterials exploit the variations in pH found in different biological environments to trigger drug release. For instance, the acidic microenvironment of tumors (pH ~6.5) or the endosomal/lysosomal compartments within cells (pH ~5.0) can be targeted using pH-sensitive polymers. Polymers such as poly(l-histidine), poly(acrylic acid), and poly(β-amino esters) undergo conformational changes or degradation at acidic pH, leading to the release of encapsulated drugs.

- **Mechanism:** In pH-sensitive systems, the polymer matrix can either swell, dissolve, or degrade in response to pH changes. For example, poly(lactic-co-glycolic acid) (PLGA) nanoparticles can be coated with pH-sensitive materials that dissolve at acidic pH, releasing the drug payload specifically at the tumor site or within cellular compartments.
- **Applications:** pH-responsive nanomaterials are particularly useful in cancer therapy, where they ensure targeted drug delivery to tumor cells while sparing healthy tissues. This specificity enhances the therapeutic index of anticancer drugs and reduces systemic toxicity.

**Temperature-Responsive Release:** Temperature-responsive nanomaterials utilize the differences in temperature between normal and pathological tissues or the externally applied thermal triggers to control drug release. Polymers like poly(N-isopropylacrylamide) (PNIPAM) exhibit a lower critical solution temperature (LCST) around body temperature, below which they are hydrophilic and swollen, and above which they become hydrophobic and collapse, releasing the drug.

- **Mechanism:** In temperature-sensitive systems, the polymer undergoes a phase transition in response to temperature changes. For instance, at temperatures above the LCST, PNIPAM-based nanoparticles shrink, expelling the encapsulated drug. Conversely, at temperatures below the LCST, the polymer swells, retaining the drug within its matrix.
- **Applications:** Temperature-responsive nanomaterials are employed in hyperthermia-based cancer treatments, where localized heating of the tumor site triggers drug release. They are also used in transdermal drug delivery systems, where the application of mild heat can enhance drug permeation through the skin.

**Light-Responsive Release:** Light-responsive nanomaterials leverage the use of specific wavelengths of light to induce drug release. These systems often incorporate photosensitive molecules such as azobenzene, spiropyran, or gold nanorods, which undergo structural changes or generate heat upon light irradiation, triggering drug release.

- **Mechanism:** Light-sensitive nanomaterials can release drugs through photothermal effects, where light absorption by nanoparticles generates localized heat, causing the polymer matrix to degrade or swell. Alternatively, photoisomerization of incorporated molecules can lead to conformational changes that release the drug.
- **Applications:** Light-responsive systems offer the advantage of non-invasive, precise control over drug release. They are used in site-specific treatments where light can be directed to the target area, such as in ocular therapies, skin treatments, or localized cancer therapy.

**Magnetic-Responsive Release:** Magnetic-responsive nanomaterials utilize externally applied magnetic fields to control drug release. These systems often include superparamagnetic iron oxide nanoparticles (SPIONs) embedded within the polymer matrix. Upon exposure to an alternating magnetic field, the nanoparticles generate heat (magnetic hyperthermia) or induce mechanical changes that trigger drug release.

- **Mechanism:** Magnetic fields can induce heating in magnetic nanoparticles, leading to thermal degradation of the polymer matrix and subsequent drug release. Alternatively, magnetic fields can cause physical deformation or movement of the nanoparticles, disrupting the polymer matrix and releasing the drug.
- **Applications:** Magnetic-responsive nanomaterials are applied in targeted drug delivery and hyperthermia therapy for cancer treatment. The ability to externally control drug release with magnetic fields allows for precise spatiotemporal delivery, reducing off-target effects and improving therapeutic outcomes.

**Enzyme-Responsive Release:** Enzyme-responsive nanomaterials are designed to release drugs in the presence of specific enzymes that are overexpressed in certain pathological conditions. These systems use substrates that are cleaved by target enzymes, leading to the degradation of the polymer matrix and drug release.

- **Mechanism:** Enzyme-sensitive linkers or polymer backbones are incorporated into the nanomaterials. When exposed to the target enzyme, these linkers are cleaved, causing the nanomaterial to disassemble and release the drug. For example, matrix metalloproteinase (MMP)-sensitive peptides can be used to design nanoparticles that release drugs in the tumor microenvironment where MMPs are abundant.
- **Applications:** Enzyme-responsive systems are particularly useful in cancer therapy, where specific enzymes like MMPs, cathepsins, or phosphatases are overexpressed. These systems ensure that drug release occurs only in the presence of the target enzyme, providing highly targeted and efficient therapy.

Stimuli-responsive release mechanisms offer significant advantages in the design of sophisticated drug delivery systems. By responding to specific triggers, these systems provide controlled, on-demand drug release, enhancing therapeutic efficacy, minimizing side effects, and improving patient outcomes. The versatility of stimuli-responsive nanomaterials holds great promise for advancing personalized medicine and developing next-generation therapies.

## *10.2.2 In Vitro Drug Release Testing*

## *Introduction:*

In vitro drug release testing is a crucial step in the evaluation of nanomaterials designed for drug delivery. This testing allows researchers to understand the release kinetics and mechanisms of drug release from nanocarriers under controlled laboratory conditions. The data obtained from in vitro studies are essential for predicting the in vivo behavior of the drug delivery system, optimizing formulations, and ensuring consistent performance.

**Setup and Equipment:**

In vitro drug release testing typically involves the use of dissolution apparatuses, dialysis methods, or diffusion cells.

1. **Dissolution Apparatuses:**

- **USP Apparatus 1 (Basket):** In this method, the nanomaterial is placed in a basket that rotates in a dissolution medium. The medium is sampled at specific time intervals to measure the amount of drug released.
- **USP Apparatus 2 (Paddle):** This apparatus uses a paddle that stirs the dissolution medium in which the nanomaterial is dispersed. Samples of the medium are taken at regular intervals to determine the drug concentration.
- **USP Apparatus 4 (Flow-Through Cell):** In this setup, the dissolution medium flows through a cell containing the nanomaterial. This method is suitable for poorly soluble drugs and provides a continuous release profile.

1. **Dialysis Methods:**

- **Dialysis Bags or Membranes:** The nanomaterial is placed inside a dialysis bag or membrane, which is then immersed in the dissolution medium. Only drug molecules can diffuse through the membrane, allowing for the measurement of drug release over time.
- **Advantages:** Dialysis methods are simple and effective for separating the drug from the nanocarrier and are commonly used for testing nanoparticle and liposome formulations.

3. **Diffusion Cells:**

- **Franz Diffusion Cells:** These cells are used for testing drug release from semi-solid formulations like gels and creams. The nanomaterial formulation is placed in the donor compartment, and the receptor compartment contains the dissolution medium. The drug diffuses across a membrane separating the two compartments, and samples are collected from the receptor compartment for analysis.

**Procedure:**

1. **Preparation of Nanomaterial:**

- The nanomaterial containing the drug is accurately weighed and dispersed in an appropriate dissolution medium. The medium is chosen based on the solubility and stability of the drug and nanomaterial.

2. **Setup and Initiation:**

- The dissolution apparatus, dialysis setup, or diffusion cell is prepared according to the specific method being used. The nanomaterial is placed in the designated compartment (e.g., basket, paddle, dialysis bag, or donor compartment).

3. **Sampling:**

- At predetermined time intervals, samples of the dissolution medium are collected to measure the concentration of the released drug. The intervals are chosen based on the expected release profile and the kinetics of the drug release.

4. **Analysis:**

- The collected samples are analyzed using appropriate analytical techniques, such as High-Performance Liquid Chromatography (HPLC), UV-Visible Spectroscopy, or Mass Spectrometry, to quantify the amount of drug released at each time point.

5. **Data Interpretation:**

- The release data are plotted as a function of time to generate release profiles. Various mathematical models (e.g., zero-order, first-order, Higuchi, Korsmeyer-Peppas) are used to analyze the release kinetics and mechanisms.

**Examples of In Vitro Drug Release Testing Methods:**

1. **Dialysis Method:**

- **Setup:** The nanomaterial containing the drug is placed inside a dialysis bag, which is then immersed in a dissolution medium.
- **Procedure:** Samples are taken from the dissolution medium at regular intervals and analyzed to determine the drug concentration.

2. **Rotating Basket Method:**

- **Setup:** The nanomaterial is placed in a rotating basket submerged in the dissolution medium.
- **Procedure:** The medium is stirred by the rotating basket, and samples are taken at specific time points to measure drug release.

3. **Franz Diffusion Cell Method:**

- **Setup:** The nanomaterial formulation is placed in the donor compartment, and the receptor compartment contains the dissolution medium.
- **Procedure:** Samples are taken from the receptor compartment at regular intervals to determine the drug concentration.

**Advantages of In Vitro Drug Release Testing:**

- **Controlled Environment:** In vitro testing provides a controlled environment where variables such as temperature, pH, and agitation can be precisely regulated.
- **Cost-Effective:** It is a cost-effective method for preliminary evaluation of drug release profiles before proceeding to in vivo studies.
- **Predictive Value:** In vitro data can provide valuable insights into the expected in vivo behavior of the drug delivery system, helping to predict its performance in biological systems.

## *10.2.2.1 Dialysis Method*

The dialysis method is a widely used technique for evaluating the in vitro drug release profiles of nanomaterials. This method employs dialysis membranes to create a barrier that mimics biological membranes, allowing the drug to diffuse from the nanomaterial into the release medium. This setup provides a controlled environment to study the release kinetics and mechanism.

**Setup and Equipment:** The dialysis method involves using a dialysis bag or membrane with a specified molecular weight cut-off (MWCO) that allows only the drug molecules to pass through while retaining the nanomaterials within the bag. The choice of MWCO depends on the size of the drug molecules and the nanocarriers. Typically, dialysis tubing made of materials like cellulose acetate or regenerated cellulose is used.

**Procedure:**

1. **Preparation of Dialysis Bag:** A section of dialysis tubing is cut to the desired length and soaked in distilled water to remove any preservatives. The ends of the tubing are securely tied after loading the drug-loaded nanomaterial solution into the bag.

2. **Immersion in Release Medium:** The dialysis bag containing the nanomaterial is immersed in a beaker or flask filled with an appropriate release medium, such as phosphate-buffered saline (PBS) or simulated body fluids. The medium is maintained at a constant temperature, usually 37°C, to mimic physiological conditions.

3. **Stirring and Sampling:** The beaker or flask is placed on a magnetic stirrer to ensure uniform mixing of the release medium. At predetermined time intervals, samples of the release medium are withdrawn for analysis. An equal volume of fresh medium is added to maintain constant volume.

4. **Analysis of Released Drug:** The withdrawn samples are analyzed using techniques such as high-performance liquid chromatography (HPLC), UV-visible spectroscopy, or mass spectrometry to quantify the amount of drug released.

**Parameters Affecting Drug Release:** Several factors influence the drug release profile in the dialysis method:

- **Molecular Weight Cut-Off (MWCO):** The MWCO of the dialysis membrane determines the size of molecules that can pass through. Choosing an appropriate MWCO is critical to ensure that only the drug molecules are released while retaining the nanomaterials.

- **Release Medium:** The composition of the release medium affects the solubility and stability of the drug. Commonly used media include PBS, simulated gastric fluid, and simulated intestinal fluid.

- **Temperature:** The release studies are usually conducted at 37°C to simulate body temperature. Temperature variations can affect the diffusion rate and solubility of the drug.
- **Stirring Speed:** Uniform mixing of the release medium is essential to maintain a consistent concentration gradient across the dialysis membrane, which drives the diffusion of the drug.

**Advantages and Limitations:**

- **Advantages:** The dialysis method is simple, cost-effective, and widely applicable to various types of nanomaterials. It provides a clear understanding of the drug release kinetics and can be easily adapted to different experimental conditions.
- **Limitations:** The method may not perfectly mimic in vivo conditions due to the absence of biological interactions. The choice of dialysis membrane and MWCO must be carefully considered to avoid interference with the release profile.

The dialysis method is a valuable tool in the preliminary assessment of drug release from nanomaterials. By providing insights into the release kinetics and mechanism, this method helps in optimizing the formulation and ensuring the consistent performance of drug delivery systems.

## *10.2.2.2 Rotating Basket Method*

The rotating basket method is a standardized in vitro technique used to assess the drug release profiles from nanomaterials. It is one of the official methods specified in pharmacopeias such as the United States Pharmacopeia (USP). This method involves using a rotating basket apparatus that facilitates uniform drug release into the dissolution medium under controlled conditions, providing valuable data on the release kinetics and mechanisms.

**Setup and Equipment:** The rotating basket method employs a dissolution apparatus, typically referred to as USP Apparatus 1. The key components of this apparatus include:

- **Rotating Basket:** A cylindrical metal mesh basket that holds the nanomaterial sample. The basket is attached to a shaft that rotates at a constant speed.
- **Dissolution Vessel:** A glass vessel containing the dissolution medium, which is placed in a water bath to maintain a constant temperature, usually at 37°C.
- **Stirring Mechanism:** The basket is rotated at a specified speed, usually 50-100 revolutions per minute (rpm), to ensure consistent mixing of the dissolution medium.

**Procedure:**

1. **Preparation of Sample:** The drug-loaded nanomaterial is placed in the rotating basket. The quantity of the sample and the volume of the dissolution medium are determined based on the experimental requirements and pharmacopeial guidelines.
2. **Immersion in Dissolution Medium:** The basket containing the sample is immersed in the dissolution vessel filled with an appropriate medium, such as phosphate-buffered saline (PBS) or simulated gastric fluid. The medium is maintained at a constant temperature to simulate physiological conditions.
3. **Rotation and Sampling:** The basket is rotated at a specified speed to ensure uniform mixing and exposure of the nanomaterial to the dissolution medium. At predetermined time intervals, samples of the dissolution medium are withdrawn for analysis. An equal volume of fresh medium is added to maintain a constant volume.
4. **Analysis of Released Drug:** The withdrawn samples are analyzed using techniques such as high-performance liquid chromatography (HPLC), UV-visible spectroscopy, or mass spectrometry to quantify the amount of drug released.

**Parameters Affecting Drug Release:** Several factors influence the drug release profile in the rotating basket method:

- **Rotation Speed:** The speed of basket rotation affects the hydrodynamic conditions and the rate of drug release. Higher speeds can enhance the dissolution rate but may also lead to mechanical stress on the nanomaterials.

- **Dissolution Medium:** The composition and pH of the dissolution medium impact the solubility and stability of the drug. Commonly used media include PBS, simulated gastric fluid, and simulated intestinal fluid.
- **Temperature:** The release studies are typically conducted at 37°C to mimic body temperature. Temperature variations can affect the solubility and diffusion rate of the drug.
- **Basket Mesh Size:** The mesh size of the basket should be appropriate to contain the nanomaterials while allowing the free flow of the dissolution medium.

**Advantages and Limitations:**

- **Advantages:** The rotating basket method is a well-established and widely accepted technique for drug release testing. It provides reproducible and reliable data, making it suitable for regulatory submissions. The method allows for the controlled study of drug release kinetics under standardized conditions.
- **Limitations:** The method may not fully replicate the complex biological environment encountered in vivo. The mechanical stress induced by rotation might affect the integrity of some sensitive nanomaterials. Additionally, the choice of dissolution medium must be carefully considered to ensure it mimics the intended site of drug release.

The rotating basket method is a valuable tool in the evaluation of drug release from nanomaterials. It offers a standardized approach to studying release kinetics, aiding in the optimization and development of effective drug delivery systems. By providing detailed insights into the release profiles, this method contributes to the formulation of nanomaterials with predictable and controlled drug release characteristics.

## 10.2.2 In Vitro Drug Release Testing

## 10.2.2.3 Franz Diffusion Cell Method

The Franz diffusion cell method is a widely used technique for evaluating the in vitro drug release profiles of nanomaterials, particularly those intended for topical and transdermal delivery. This method employs a diffusion cell apparatus to simulate the conditions of drug release through a semi-permeable membrane, providing valuable insights into the release kinetics and mechanisms.

**Setup and Equipment:** The Franz diffusion cell apparatus consists of several key components:

- **Donor Compartment:** The upper chamber where the drug-loaded nanomaterial is placed.
- **Receptor Compartment:** The lower chamber filled with a suitable receptor medium that receives the released drug.
- **Semi-Permeable Membrane:** A membrane, such as synthetic or biological skin, that separates the donor and receptor compartments. This membrane mimics the barrier properties of skin or other biological tissues.
- **Magnetic Stirrer:** Ensures uniform mixing of the receptor medium to maintain a constant concentration gradient.

**Procedure:**

1. **Preparation of Membrane and Sample:** The semi-permeable membrane is pre-treated (hydrated) according to experimental requirements and placed between the donor and receptor compartments. The drug-loaded nanomaterial is then applied to the surface of the membrane in the donor compartment.
2. **Filling the Receptor Compartment:** The receptor compartment is filled with an appropriate receptor medium, such as phosphate-buffered saline (PBS) or simulated body fluids, and maintained at a constant temperature, usually 37°C, to simulate physiological conditions.
3. **Diffusion and Sampling:** The diffusion cell is assembled, ensuring that the donor and receptor compartments are securely fastened. The receptor medium is stirred continuously using a magnetic stirrer. At predetermined time intervals, samples of the receptor medium are withdrawn for analysis. An equal volume of fresh medium is added to maintain constant volume and concentration.
4. **Analysis of Released Drug:** The withdrawn samples are analyzed using techniques such as high-performance liquid chromatography (HPLC), UV-visible spectroscopy, or mass spectrometry to quantify the amount of drug released.

**Parameters Affecting Drug Release:** Several factors influence the drug release profile in the Franz diffusion cell method:

- **Membrane Type:** The choice of membrane is crucial as it mimics the biological barrier. Commonly used membranes include synthetic membranes (e.g., cellulose acetate) and biological membranes (e.g., excised animal skin).
- **Receptor Medium Composition:** The receptor medium should be chosen to maintain the drug's solubility and stability. PBS, simulated gastric fluid, and simulated intestinal fluid are commonly used.
- **Temperature:** The release studies are typically conducted at 37°C to mimic body temperature. Variations in temperature can affect the diffusion rate and solubility of the drug.
- **Stirring Rate:** Uniform mixing of the receptor medium is essential to maintain a consistent concentration gradient across the membrane, which drives the diffusion of the drug.

**Advantages and Limitations:**

- **Advantages:** The Franz diffusion cell method provides a controlled and reproducible environment for studying drug release from nanomaterials. It is particularly useful for evaluating topical and transdermal delivery systems. The method allows for the investigation of drug permeation through biological or synthetic membranes.
- **Limitations:** The method may not fully replicate in vivo conditions due to the absence of complex biological interactions. The choice of membrane and receptor medium must be carefully considered to ensure they accurately represent the intended application site.

The Franz diffusion cell method is an essential tool in the preliminary assessment of drug release from nanomaterials intended for topical and transdermal applications. By providing detailed insights into the release kinetics and mechanisms, this method aids in optimizing the formulation and ensuring consistent performance of drug delivery systems.

## *10.2.2.4 HPLC Analysis*

High-performance liquid chromatography (HPLC) analysis is a crucial technique used to quantify the amount of drug released from nanomaterials during in vitro drug release testing. This method provides accurate and reliable data on drug concentrations, enabling the assessment of release profiles and kinetics. HPLC analysis involves the separation, identification, and quantification of drug molecules in the samples collected from various in vitro release methods such as the dialysis method, rotating basket method, and Franz diffusion cell method.

**Principle and Equipment:** HPLC operates on the principle of liquid chromatography, where a liquid mobile phase carries the sample through a stationary phase (column) packed with a solid adsorbent material. The drug molecules interact with the stationary phase and are separated based on their different affinities. Key components of the HPLC system include:

- **Pump:** Delivers the mobile phase at a constant flow rate, ensuring reproducible chromatography conditions.
- **Injector:** Introduces the sample into the mobile phase stream.
- **Column:** Packed with adsorbent material (e.g., silica) that separates the drug molecules based on their chemical properties.
- **Detector:** Detects the separated drug molecules and generates a signal proportional to their concentration. Common detectors include UV-visible spectrophotometers and mass spectrometers.
- **Data System:** Collects and analyzes the detector signals, providing quantitative and qualitative information about the drug.

**Procedure:**

1. **Sample Preparation:** Samples collected from the in vitro release methods are prepared for HPLC analysis. This involves filtration to remove any particulate matter and, if necessary, dilution to bring the drug concentration within the linear range of the detector.
2. **Mobile Phase Selection:** The mobile phase is selected based on the solubility and chemical properties of the drug. It typically consists of a mixture of solvents such as water, methanol, acetonitrile, and buffer solutions. The pH and ionic strength of the mobile phase are adjusted to optimize separation.
3. **Chromatographic Conditions:** The HPLC system is set up with appropriate chromatographic conditions, including the choice of

column, flow rate, and detection wavelength. These parameters are optimized to achieve the best resolution and sensitivity for the drug.

4. **Injection and Separation:** The prepared sample is injected into the HPLC system. The mobile phase carries the sample through the column, where the drug molecules are separated based on their interaction with the stationary phase.

5. **Detection and Quantification:** As the separated drug molecules elute from the column, they are detected by the detector. The detector generates a chromatogram, displaying peaks corresponding to the drug and any impurities. The area under the peak is proportional to the drug concentration, which is quantified using a calibration curve prepared with known concentrations of the drug.

**Parameters Affecting HPLC Analysis:** Several factors influence the accuracy and precision of HPLC analysis:

- **Column Selection:** The choice of column, including its length, diameter, and particle size, affects the separation efficiency and resolution. Columns with smaller particle sizes generally provide better resolution but require higher pressure.
- **Mobile Phase Composition:** The composition, pH, and ionic strength of the mobile phase influence the retention time and separation of the drug. Gradient elution, where the mobile phase composition changes during the run, can improve separation for complex mixtures.
- **Flow Rate:** The flow rate of the mobile phase affects the separation and analysis time. Optimal flow rates balance resolution and analysis speed.
- **Detection Wavelength:** The wavelength selected for detection should correspond to the maximum absorbance of the drug to ensure sensitive and accurate quantification.

**Advantages and Limitations:**

- **Advantages:** HPLC analysis offers high sensitivity, specificity, and accuracy for quantifying drug release. It can separate and identify multiple components in a sample, providing detailed information about the drug and any degradation products or impurities. HPLC is widely applicable to various types of drugs and formulations.

- **Limitations:** HPLC analysis requires sophisticated equipment and skilled operators. The method development and optimization process can be time-consuming. Additionally, the choice of mobile phase and chromatographic conditions may require extensive trial and error to achieve optimal separation.

HPLC analysis is an indispensable tool in the evaluation of drug release from nanomaterials. It provides precise and reliable quantitative data, enabling the characterization of release profiles and supporting the development of effective drug delivery systems. By ensuring accurate measurement of drug concentrations, HPLC analysis contributes to the optimization and validation of in vitro drug release testing methods.

## *10.2.3 In Vivo Drug Release Studies*

In vivo drug release studies are essential for understanding the behavior of drug-loaded nanomaterials within a living organism. These studies provide critical data on the pharmacokinetics, biodistribution, efficacy, and safety of the nanomaterials, which are crucial for the translation of laboratory findings to clinical applications. Unlike in vitro studies, in vivo studies offer a more comprehensive assessment of how the drug is released, distributed, metabolized, and excreted in the body.

**Study Design and Animal Models:** In vivo drug release studies are typically conducted using animal models that closely mimic human physiology and disease conditions. Commonly used animal models include rodents (mice and rats), rabbits, and larger animals such as dogs and primates, depending on the specific requirements of the study. The choice of animal model depends on factors such as the drug's intended use, the complexity of the disease model, and ethical considerations.

**Procedure:**

1. **Preparation of Drug-Loaded Nanomaterials:** The nanomaterials are synthesized and characterized for their physicochemical properties, such as size, shape, surface charge, and drug loading efficiency. This step ensures consistency and reproducibility of the nanomaterials used in the study.

2. **Dosing and Administration:** The drug-loaded nanomaterials are administered to the animal models via appropriate routes, such as

intravenous, intraperitoneal, subcutaneous, oral, or topical. The dosing regimen, including the dose, frequency, and duration, is designed based on the drug's pharmacokinetic profile and therapeutic goals.

3. **Sample Collection:** Biological samples, including blood, urine, feces, and tissues, are collected at predetermined time points following administration. These samples provide data on the drug's absorption, distribution, metabolism, and excretion (ADME).

4. **Drug Analysis:** The collected samples are analyzed using advanced analytical techniques, such as high-performance liquid chromatography (HPLC), liquid chromatography-mass spectrometry (LC-MS), or enzyme-linked immunosorbent assay (ELISA), to quantify the drug concentration in various biological matrices. These analyses provide time-dependent concentration profiles that describe the drug's pharmacokinetics.

5. **Pharmacokinetic Analysis:** The pharmacokinetic parameters, including the area under the curve (AUC), peak plasma concentration (Cmax), time to peak concentration (Tmax), half-life (t1/2), and clearance (CL), are calculated from the concentration-time data. These parameters help in understanding the drug's release rate, bioavailability, and elimination kinetics.

**Parameters Affecting In Vivo Drug Release:** Several factors influence the drug release and pharmacokinetic behavior of nanomaterials in vivo:

- **Nanomaterial Properties:** The size, shape, surface charge, and hydrophobicity/hydrophilicity of the nanomaterials affect their interaction with biological systems, including circulation time, cellular uptake, and clearance.
- **Drug Properties:** The physicochemical properties of the drug, such as solubility, stability, and binding affinity, impact its release rate and bioavailability.
- **Administration Route:** The route of administration influences the absorption and distribution of the drug. For example, intravenous administration provides direct access to the bloodstream, while oral administration involves absorption through the gastrointestinal tract.
- **Biological Barriers:** Biological barriers, such as the blood-brain barrier, intestinal epithelium, and skin, can affect the drug's penetration and distribution in target tissues.

- **Physiological Conditions:** Factors such as blood flow, pH, enzyme activity, and disease state can modulate the drug's release and pharmacokinetics.

**Advantages and Limitations:**

- **Advantages:** In vivo studies provide a realistic assessment of the drug's behavior in a living organism, including its pharmacokinetics, biodistribution, and therapeutic efficacy. They help identify potential side effects and toxicity, guiding the safe and effective use of the drug in humans.
- **Limitations:** In vivo studies are complex, time-consuming, and expensive. They require ethical approval and adherence to animal welfare guidelines. Additionally, differences in physiology between animal models and humans can limit the direct translation of findings to clinical applications. Nevertheless, in vivo studies are indispensable for bridging the gap between laboratory research and clinical use.

**Applications and Case Studies:** In vivo drug release studies have been extensively applied in various therapeutic areas, including cancer treatment, infectious diseases, and chronic conditions. For example, in cancer therapy, drug-loaded nanomaterials are designed to enhance the delivery of chemotherapeutic agents to tumor sites while minimizing systemic toxicity. In vivo studies in animal models of cancer have demonstrated improved targeting and efficacy of these nanomaterials compared to conventional chemotherapy.

In the field of infectious diseases, nanomaterials are employed to deliver antibiotics and antiviral drugs more effectively. In vivo studies have shown that these nanomaterials can improve the pharmacokinetics and therapeutic outcomes of the drugs, reducing the required dose and frequency of administration.

**Regulatory and Ethical Considerations:** Conducting in vivo studies requires compliance with regulatory guidelines and ethical standards to ensure the welfare of the animal models. Researchers must obtain approval from institutional animal care and use committees (IACUC) or equivalent ethical review boards before initiating studies. The design and conduct of the studies must adhere to the principles of the 3Rs: Replacement (using alternatives to animal models where possible), Reduction (minimizing the number of animals used), and Refinement (enhancing animal welfare through improved techniques and conditions).

**Future Perspectives:** Advancements in in vivo imaging and monitoring technologies, such as positron emission tomography (PET), magnetic resonance imaging (MRI), and fluorescence imaging, are enhancing the ability to study drug release and distribution in real-time within living organisms. These technologies provide non-invasive, detailed insights into the pharmacokinetics and biodistribution of nanomaterials, facilitating the development of more effective and safer drug delivery systems.

Additionally, the integration of computational modeling and simulation with in vivo studies is emerging as a powerful approach to predict drug release and pharmacokinetics, optimize formulation design, and reduce the reliance on extensive animal testing. By combining experimental data with computational tools, researchers can gain a deeper understanding of the complex interactions between nanomaterials and biological systems, accelerating the translation of nanomedicine from bench to bedside.

In vivo drug release studies remain a cornerstone of nanomaterial research, providing essential data on the pharmacokinetics, biodistribution, efficacy, and safety of drug-loaded nanomaterials. Through careful design, ethical conduct, and integration with advanced technologies, these studies continue to drive the development of innovative drug delivery systems that hold the promise of transforming modern medicine.

## *10.2.3 In Vivo Drug Release Studies*

## *10.2.3.2 Pharmacokinetic Studies*

Pharmacokinetic studies are fundamental to understanding the behavior of drug-loaded nanomaterials in vivo. These studies provide critical insights into the absorption, distribution, metabolism, and excretion (ADME) of drugs, which are essential for optimizing drug delivery systems and ensuring their safety and efficacy. By analyzing how nanomaterials interact with biological systems over time, researchers can tailor the design of these systems to achieve desired therapeutic outcomes.

**Study Design and Methodology:** Pharmacokinetic studies typically involve administering the drug-loaded nanomaterials to animal models and collecting biological samples at various time points to measure drug concentrations. Commonly used animal models include mice, rats, rabbits, and larger animals such as dogs or primates, depending on the study's complexity and objectives. The choice of model is guided by the similarity of the animal's physiology to humans and the ethical considerations involved.

**Pharmacokinetic Parameters:**

1. **Absorption:** This phase involves the uptake of the drug from the site of administration into the bloodstream. The rate and extent of absorption are influenced by the route of administration (e.g., intravenous, oral, subcutaneous) and the properties of the nanomaterials.
2. **Distribution:** Once absorbed, the drug is distributed throughout the body. This distribution depends on the drug's affinity for different tissues and the nanomaterials' ability to target specific sites. Key parameters include the volume of distribution (Vd) and the drug's concentration in various tissues.
3. **Metabolism:** The drug undergoes biotransformation, primarily in the liver, where it is converted into metabolites. The rate of metabolism affects the drug's half-life and overall efficacy. Enzymes involved in metabolism can be influenced by the nanomaterials' design, potentially altering the drug's pharmacokinetic profile.
4. **Excretion:** The elimination of the drug and its metabolites occurs primarily through the kidneys (urine) and, to a lesser extent, the liver (bile). The clearance (CL) rate is a critical parameter that determines how quickly the drug is removed from the body.

**Key Parameters in Pharmacokinetic Analysis:**

- **Area Under the Curve (AUC):** Represents the total drug exposure over time. It is a measure of the extent of absorption and provides insights into the drug's bioavailability.
- **Peak Plasma Concentration (Cmax):** The highest concentration of the drug observed in the bloodstream, indicating the rate of absorption.
- **Time to Peak Concentration (Tmax):** The time taken to reach Cmax, reflecting the absorption rate.
- **Half-Life (t1/2):** The time required for the drug's plasma concentration to reduce by half, indicating the duration of action and the rate of elimination.

- **Clearance (CL):** The volume of plasma from which the drug is completely removed per unit time, representing the efficiency of elimination.

**Analytical Techniques:** To quantify the drug concentrations in biological samples, advanced analytical techniques are employed. High-Performance Liquid Chromatography (HPLC) and Liquid Chromatography-Mass Spectrometry (LC-MS) are commonly used due to their high sensitivity and specificity. These techniques allow for accurate measurement of drug levels in plasma, tissues, urine, and other biological matrices, providing detailed pharmacokinetic profiles.

**Factors Affecting Pharmacokinetics:**

1. **Nanomaterial Characteristics:** The size, shape, surface charge, and hydrophobicity of nanomaterials influence their pharmacokinetic behavior. Smaller particles typically have a larger surface area for interaction and faster clearance, while surface modifications can enhance targeting and reduce nonspecific uptake.

2. **Drug Properties:** The solubility, stability, and affinity of the drug for the nanomaterial matrix affect its release rate and bioavailability. Hydrophobic drugs may benefit from encapsulation in lipophilic nanomaterials to enhance solubility and retention.

3. **Biological Environment:** The physiological and pathological conditions of the host, such as pH, enzyme activity, and disease state, can alter the drug's pharmacokinetics. For instance, tumor microenvironments with acidic pH may enhance the release of certain drugs from pH-sensitive nanomaterials.

4. **Administration Route:** The route of administration affects the absorption and initial distribution of the drug. Intravenous administration provides immediate systemic circulation, while oral delivery involves absorption through the gastrointestinal tract and first-pass metabolism in the liver.

**Applications and Case Studies:** Pharmacokinetic studies are crucial in the development of nanomedicines for various therapeutic areas. For example, in cancer therapy, drug-loaded nanomaterials are designed to enhance the delivery of chemotherapeutic agents to tumor sites while minimizing systemic toxicity. Pharmacokinetic studies in animal models of cancer have demonstrated improved targeting and prolonged circulation times, leading to better therapeutic outcomes.

In infectious diseases, nanomaterials are used to deliver antibiotics and antiviral drugs more effectively. Pharmacokinetic studies have shown that these nanomaterials can improve drug bioavailability, reduce dosing frequency, and enhance treatment efficacy.

**Regulatory and Ethical Considerations:** Conducting pharmacokinetic studies requires adherence to regulatory guidelines and ethical standards. Researchers must obtain approval from institutional animal care and use committees (IACUC) or equivalent ethical review boards before initiating studies. The design and conduct of the studies must follow the principles of the 3Rs: Replacement, Reduction, and Refinement, to ensure ethical and responsible use of animal models.

**Future Perspectives:** Advancements in pharmacokinetic modeling and simulation are enhancing the ability to predict drug behavior in vivo, reducing the reliance on extensive animal testing. By integrating experimental data with computational models, researchers can gain deeper insights into the complex interactions between nanomaterials and biological systems, accelerating the development of safer and more effective drug delivery systems.

Pharmacokinetic studies remain a cornerstone of nanomedicine research, providing essential data on the ADME properties of drug-loaded nanomaterials. Through careful design, ethical conduct, and the integration of advanced technologies, these studies continue to drive the development of innovative drug delivery systems that hold the promise of transforming modern medicine.

## 10.3 Stability Studies of Nanomaterials

### 10.3.1 Physical Stability

Physical stability studies of nanomaterials are critical for ensuring the consistency, safety, and efficacy of nanotechnology-based products. These studies focus on the ability of nanomaterials to maintain their size, shape, surface properties, and dispersibility over time and under various environmental conditions. Physical stability is a crucial determinant of the performance of nanomaterials in both laboratory and clinical settings.

**Nanomaterial Characteristics and Stability:** The physical stability of nanomaterials depends on several intrinsic properties, including particle size, shape, surface charge, and coating. For example, smaller nanoparticles tend to aggregate more easily due to higher surface energy, while larger particles may settle out of suspension over time. Similarly, spherical nanoparticles may behave differently in stability tests compared to rod-shaped or irregularly shaped particles.

**Factors Influencing Physical Stability:**

1. **Aggregation and Agglomeration:**

   - **Aggregation** refers to the reversible clumping of nanoparticles, usually due to van der Waals forces or hydrophobic interactions.
   - **Agglomeration** is the irreversible fusion of particles, often caused by strong chemical bonding or sintering.
   - Both processes can significantly alter the size distribution and surface area of nanomaterials, impacting their functionality.

1. **Sedimentation:**

   - Over time, nanoparticles in suspension may settle due to gravity, leading to non-uniform distribution.
   - Sedimentation can be influenced by particle size, density, and the viscosity of the suspension medium.

3. **Ostwald Ripening:**

   - This process involves the growth of larger particles at the expense of smaller ones, driven by the reduction in total surface energy.
   - Ostwald ripening can lead to changes in particle size distribution and is affected by factors such as temperature and solubility of the nanoparticles.

4. **Surface Chemistry:**

   - The presence and nature of surface coatings or functional groups can stabilize nanoparticles by providing steric or electrostatic repulsion.

- For instance, surfactants, polymers, or ligands attached to the nanoparticle surface can prevent aggregation and improve dispersibility.

**Stability Testing Methods:**

1. **Dynamic Light Scattering (DLS):**

   - DLS measures the size distribution of nanoparticles in suspension by analyzing the scattering of light.
   - Changes in the average particle size or polydispersity index over time can indicate aggregation or sedimentation.

2. **Zeta Potential Analysis:**

   - Zeta potential measures the surface charge of nanoparticles, which is an indicator of electrostatic stability.
   - A high absolute value of zeta potential (positive or negative) typically suggests good stability due to repulsion between particles.

3. **Transmission Electron Microscopy (TEM) and Scanning Electron Microscopy (SEM):**

   - TEM and SEM provide detailed images of nanoparticle morphology and size distribution.
   - These techniques can reveal changes in particle size, shape, and aggregation state over time.

4. **Centrifugation and Ultracentrifugation:**

   - These methods separate nanoparticles based on size and density, allowing for the assessment of sedimentation behavior.
   - By analyzing the sediment and supernatant, researchers can determine the extent of aggregation and stability of the dispersion.

5. **Spectroscopic Techniques:**

- Ultraviolet-Visible (UV-Vis) spectroscopy and Fourier Transform Infrared (FTIR) spectroscopy can monitor changes in optical properties and surface chemistry.
- These techniques help detect alterations in nanoparticle stability and surface modifications.

**Environmental Conditions Affecting Stability:**

1. **Temperature:**

- Elevated temperatures can accelerate aggregation, sedimentation, and Ostwald ripening.
- Stability studies often include thermal cycling or storage at different temperatures to evaluate the impact on nanoparticle integrity.

2. **pH:**

- The pH of the suspension medium can influence the surface charge and stability of nanoparticles.
- Stability tests typically involve exposing nanomaterials to a range of pH conditions to assess their behavior in different environments.

3. **Ionic Strength:**

- High ionic strength in the medium can shield electrostatic repulsion, promoting aggregation.
- Stability studies may include varying salt concentrations to understand their effects on nanoparticle dispersibility.

4. **Light Exposure:**

- Photoreactive nanoparticles may undergo changes upon exposure to light, affecting their stability.
- Stability testing often includes light exposure studies to determine the impact on nanoparticle properties.

**Applications and Implications:** Ensuring the physical stability of nanomaterials is essential for their effective application in various fields, including drug delivery, diagnostics, and materials science. Stable nanomaterials can achieve consistent performance, reduced toxicity, and prolonged shelf life. For instance, in drug delivery, physically stable nanoparticles ensure uniform dosing and predictable therapeutic outcomes. In diagnostics, stable nanoparticles maintain their optical or magnetic properties, providing reliable and reproducible results.

**Regulatory and Quality Control:** Regulatory agencies require comprehensive stability data for the approval of nanomaterial-based products. Stability studies are an integral part of quality control processes, ensuring that products meet safety and efficacy standards throughout their shelf life. Continuous monitoring and adherence to good manufacturing practices (GMP) are essential for maintaining the stability and quality of nanomaterials.

## *10.3.1.1 Agglomeration and Sedimentation*

Agglomeration and sedimentation are two critical aspects that significantly impact the physical stability of nanomaterials. These processes can alter the size distribution, surface area, and dispersibility of nanoparticles, ultimately affecting their functionality and efficacy in various applications.

**Agglomeration:**

Agglomeration refers to the clustering of nanoparticles into larger assemblies due to interparticle forces such as van der Waals forces, hydrophobic interactions, or magnetic attractions. This process can be either reversible or irreversible. Reversible agglomeration allows for the redispersion of nanoparticles upon the application of external energy, such as ultrasonication or vigorous stirring. In contrast, irreversible agglomeration results in the permanent fusion of particles, which is often driven by strong chemical bonding or sintering.

Several factors influence the tendency of nanoparticles to agglomerate:

1. **Surface Energy:**

   - Nanoparticles possess high surface energy due to their large surface-to-volume ratio, making them thermodynamically unstable and prone to agglomeration.
   - Surface modifications, such as coating with surfactants or polymers, can reduce surface energy and prevent agglomeration by providing

steric or electrostatic stabilization.

## 2. Particle Size and Shape:

- Smaller nanoparticles have higher surface energy and a greater tendency to agglomerate compared to larger particles.
- The shape of nanoparticles also plays a role, with spherical particles generally exhibiting lower agglomeration propensity than rod-shaped or irregularly shaped particles.

## 3. Concentration:

- Higher concentrations of nanoparticles in a suspension increase the likelihood of particle collisions, leading to agglomeration.
- Diluting the suspension can reduce the frequency of collisions and mitigate agglomeration.

## 4. Medium Properties:

- The properties of the suspension medium, such as viscosity and dielectric constant, can influence agglomeration behavior.
- Higher viscosity mediums slow down particle movement, reducing the collision rate and agglomeration.

### Sedimentation:

Sedimentation is the process by which nanoparticles settle out of suspension due to gravitational forces. This phenomenon is influenced by the size, density, and shape of the nanoparticles, as well as the viscosity of the suspension medium. Sedimentation can lead to non-uniform distribution of nanoparticles, affecting the consistency and performance of nanomaterial-based products.

Key factors affecting sedimentation include:

## 1. Particle Size and Density:

- Larger and denser nanoparticles settle faster than smaller and less dense particles.

- The sedimentation rate can be described by Stokes' law, which relates the settling velocity to particle size, density, and medium viscosity.

2. **Medium Viscosity:**

- Higher viscosity mediums slow down sedimentation by increasing the resistance to particle movement.
- Adjusting the viscosity of the suspension medium can help control the sedimentation rate.

3. **Particle Shape:**

- Non-spherical particles, such as rods or platelets, experience different drag forces compared to spherical particles, affecting their sedimentation behavior.
- The orientation and aspect ratio of anisotropic particles can influence their settling velocity.

**Mitigation Strategies:**

To prevent agglomeration and sedimentation, various strategies can be employed:

1. **Surface Modification:**

- Coating nanoparticles with surfactants, polymers, or other stabilizing agents can provide steric or electrostatic barriers, preventing agglomeration.
- Surface modifications can also enhance the dispersibility and stability of nanoparticles in suspension.

2. **pH and Ionic Strength Adjustment:**

- Controlling the pH and ionic strength of the suspension medium can influence the surface charge and zeta potential of nanoparticles, affecting their stability.
- Optimal pH and ionic strength conditions can reduce agglomeration and improve dispersion stability.

3. **Use of Stabilizing Agents:**

- Incorporating stabilizing agents such as citrate ions, polyvinylpyrrolidone (PVP), or thiol compounds can prevent agglomeration by providing electrostatic or steric stabilization.
- These agents can also enhance the long-term stability of nanoparticle suspensions.

4. **Mechanical Dispersion:**

- Techniques such as ultrasonication, high-shear mixing, or ball milling can break up agglomerates and ensure uniform dispersion of nanoparticles.
- Regular agitation or mixing can prevent sedimentation by maintaining nanoparticles in suspension.

**Analytical Techniques for Monitoring:**

To assess agglomeration and sedimentation, several analytical techniques are employed:

1. **Dynamic Light Scattering (DLS):**

- DLS measures the size distribution and polydispersity index of nanoparticles in suspension, providing insights into agglomeration behavior.
- Changes in particle size over time can indicate the extent of agglomeration.

2. **Zeta Potential Analysis:**

- Zeta potential measurements provide information on the surface charge and stability of nanoparticles.
- High absolute values of zeta potential suggest good electrostatic stability and reduced agglomeration.

3. **Sedimentation Analysis:**

- Techniques such as centrifugation and sedimentation velocity analysis can quantify the sedimentation rate and stability of nanoparticle suspensions.
- Monitoring the sediment and supernatant fractions can provide insights into particle distribution and stability.

## 10.3.1.2 Changes in Particle Size and Morphology

Changes in particle size and morphology are pivotal indicators of the physical stability of nanomaterials. These alterations can profoundly impact the functional properties, performance, and applications of nanoparticles in various fields such as drug delivery, diagnostics, and materials science. Monitoring and controlling these changes are essential to maintain the desired characteristics of nanoparticles over time.

**Factors Influencing Particle Size and Morphology Changes:**

1. **Aggregation and Agglomeration:**

   - **Aggregation** refers to the reversible clustering of nanoparticles due to interparticle interactions such as van der Waals forces and hydrogen bonding.
   - **Agglomeration** involves the irreversible fusion of nanoparticles, often leading to larger and irregularly shaped aggregates.
   - These processes can result in an increase in the effective particle size and changes in morphology, affecting the dispersion stability and functionality of the nanoparticles.

2. **Surface Modifications:**

   - Surface modifications with stabilizing agents such as surfactants, polymers, or ligands can influence the size and shape of nanoparticles.
   - Properly designed surface modifications can prevent agglomeration and maintain the desired particle size and morphology.
   - Conversely, inadequate or unstable surface coatings can lead to changes in particle size and morphology due to loss of stabilization.

3.  **Environmental Conditions:**

- **pH and Ionic Strength:** The pH and ionic strength of the suspension medium can alter the surface charge and electrostatic interactions of nanoparticles, leading to changes in particle size and morphology.
- **Temperature:** Elevated temperatures can enhance the kinetic energy of nanoparticles, increasing the likelihood of collisions and agglomeration. Temperature fluctuations can also affect the stability of surface coatings, leading to morphological changes.
- **Mechanical Stress:** Shear forces and agitation during processing or handling can induce aggregation or break up larger particles, resulting in changes in particle size distribution and morphology.

**Monitoring Changes in Particle Size and Morphology:**

1.  **Dynamic Light Scattering (DLS):**

- DLS is a widely used technique for measuring the hydrodynamic diameter and size distribution of nanoparticles in suspension.
- It provides real-time monitoring of changes in particle size, offering insights into aggregation or agglomeration processes.
- DLS can detect subtle changes in size distribution, which can indicate the onset of instability or morphological alterations.

2.  **Transmission Electron Microscopy (TEM):**

- TEM provides high-resolution imaging of nanoparticles, allowing for detailed examination of their size and morphology.
- It can reveal changes in shape, surface texture, and aggregation state, providing direct visual evidence of morphological alterations.
- TEM is particularly useful for characterizing complex nanostructures and identifying the presence of agglomerates.

3.  **Scanning Electron Microscopy (SEM):**

- SEM offers detailed surface imaging of nanoparticles, complementing TEM by providing information on surface morphology and particle interactions.

- It can visualize changes in particle shape and surface characteristics, which are critical for understanding morphological stability.
- SEM is valuable for examining larger aggregates and surface modifications that may not be apparent in TEM images.

## 4. Atomic Force Microscopy (AFM):

- AFM provides three-dimensional surface profiles of nanoparticles, allowing for precise measurement of size and morphology.
- It can detect changes in surface roughness, particle height, and aggregation state, offering insights into morphological stability.
- AFM is particularly useful for examining nanoparticles on substrates or in dry conditions, complementing other imaging techniques.

**Implications of Changes in Particle Size and Morphology:**

## 1. Functional Properties:

- Changes in particle size and morphology can significantly impact the optical, magnetic, and catalytic properties of nanoparticles.
- For example, variations in size can affect the plasmonic properties of gold nanoparticles, altering their color and optical behavior.
- Morphological changes can influence the surface area and reactivity of nanoparticles, affecting their performance in catalytic and sensing applications.

## 2. Biocompatibility and Biodistribution:

- In biomedical applications, particle size and morphology are critical determinants of biocompatibility, cellular uptake, and biodistribution.
- Smaller nanoparticles generally exhibit better cellular uptake and deeper tissue penetration, while larger aggregates may be rapidly cleared by the reticuloendothelial system.
- Morphological stability ensures consistent interactions with biological systems, enhancing the efficacy and safety of nanoparticle-based therapies.

## 3. Formulation Stability:

- In pharmaceutical formulations, maintaining the size and morphology of nanoparticles is essential for consistent drug release, targeting, and therapeutic efficacy.
- Changes in particle size can affect the dissolution rate and bioavailability of encapsulated drugs, impacting their therapeutic outcomes.
- Morphological stability ensures uniform distribution and dosing, reducing variability and enhancing patient compliance.

**Strategies to Mitigate Changes in Particle Size and Morphology:**

## 1. Optimized Surface Coatings:

- Employing robust and stable surface coatings can prevent aggregation and maintain the desired size and shape of nanoparticles.
- Coatings such as PEGylation (attachment of polyethylene glycol) provide steric stabilization and enhance colloidal stability in biological environments.

## 2. Controlled Processing Conditions:

- Maintaining consistent pH, ionic strength, and temperature during synthesis and storage can minimize changes in particle size and morphology.
- Avoiding excessive mechanical stress and optimizing mixing conditions can prevent aggregation and ensure uniform particle dispersion.

## 3. Use of Stabilizing Agents:

- Incorporating stabilizing agents such as surfactants, polymers, or small molecules can enhance the stability of nanoparticles by providing electrostatic or steric barriers to aggregation.
- Selecting appropriate stabilizers based on the application and environmental conditions can ensure long-term stability and functionality of nanomaterials.

## *10.3.2 Chemical Stability*

Chemical stability is a critical aspect of nanomaterials that determines their longevity, functionality, and overall performance in various applications. It refers to the ability of nanoparticles to resist chemical changes such as oxidation, reduction, dissolution, or chemical reactions with their environment over time. Maintaining chemical stability is essential to ensure that nanomaterials retain their desired properties and functionality throughout their intended use.

**Factors Influencing Chemical Stability:**

1. **Surface Chemistry:**

   - The surface chemistry of nanoparticles, including the presence of functional groups, surface coatings, and ligands, plays a pivotal role in their chemical stability.
   - Surface modifications can provide a protective layer that prevents unwanted chemical reactions with environmental agents such as oxygen, moisture, or other reactive species.
   - For instance, gold nanoparticles are often coated with citrate ions, polymers, or thiol groups to enhance their chemical stability and prevent oxidation.

2. **Environmental Conditions:**

   - **pH:** The pH of the surrounding medium can significantly influence the chemical stability of nanoparticles. Acidic or basic conditions can lead to the dissolution or chemical alteration of nanoparticles.
   - **Temperature:** Elevated temperatures can accelerate chemical reactions, leading to the degradation or transformation of nanoparticles. Maintaining a stable temperature is crucial to preserving their chemical stability.
   - **Oxidizing and Reducing Agents:** The presence of oxidizing or reducing agents in the environment can induce chemical changes in nanoparticles. For example, silver nanoparticles can undergo oxidation to form silver oxide in the presence of oxidizing agents.

3. **Intrinsic Properties:**

- The intrinsic properties of the nanomaterials, such as their composition, crystallinity, and size, influence their chemical stability.
- Nanoparticles with higher surface area-to-volume ratios are more susceptible to chemical reactions due to their increased surface reactivity.
- The crystalline structure of nanoparticles can also affect their stability, with certain crystal facets being more reactive than others.

**Monitoring Chemical Stability:**

1. **Spectroscopic Techniques:**

- **UV-Vis Spectroscopy:** UV-Vis spectroscopy is commonly used to monitor the chemical stability of nanoparticles by observing changes in their absorption spectra. Shifts in the plasmon resonance peaks indicate chemical alterations such as oxidation or aggregation.
- **FTIR Spectroscopy:** Fourier-transform infrared (FTIR) spectroscopy provides information on the chemical bonds and functional groups present on the surface of nanoparticles. Changes in the FTIR spectra can indicate chemical modifications or degradation.

2. **X-ray Diffraction (XRD):**

- XRD is used to study the crystalline structure of nanoparticles and detect changes in their phase composition. It can reveal the formation of new crystalline phases resulting from chemical reactions.
- Monitoring the XRD patterns over time can provide insights into the chemical stability and structural integrity of nanomaterials.

3. **Electron Microscopy:**

- **Transmission Electron Microscopy (TEM):** TEM provides high-resolution images that can reveal changes in the morphology and composition of nanoparticles due to chemical reactions.
- **Energy-Dispersive X-ray Spectroscopy (EDS):** EDS, coupled with TEM or SEM, allows for elemental analysis and mapping, providing

information on the chemical composition and distribution of elements within the nanoparticles.

**Implications of Chemical Instability:**

1. **Loss of Functionality:**

   - Chemical instability can lead to the loss of the unique properties that make nanoparticles suitable for specific applications. For example, oxidation of metallic nanoparticles can diminish their electrical conductivity, catalytic activity, or optical properties.
   - In drug delivery systems, chemical changes can affect the encapsulation efficiency, release profile, and therapeutic efficacy of the nanocarriers.

2. **Safety Concerns:**

   - Chemical instability can result in the release of toxic degradation products or ions, posing safety risks to humans and the environment.
   - Ensuring the chemical stability of nanoparticles is crucial to prevent unintended exposure to harmful substances and ensure their safe use in biomedical and environmental applications.

3. **Performance Degradation:**

   - The degradation of nanoparticles due to chemical instability can lead to reduced performance in applications such as sensors, catalysts, and electronic devices.
   - For instance, the oxidation of silver nanoparticles can impair their antimicrobial activity, limiting their effectiveness in medical and consumer products.

**Strategies to Enhance Chemical Stability:**

1. **Surface Passivation:**

   - Coating nanoparticles with stable and inert materials can prevent chemical reactions with the environment. Common passivating agents include silica, polymers, and thiol-containing molecules.

- For example, silica coating on metal nanoparticles provides a robust barrier that protects against oxidation and other chemical changes.

## 2. Controlled Synthesis:

- Optimizing the synthesis conditions to produce nanoparticles with well-defined sizes, shapes, and crystallinity can enhance their chemical stability.
- Using high-purity precursors and controlled reaction environments minimizes the presence of impurities that could catalyze unwanted chemical reactions.

## 3. Environmental Control:

- Storing nanoparticles under inert or controlled environments, such as in the presence of inert gases (e.g., nitrogen or argon) or in vacuum-sealed containers, can prevent exposure to reactive species.
- Maintaining stable pH and temperature conditions during storage and use can also mitigate chemical degradation.

# *10.3.2.1 Degradation in Biological Environments*

Nanomaterials used in biomedical applications must exhibit stability in biological environments to ensure their effectiveness and safety. Degradation in biological environments is a complex process influenced by various factors such as the presence of enzymes, pH variations, ionic strength, and interactions with biological molecules. Understanding the mechanisms of degradation and the factors affecting it is crucial for designing nanomaterials that can maintain their integrity and functionality in vivo.

**Mechanisms of Degradation:**

## 1. Enzymatic Degradation:

- Enzymes present in biological systems can catalyze the breakdown of nanomaterials. For instance, esterases, proteases, and phosphatases can degrade polymeric nanoparticles by cleaving ester, amide, or phosphate bonds, respectively.

- Enzymatic degradation is particularly relevant for biodegradable polymers like poly(lactic-co-glycolic acid) (PLGA) and polycaprolactone (PCL), which are designed to be broken down by specific enzymes in the body.

## 2. Hydrolytic Degradation:

- Hydrolysis is a chemical reaction involving the cleavage of bonds by the addition of water. In biological environments, hydrolytic degradation can occur due to the presence of water and biological fluids.
- Hydrolytic degradation is common in materials containing hydrolyzable bonds such as esters, anhydrides, and amides. For example, PLGA nanoparticles undergo hydrolysis of ester bonds, leading to the gradual breakdown of the polymer.

## 3. Oxidative Degradation:

- Reactive oxygen species (ROS) generated in biological systems can oxidize nanomaterials, leading to their degradation. Oxidative stress is particularly significant for metallic nanoparticles like silver and iron oxide, which can undergo oxidation in the presence of ROS.
- Antioxidant coatings or incorporation of antioxidant molecules can help mitigate oxidative degradation and enhance the stability of nanomaterials in biological environments.

## 4. Dissolution:

- Some nanomaterials, particularly inorganic ones like zinc oxide and calcium phosphate, can dissolve in biological fluids, leading to their degradation. The dissolution rate depends on factors such as pH, ionic strength, and the presence of chelating agents.
- The dissolution of nanomaterials can release ions that may have therapeutic effects or, conversely, toxic effects, necessitating careful control over the dissolution behavior.

**Factors Affecting Degradation:**

1. **Surface Chemistry:**

   - The surface properties of nanomaterials, including functional groups, coatings, and surface charge, significantly influence their degradation in biological environments.
   - Surface modifications can provide steric or electrostatic stabilization, reducing interactions with degrading agents and enhancing stability.

2. **Particle Size and Shape:**

   - The size and shape of nanoparticles affect their surface area-to-volume ratio, which in turn influences their degradation rate. Smaller nanoparticles with higher surface area are more prone to rapid degradation.
   - Shape also plays a role, as certain shapes may be more resistant to degradation due to their geometric configuration and surface exposure.

3. **Biological Interactions:**

   - Interactions with proteins, cells, and other biological molecules can affect the stability of nanomaterials. Protein corona formation, for example, can either protect nanoparticles from degradation or promote it, depending on the nature of the proteins adsorbed.
   - Cellular uptake and intracellular trafficking can expose nanomaterials to different intracellular environments, such as acidic lysosomes, where degradation is accelerated.

**Monitoring Degradation:**

1. **In Vitro Studies:**

   - In vitro degradation studies involve exposing nanomaterials to simulated biological conditions, such as buffered solutions, enzymes, or cell cultures, and monitoring changes over time.

- Techniques such as dynamic light scattering (DLS), transmission electron microscopy (TEM), and high-performance liquid chromatography (HPLC) can be used to assess changes in particle size, morphology, and chemical composition.

2. **In Vivo Studies:**

- In vivo studies provide insights into the degradation behavior of nanomaterials in actual biological environments. Animal models are used to evaluate the biodistribution, degradation, and clearance of nanomaterials.
- Imaging techniques like fluorescence imaging, magnetic resonance imaging (MRI), and positron emission tomography (PET) can track the fate of nanomaterials in vivo, providing valuable data on their stability and degradation.

**Implications of Degradation:**

1. **Therapeutic Efficacy:**

- Controlled degradation is essential for the sustained release of therapeutics from nanocarriers. Rapid degradation may lead to burst release, while slow degradation may result in prolonged therapeutic action.
- Understanding degradation kinetics helps in designing nanocarriers with optimized release profiles to achieve desired therapeutic outcomes.

2. **Toxicity:**

- Degradation products of nanomaterials can exhibit toxicity, necessitating careful evaluation of the biocompatibility and safety of both the nanomaterials and their degradation byproducts.
- Ensuring that degradation products are non-toxic and can be readily metabolized or excreted is crucial for the safe use of nanomaterials in biomedical applications.

3. **Regulatory Considerations:**

- Regulatory guidelines require comprehensive characterization of the degradation behavior of nanomaterials to ensure their safety and efficacy. Detailed studies on degradation mechanisms, kinetics, and biocompatibility are essential for regulatory approval.
- Stability and degradation studies are integral parts of the safety assessment and quality control processes for nanomaterial-based products.

# 10.3.2.2 Oxidation and Hydrolysis

## Oxidation and Hydrolysis as Degradation Mechanisms:

Nanomaterials are subject to various degradation mechanisms in biological environments, with oxidation and hydrolysis being two of the most significant processes. These degradation pathways can profoundly influence the stability, efficacy, and safety of nanomaterials used in medical and industrial applications.

**Oxidation:**

1. **Mechanism of Oxidation:**

- Oxidation involves the loss of electrons from a material, often facilitated by reactive oxygen species (ROS) such as superoxide anions (O2-), hydroxyl radicals ($\cdot$OH), and hydrogen peroxide (H2O2). These ROS are commonly found in biological environments, particularly under conditions of oxidative stress.
- Metals like silver and iron, and even certain polymers, are susceptible to oxidative degradation. For instance, silver nanoparticles can oxidize to form silver ions (Ag+), which can impact their antimicrobial efficacy and cytotoxicity.

2. **Factors Influencing Oxidation:**

- **Surface Chemistry:** The presence of surface coatings or functional groups can either mitigate or exacerbate oxidative degradation. Protective coatings, such as polyethylene glycol (PEG) or thiol-based ligands, can shield nanoparticles from direct exposure to ROS.

- **Particle Size and Morphology:** Smaller nanoparticles with larger surface area-to-volume ratios are more prone to oxidation due to increased surface reactivity. Morphological features, such as edges and corners, also provide sites for oxidative attack.

3. **Consequences of Oxidation:**

- Oxidative degradation can lead to the loss of structural integrity and functionality of nanomaterials. For example, the oxidation of iron oxide nanoparticles ($Fe_3O_4$) to ferric oxide ($Fe_2O_3$) can alter their magnetic properties, affecting their performance in magnetic resonance imaging (MRI).
- The generation of metal ions or other degradation products can also pose toxicity risks, necessitating thorough evaluation of oxidative stability for safe biomedical use.

**Hydrolysis:**

1. **Mechanism of Hydrolysis:**

- Hydrolysis is the chemical breakdown of materials through reaction with water, resulting in the cleavage of chemical bonds. This process is particularly relevant for nanomaterials containing hydrolyzable bonds such as esters, amides, and anhydrides.
- In biological environments, hydrolysis is often catalyzed by enzymes such as esterases, which accelerate the degradation of polymeric nanoparticles like poly(lactic-co-glycolic acid) (PLGA) and polycaprolactone (PCL).

2. **Factors Influencing Hydrolysis:**

- **Environmental Conditions:** The rate of hydrolysis is influenced by the pH, temperature, and ionic strength of the surrounding environment. Acidic or basic conditions can significantly enhance hydrolytic degradation.
- **Material Composition:** The chemical structure of the nanomaterial determines its susceptibility to hydrolysis. Materials with more labile

bonds, such as ester linkages, degrade more readily compared to those with more stable bonds.

## 3. Consequences of Hydrolysis:

- Hydrolytic degradation leads to the breakdown of nanomaterials into smaller fragments or monomers, which can affect their mechanical and functional properties. For instance, the hydrolysis of PLGA nanoparticles releases lactic and glycolic acids, which can alter the local pH and affect surrounding tissues.
- The products of hydrolysis need to be biocompatible and non-toxic to ensure safe use in biomedical applications. Understanding hydrolysis kinetics helps in designing nanocarriers with controlled release profiles for drug delivery.

**Combined Effects of Oxidation and Hydrolysis:**

## 1. Synergistic Degradation:

- In many cases, oxidation and hydrolysis can occur simultaneously, leading to synergistic degradation effects. For example, oxidative stress can generate ROS that not only oxidize nanomaterials but also promote hydrolytic reactions.
- The interplay between these mechanisms can complicate the stability profile of nanomaterials, requiring comprehensive studies to fully understand their degradation behavior.

## 2. Stability Enhancements:

- Strategies to enhance the stability of nanomaterials against oxidation and hydrolysis include surface modifications, the use of stabilizing agents, and the development of more robust materials. For example, coating nanoparticles with antioxidants can mitigate oxidative degradation, while hydrophobic coatings can reduce hydrolytic degradation.
- Nanomaterials can be engineered to degrade in a controlled manner, releasing therapeutic agents in response to specific triggers like pH changes or the presence of certain enzymes.

**Monitoring and Characterization:**

1. **Analytical Techniques:**

   - Various analytical techniques are employed to monitor oxidation and hydrolysis of nanomaterials. Spectroscopic methods such as Fourier-transform infrared spectroscopy (FTIR) and X-ray photoelectron spectroscopy (XPS) can identify chemical changes indicative of oxidation or hydrolysis.
   - Microscopy techniques like transmission electron microscopy (TEM) and scanning electron microscopy (SEM) provide insights into morphological changes associated with degradation.

2. **In Vitro and In Vivo Studies:**

   - In vitro studies under controlled conditions help elucidate the degradation mechanisms and kinetics of nanomaterials. These studies often use simulated biological fluids or enzyme solutions to replicate in vivo conditions.
   - In vivo studies in animal models provide a more realistic assessment of degradation behavior in complex biological environments, helping to predict the stability and safety of nanomaterials in clinical applications.

Understanding the degradation mechanisms of oxidation and hydrolysis is essential for the design and development of stable, effective, and safe nanomaterials for biomedical applications. Comprehensive stability studies guide the optimization of nanomaterial properties to meet the specific requirements of various therapeutic and diagnostic applications.

## *10.3.3 Environmental Stability*

## *Environmental Stability of Nanomaterials:*

Environmental stability refers to the ability of nanomaterials to maintain their structural and functional integrity when exposed to various environmental conditions. This aspect is crucial for the long-term performance and safety of nanomaterials, particularly in applications where they are subjected to varying external factors such as temperature, humidity, light, and biological agents.

**Factors Influencing Environmental Stability:**

## 1. Temperature:

- Temperature fluctuations can significantly impact the stability of nanomaterials. Elevated temperatures may accelerate degradation processes such as oxidation, hydrolysis, and thermal decomposition. For instance, polymeric nanoparticles like poly(lactic-co-glycolic acid) (PLGA) can undergo faster hydrolytic degradation at higher temperatures.
- Conversely, low temperatures can affect the solubility and dispersion stability of nanomaterials, potentially leading to agglomeration or phase separation.

## 2. Humidity:

- Humidity, or the presence of moisture in the environment, can facilitate hydrolytic degradation of nanomaterials. Hygroscopic materials, which absorb moisture from the air, are particularly susceptible to humidity-induced degradation.
- Nanoparticles stored in high-humidity conditions may experience increased rates of hydrolysis and other moisture-driven reactions, affecting their long-term stability and efficacy.

## 3. Light Exposure:

- Exposure to light, especially ultraviolet (UV) radiation, can induce photodegradation of nanomaterials. UV light can generate reactive oxygen species (ROS) and free radicals, leading to oxidative degradation of materials such as metal nanoparticles and polymers.
- Photodegradation can result in changes to the optical properties, color, and structural integrity of nanomaterials, impacting their performance in applications like drug delivery and imaging.

## 4. Biological Agents:

- Biological environments present additional challenges to the stability of nanomaterials. Enzymes, proteins, and other biological molecules can interact with nanomaterials, catalyzing degradation processes such as enzymatic hydrolysis and oxidation.
- For example, enzymes like esterases and proteases can degrade polymeric nanoparticles, while macrophages and other immune cells can engulf and break down nanomaterials, affecting their biodistribution and therapeutic efficacy.

**Strategies to Enhance Environmental Stability:**

1. **Surface Modifications:**

- Surface modifications, such as coating nanoparticles with stabilizing agents, can enhance their resistance to environmental degradation. Coatings like polyethylene glycol (PEG), silica, and gold can provide a protective barrier against oxidative and hydrolytic attacks.
- Functionalizing the surface with antioxidants or UV-blocking agents can mitigate photodegradation, extending the shelf life and functional performance of nanomaterials.

2. **Material Selection:**

- Choosing materials with inherent stability under environmental conditions is a critical strategy. For instance, using more stable polymers like polystyrene or poly(methyl methacrylate) (PMMA) instead of biodegradable polymers can improve stability in certain applications.
- Inorganic nanomaterials, such as silica and cerium oxide nanoparticles, often exhibit greater environmental stability compared to their organic counterparts.

3. **Environmental Control:**

- Controlling storage and handling conditions can significantly enhance the stability of nanomaterials. Storing nanomaterials in sealed, low-humidity environments, away from light and at controlled temperatures, can prevent degradation.

- Employing inert atmospheres, such as nitrogen or argon, for the storage of sensitive nanomaterials can reduce oxidative degradation.

**Assessment of Environmental Stability:**

1. **Accelerated Aging Tests:**

- Accelerated aging tests simulate environmental conditions to predict the long-term stability of nanomaterials. These tests involve exposing nanomaterials to elevated temperatures, humidity, and light for extended periods to observe changes in their properties.
- Parameters such as particle size, morphology, chemical composition, and functional performance are monitored to assess stability.

2. **Analytical Techniques:**

- Techniques like dynamic light scattering (DLS) and zeta potential measurements assess changes in particle size and surface charge, providing insights into agglomeration and dispersion stability.
- Spectroscopic methods, including UV-Vis spectroscopy, Fourier-transform infrared spectroscopy (FTIR), and X-ray photoelectron spectroscopy (XPS), detect chemical and structural changes indicative of degradation.

3. **Real-Time Monitoring:**

- Real-time monitoring of nanomaterials in their intended application environments provides valuable data on their stability and performance. In vivo studies and field tests can reveal how nanomaterials behave under actual usage conditions, guiding the optimization of their design and storage.

Ensuring the environmental stability of nanomaterials is essential for their successful application in various fields, including biomedicine, electronics, and environmental remediation. By understanding the factors influencing stability and employing strategies to enhance resistance to degradation, researchers can develop robust nanomaterials that maintain their functionality and safety over time.

## *10.3.3.1 Impact of Temperature, pH, and Light*

**Temperature:**

Temperature plays a pivotal role in the environmental stability of nanomaterials. Elevated temperatures can accelerate the degradation processes, leading to the breakdown of nanomaterials. For example, polymeric nanoparticles such as those made from poly(lactic-co-glycolic acid) (PLGA) are prone to faster hydrolytic degradation at higher temperatures. This is due to the increased kinetic energy at elevated temperatures, which enhances molecular mobility and reaction rates, facilitating processes such as hydrolysis, oxidation, and thermal decomposition. For metallic nanoparticles, higher temperatures can induce sintering, where particles fuse together, leading to a loss of nanoscale properties. Conversely, low temperatures can affect the solubility and dispersion stability of nanomaterials. For instance, liposomal formulations may experience phase transitions in their lipid bilayers at lower temperatures, potentially leading to aggregation or leakage of encapsulated drugs.

**pH:**

The pH of the environment can significantly impact the stability of nanomaterials, particularly those composed of polymers and proteins. Nanoparticles in acidic or basic conditions may undergo pH-induced degradation. For instance, in acidic environments, the ester bonds in PLGA nanoparticles can be hydrolyzed more rapidly, leading to faster degradation. Similarly, the stability of protein-based nanoparticles can be compromised at extreme pH levels due to denaturation and aggregation. Gold nanoparticles stabilized with citrate ions can experience desorption of the citrate at lower pH levels, resulting in aggregation and loss of stability. Maintaining an optimal pH is crucial for ensuring the integrity and functionality of nanomaterials, especially in biological applications where pH varies across different tissues and cellular compartments.

**Light:**

Exposure to light, particularly ultraviolet (UV) radiation, can induce photodegradation of nanomaterials. UV light can generate reactive oxygen species (ROS) and free radicals, which can lead to oxidative degradation of both organic and inorganic nanomaterials. For example, silver nanoparticles are susceptible to oxidation when exposed to light, resulting in the formation of silver oxide and a decrease in antimicrobial activity. Similarly, polymeric nanoparticles can undergo photo-oxidative degradation, leading to changes in molecular weight, mechanical properties, and overall stability. Photodegradation can also affect the optical properties of nanomaterials, such as the surface plasmon resonance of gold nanoparticles, which is sensitive to changes in particle size and surface chemistry. Protecting nanomaterials from light exposure, using UV-blocking agents, and storing them in dark conditions can mitigate these adverse effects and enhance their stability.

Understanding the impact of temperature, pH, and light on the stability of nanomaterials is crucial for their successful application and long-term performance. By controlling these environmental factors and employing stabilization strategies, researchers can ensure the robustness and efficacy of nanomaterials in various applications, ranging from drug delivery to environmental remediation.

### 10.3.3.2 Long-Term Storage Conditions

**Long-Term Storage Conditions of Nanomaterials:**

Ensuring the long-term stability of nanomaterials requires meticulous control over storage conditions. Various factors such as temperature, humidity, light exposure, and the presence of reactive agents must be managed to prevent degradation and preserve the functional integrity of nanomaterials over extended periods.

**Temperature Control:**

Maintaining an optimal storage temperature is crucial for preserving the stability of nanomaterials. For many nanomaterials, particularly those made from polymers and biological molecules, storing at lower temperatures can slow down degradation processes such as hydrolysis and oxidation. Refrigerated storage (typically at 4°C) is commonly used for polymeric and protein-based nanoparticles to minimize thermal degradation. For certain sensitive nanomaterials, ultra-low temperature storage (e.g., -20°C or -80°C) might be necessary to ensure stability. However, repeated freeze-thaw cycles should be avoided as they can cause aggregation or denaturation of nanomaterials. Temperature fluctuations can also induce phase transitions, particularly in lipid-based nanoparticles like liposomes, affecting their structural integrity and encapsulation efficiency.

**Humidity Control:**

Humidity, or the presence of moisture in the storage environment, can significantly impact the stability of nanomaterials, especially those that are hygroscopic or prone to hydrolytic degradation. High humidity levels can facilitate hydrolysis and other moisture-induced reactions, leading to the breakdown of nanomaterials. To prevent this, nanomaterials should be stored in low-humidity environments. Desiccators or sealed containers with desiccant packs (e.g., silica gel) are commonly used to maintain a dry storage atmosphere. For highly sensitive nanomaterials, vacuum-sealed packaging or the use of inert gas (e.g., nitrogen or argon) can further protect against moisture-induced degradation.

**Light Protection:**

Exposure to light, particularly ultraviolet (UV) radiation, can induce photodegradation of nanomaterials. UV light can generate reactive oxygen species (ROS) and free radicals, leading to oxidative degradation of both organic and inorganic nanomaterials. To mitigate photodegradation, nanomaterials should be stored in dark or opaque containers that block light exposure. Amber-colored glass or UV-blocking plastic containers are effective in protecting against UV radiation. Additionally, storage in dark conditions or within cabinets that restrict light exposure can further enhance the long-term stability of light-sensitive nanomaterials.

**Chemical Environment:**

The chemical environment surrounding nanomaterials during storage can also affect their stability. Reactive gases such as oxygen and carbon dioxide can induce oxidation and other chemical reactions. For instance, metallic nanoparticles like silver and copper are prone to oxidation when exposed to air, leading to the formation of oxide layers that can alter their properties. To prevent this, storing nanomaterials in an inert atmosphere, such as argon or nitrogen, can significantly reduce the risk of oxidation. Additionally, the presence of volatile organic compounds (VOCs) or other reactive chemicals should be avoided as they can interact with nanomaterials, causing degradation.

**Encapsulation and Stabilization:**

Encapsulation or surface modification of nanomaterials can enhance their stability during long-term storage. Coating nanomaterials with protective layers such as polyethylene glycol (PEG), silica, or gold can create a barrier against environmental factors like moisture, oxygen, and light. These coatings can also prevent aggregation by providing steric or electrostatic stabilization. Encapsulation in polymer matrices or hydrogels can further protect nanomaterials from environmental stressors, maintaining their functional properties over extended periods.

**Monitoring and Quality Control:**

Regular monitoring of nanomaterials during storage is essential to ensure their stability. Analytical techniques such as dynamic light scattering (DLS), zeta potential measurements, and spectroscopic methods (e.g., UV-Vis, FTIR) can be used to assess changes in particle size, surface charge, and chemical composition. By conducting periodic quality control checks, any signs of degradation can be detected early, allowing for corrective measures to be taken to preserve the nanomaterials' integrity.

Optimal long-term storage conditions are critical for maintaining the stability and functionality of nanomaterials. By controlling temperature, humidity, light exposure, and the chemical environment, and by employing encapsulation and regular monitoring, researchers can ensure that nanomaterials retain their desired properties and efficacy throughout their intended shelf life.

### 10.3.4 Stability Testing Protocols

**Overview of Stability Testing Protocols:**

Stability testing protocols are essential for assessing the durability and longevity of nanomaterials under various environmental conditions. These protocols involve systematic procedures to evaluate the physical, chemical, and biological stability of nanomaterials over time. By simulating different storage and usage conditions, stability testing helps predict the shelf life and performance of nanomaterials in real-world applications.

**Physical Stability Testing:**

Physical stability testing focuses on assessing changes in the physical properties of nanomaterials, such as particle size, shape, and dispersibility. Key methods include:

- **Dynamic Light Scattering (DLS):** This technique measures the size distribution and polydispersity index (PDI) of nanoparticles. Regular DLS measurements can detect aggregation or changes in particle size over time.
- **Transmission Electron Microscopy (TEM) and Scanning Electron Microscopy (SEM):** These imaging techniques provide detailed visual information about the morphology and structural integrity of nanomaterials.
- **Zeta Potential Analysis:** This measures the surface charge of nanoparticles, which is critical for understanding their colloidal stability. A significant change in zeta potential can indicate instability and

potential aggregation.

**Chemical Stability Testing:**

Chemical stability testing evaluates the chemical integrity of nanomaterials, including their resistance to oxidation, hydrolysis, and other degradation processes. Common methods include:

- **Fourier Transform Infrared Spectroscopy (FTIR):** FTIR can detect changes in the chemical bonds and functional groups of nanomaterials, indicating chemical degradation.
- **UV-Vis Spectroscopy:** This technique monitors the optical properties of nanomaterials, which can change due to chemical reactions such as oxidation. For example, a shift in the surface plasmon resonance peak of gold nanoparticles can indicate oxidation or aggregation.
- **High-Performance Liquid Chromatography (HPLC):** HPLC is used to analyze the purity and composition of nanomaterials, detecting any degradation products or impurities that may form over time.

**Biological Stability Testing:**

For nanomaterials intended for biomedical applications, biological stability testing is crucial. This involves evaluating the interaction of nanomaterials with biological environments, such as blood, tissues, and cells. Key methods include:

- **In Vitro Stability Testing:** This involves incubating nanomaterials in simulated biological fluids (e.g., phosphate-buffered saline, serum) and monitoring changes in their properties. Techniques such as DLS, TEM, and UV-Vis spectroscopy can be used to assess stability.
- **Cell Viability Assays:** These assays evaluate the cytotoxicity of nanomaterials over time, using cell lines relevant to the intended application. The MTT or Alamar Blue assays are common methods for assessing cell viability and proliferation.
- **Protein Binding Studies:** These studies assess the interaction of nanomaterials with proteins in biological fluids, which can affect their stability and biodistribution. Techniques such as surface plasmon resonance (SPR) and enzyme-linked immunosorbent assay (ELISA) can be used for this purpose.

**Environmental Stability Testing:**

Environmental stability testing simulates different storage conditions to evaluate the robustness of nanomaterials. Key parameters include:

- **Temperature Cycling:** Nanomaterials are subjected to repeated cycles of heating and cooling to assess their thermal stability. This can reveal potential issues with phase transitions or thermal degradation.
- **Humidity Exposure:** Nanomaterials are exposed to controlled humidity levels to evaluate their resistance to moisture-induced degradation. Desiccators or humidity chambers are used for this purpose.
- **Light Exposure:** Nanomaterials are subjected to controlled light exposure, including UV light, to assess their photostability. This helps identify any susceptibility to photodegradation.

**Long-Term Stability Studies:**

Long-term stability studies involve storing nanomaterials under predefined conditions for extended periods and periodically testing their stability. This provides a comprehensive understanding of their shelf life and potential changes in properties over time.

**Accelerated Stability Testing:**

Accelerated stability testing involves exposing nanomaterials to exaggerated stress conditions, such as higher temperatures and humidity levels, to accelerate the degradation processes. This approach helps predict the long-term stability of nanomaterials in a shorter time frame.

**Documentation and Compliance:**

Stability testing protocols must be thoroughly documented, including the testing conditions, methods used, and results obtained. Compliance with regulatory guidelines and standards, such as those set by the International Conference on Harmonisation (ICH) and the U.S. Food and Drug Administration (FDA), is crucial for ensuring the reliability and validity of stability data.

Implementing robust stability testing protocols is essential for ensuring the quality, safety, and efficacy of nanomaterials in various applications. By systematically assessing their physical, chemical, biological, and environmental stability, researchers can predict the behavior of nanomaterials over time and ensure their suitability for intended uses.

**10.3.4.1 Accelerated Stability Testing**

**Concept and Importance:**

Accelerated stability testing is a vital process designed to predict the long-term stability of nanomaterials in a shorter time frame by subjecting them to exaggerated stress conditions. These conditions typically include higher temperatures, increased humidity, and intense light exposure, which accelerate the degradation processes. The primary goal is to identify potential stability issues quickly, ensuring that nanomaterials maintain their desired properties throughout their intended shelf life.

**Procedure for Accelerated Stability Testing:**

The procedure for accelerated stability testing involves several key steps, each carefully designed to simulate and accelerate the conditions that nanomaterials might encounter over an extended period:

1. **Selection of Stress Conditions:**

   - **Temperature:** Elevated temperatures are chosen based on the thermal stability of the nanomaterial. Commonly used temperatures range from 40°C to 60°C.
   - **Humidity:** Relative humidity levels are increased, often to 75% or higher, to test the moisture sensitivity of the nanomaterial.
   - **Light Exposure:** Nanomaterials are exposed to intense light, including UV light, to simulate the effects of sunlight and indoor lighting.

2. **Preparation of Samples:**

   - Nanomaterials are prepared in their final formulation, ensuring that the conditions mimic those they will experience during storage and use.
   - Samples are placed in suitable containers, such as glass vials, plastic containers, or aluminum foil, depending on the specific requirements of the test.

3. **Exposure to Stress Conditions:**

   - Prepared samples are subjected to the selected stress conditions for a predefined period, typically ranging from weeks to a few months.
   - Samples are stored in stability chambers, which precisely control temperature, humidity, and light exposure.

4. **Periodic Testing and Analysis:**

- At regular intervals, samples are removed from the stability chamber and analyzed for any changes in their properties.
- **Physical Stability:** Techniques such as dynamic light scattering (DLS) and electron microscopy (TEM/SEM) are used to detect changes in particle size, shape, and morphology.
- **Chemical Stability:** Methods such as Fourier transform infrared spectroscopy (FTIR), UV-Vis spectroscopy, and high-performance liquid chromatography (HPLC) are employed to identify chemical degradation and changes in composition.
- **Biological Stability:** For nanomaterials intended for biomedical applications, in vitro assays and protein binding studies are conducted to assess biocompatibility and interaction with biological molecules.

5. **Data Interpretation and Shelf-Life Prediction:**

- The data obtained from periodic testing are analyzed to identify trends and patterns in the degradation of nanomaterials.
- Mathematical models, such as the Arrhenius equation, are used to extrapolate the results from accelerated conditions to predict the long-term stability under normal storage conditions.

**Benefits of Accelerated Stability Testing:**

- **Time Efficiency:** By accelerating the degradation processes, stability issues can be identified much faster than through real-time stability testing, enabling quicker decision-making and product development.
- **Cost-Effectiveness:** Reducing the time required for stability testing lowers overall research and development costs, allowing for more efficient resource allocation.
- **Early Detection of Problems:** Accelerated stability testing helps identify potential stability issues early in the development process, allowing for timely formulation adjustments and improvements.
- **Regulatory Compliance:** Conducting thorough stability testing, including accelerated studies, is often required for regulatory approval, ensuring that nanomaterials meet quality and safety standards.

**Challenges and Considerations:**

- **Extrapolation Accuracy:** While accelerated stability testing provides valuable insights, the extrapolation of results to predict long-term stability must be done carefully. Differences in degradation mechanisms under accelerated and real-time conditions can lead to inaccuracies.
- **Selection of Stress Conditions:** Choosing appropriate stress conditions that accurately simulate real-world scenarios without causing unrealistic degradation is crucial for reliable results.
- **Comprehensive Analysis:** A thorough and multidisciplinary approach is needed, combining physical, chemical, and biological analyses to obtain a complete understanding of nanomaterial stability.

Accelerated stability testing is a crucial component of the stability assessment of nanomaterials. It provides a rapid and effective means to predict the long-term behavior of nanomaterials, ensuring their quality, safety, and efficacy for various applications. By carefully selecting stress conditions, conducting periodic testing, and interpreting the data accurately, researchers can make informed decisions about the formulation and storage of nanomaterials.

### 10.3.4.2 Real-Time Stability Testing

**Concept and Significance:**

Real-time stability testing is a fundamental process that involves storing nanomaterials under recommended storage conditions for an extended period to observe any changes in their physical, chemical, and biological properties over time. Unlike accelerated stability testing, which uses stress conditions to predict long-term stability, real-time testing provides actual data on how nanomaterials behave under typical storage environments. This method is essential for confirming the shelf-life, ensuring quality control, and meeting regulatory requirements.

**Procedure for Real-Time Stability Testing:**

The procedure for real-time stability testing involves a series of meticulously planned steps, which ensure that nanomaterials are evaluated under conditions that accurately reflect their intended storage and usage environments:

1. **Selection of Storage Conditions:**

- **Temperature:** Storage temperatures are chosen based on the recommended conditions for the specific nanomaterial, typically ranging from room temperature (25°C) to refrigerated conditions (2-8°C).
- **Humidity:** Relative humidity levels are set according to the expected storage environment, often maintained at 60% RH.
- **Light Exposure:** Depending on the sensitivity of the nanomaterials, exposure to light can be controlled, with some samples stored in the dark to prevent photodegradation.

2. **Preparation of Samples:**

- Nanomaterials are prepared in their final formulation and packaged in appropriate containers that simulate real-world storage conditions, such as glass vials, plastic bottles, or aluminum pouches.

3. **Long-Term Storage:**

- Prepared samples are placed in controlled storage chambers that maintain the selected temperature, humidity, and light conditions over the duration of the study.
- The storage period typically extends over several months to years, providing a comprehensive understanding of the stability profile.

4. **Periodic Sampling and Testing:**

- At predefined intervals, samples are withdrawn from the storage chamber and analyzed for any changes in their properties.
- **Physical Stability:** Techniques such as dynamic light scattering (DLS), transmission electron microscopy (TEM), and scanning electron microscopy (SEM) are used to monitor particle size, shape, and morphology.
- **Chemical Stability:** Analytical methods such as high-performance liquid chromatography (HPLC), Fourier transform infrared spectroscopy (FTIR), and UV-Vis spectroscopy are employed to detect chemical degradation or changes in composition.
- **Biological Stability:** For nanomaterials intended for biomedical applications, assays assessing biocompatibility, protein binding, and

biological activity are performed.

5. **Data Analysis and Shelf-Life Determination:**

- The data obtained from periodic testing are analyzed to identify trends and patterns in the stability of nanomaterials over time.
- Based on the observed stability profile, the shelf-life of the nanomaterial is determined, providing crucial information for labeling, packaging, and regulatory submissions.

**Benefits of Real-Time Stability Testing:**

- **Accurate Shelf-Life Determination:** Real-time stability testing provides precise data on the long-term stability of nanomaterials under recommended storage conditions, ensuring reliable shelf-life estimation.
- **Regulatory Compliance:** Compliance with regulatory guidelines often requires real-time stability data, making this testing essential for obtaining approval from regulatory bodies.
- **Quality Assurance:** Continuous monitoring of stability ensures that nanomaterials maintain their intended quality, efficacy, and safety throughout their shelf-life.
- **Risk Management:** Early detection of stability issues during real-time testing allows for timely corrective actions, minimizing the risk of product failure.

**Challenges and Considerations:**

- **Time-Intensive Process:** Real-time stability testing is inherently time-consuming, often taking several years to complete, which can delay the time-to-market for new nanomaterials.
- **Comprehensive Analysis Required:** A thorough and multidisciplinary approach is needed, combining physical, chemical, and biological analyses to obtain a complete stability profile.
- **Cost Implications:** Long-term storage and periodic testing involve significant costs, which must be accounted for in the overall project budget.

**Integration with Accelerated Testing:**

While real-time stability testing provides essential data on the actual long-term behavior of nanomaterials, it is often complemented by accelerated stability testing. Accelerated tests help predict potential stability issues more quickly, guiding the design and interpretation of real-time studies. Together, these testing methods offer a comprehensive stability assessment, ensuring that nanomaterials meet the required quality standards and regulatory criteria.

Real-time stability testing is a cornerstone of the stability evaluation process for nanomaterials. It provides critical insights into how nanomaterials maintain their properties under typical storage conditions, ensuring their quality, efficacy, and safety over their intended shelf life. By following a rigorous testing protocol and analyzing data comprehensively, researchers and manufacturers can make informed decisions about the formulation, packaging, and storage of nanomaterials.

### 10.3.4.3 Use of Stabilizers and Coatings

**Role of Stabilizers and Coatings in Stability:**

The application of stabilizers and coatings is a pivotal strategy in enhancing the stability of nanomaterials. These substances serve multiple functions, including preventing agglomeration, improving dispersibility, and protecting nanomaterials from environmental degradation. By forming a protective layer around nanoparticles, stabilizers and coatings help maintain the physical, chemical, and biological integrity of nanomaterials during storage and use.

**Types of Stabilizers:**

1. **Polymeric Stabilizers:**

   - **Polyvinylpyrrolidone (PVP):** PVP is widely used to stabilize nanoparticles due to its excellent solubility in water and ability to form strong hydrogen bonds with nanoparticle surfaces. This prevents aggregation and improves colloidal stability.
   - **Polyethylene glycol (PEG):** PEGylation, the process of attaching PEG chains to nanoparticles, provides steric stabilization by creating a hydrophilic barrier that repels other particles, thereby preventing agglomeration.

2. **Surfactants:**

- **Sodium dodecyl sulfate (SDS):** Anionic surfactants like SDS reduce surface tension and promote the dispersion of nanoparticles in aqueous media, preventing aggregation.
- **Cetyltrimethylammonium bromide (CTAB):** As a cationic surfactant, CTAB offers electrostatic stabilization by imparting a positive charge to nanoparticles, which repels other positively charged particles.

3. **Small Molecule Stabilizers:**

- **Citrate Ions:** Citrate ions are commonly used in the synthesis of gold nanoparticles. They act as reducing agents and stabilizers, forming a negatively charged layer on nanoparticle surfaces that provides electrostatic stabilization.

**Types of Coatings:**

1. **Inorganic Coatings:**

- **Silica Coating:** Silica shells can be coated onto nanoparticles to improve their chemical stability and biocompatibility. Silica is inert, biocompatible, and provides a protective barrier against oxidation and degradation.
- **Metal Oxide Coatings:** Coatings such as titanium dioxide ($TiO_2$) or zinc oxide ($ZnO$) enhance the photostability and chemical resistance of nanoparticles, making them suitable for various applications.

2. **Organic Coatings:**

- **Lipids:** Lipid bilayers can encapsulate nanoparticles, mimicking biological membranes and providing a biocompatible interface for drug delivery applications.
- **Polysaccharides:** Coatings like chitosan and dextran are used for their biocompatibility and ability to form stable interactions with nanoparticles, improving their stability in biological environments.

**Mechanisms of Stabilization:**

## 1. Electrostatic Stabilization:

- Electrostatic stabilization occurs when nanoparticles are coated with charged molecules or ions. These charges create a repulsive force between particles, preventing agglomeration. For example, citrate ions provide a negative charge to gold nanoparticles, ensuring they remain dispersed in solution.

## 2. Steric Stabilization:

- Steric stabilization involves the use of large, bulky molecules that physically prevent nanoparticles from coming into close contact. PEGylation is a common technique where PEG chains create a steric barrier around nanoparticles, enhancing their stability in biological fluids and reducing non-specific interactions.

## 3. Combination of Both Mechanisms:

- In many cases, a combination of electrostatic and steric stabilization is employed to achieve optimal stability. For instance, nanoparticles can be stabilized using surfactants that provide both electrostatic repulsion and steric hindrance.

**Procedure for Applying Stabilizers and Coatings:**

## 1. Selection of Appropriate Stabilizer/Coating:

- The choice of stabilizer or coating depends on the specific application, desired properties, and environmental conditions the nanomaterials will be exposed to. Factors such as solubility, biocompatibility, and the potential for functionalization are considered.

## 2. Preparation of Stabilizer/Coating Solution:

- A solution of the selected stabilizer or coating material is prepared at the required concentration. The concentration is optimized to ensure complete coverage of nanoparticle surfaces without excessive use of materials.

3. **Mixing with Nanoparticles:**

   - Nanoparticles are dispersed in the stabilizer or coating solution, and the mixture is stirred or sonicated to ensure uniform coating. The process parameters, such as temperature, pH, and mixing speed, are carefully controlled to achieve consistent results.

4. **Purification and Characterization:**

   - The stabilized or coated nanoparticles are purified to remove excess stabilizer or coating material. Techniques such as centrifugation, filtration, and dialysis are employed. The nanoparticles are then characterized using methods like DLS, TEM, and zeta potential measurement to confirm successful stabilization and coating.

**Benefits of Using Stabilizers and Coatings:**

- **Enhanced Stability:** Stabilizers and coatings significantly improve the stability of nanomaterials by preventing agglomeration, oxidation, and degradation.
- **Improved Biocompatibility:** Coatings like PEG and lipid bilayers enhance the biocompatibility of nanoparticles, making them suitable for biomedical applications.
- **Controlled Release:** Stabilizers and coatings can be designed to release their payloads in response to specific stimuli, providing controlled drug delivery.
- **Functionalization Potential:** Stabilizers and coatings offer sites for further functionalization, enabling targeted delivery and specific interactions with biological targets.

**Challenges and Considerations:**

- **Compatibility:** The choice of stabilizer or coating must be compatible with the core nanomaterial and the intended application. Incompatibility can lead to reduced efficacy or adverse effects.

- **Cost and Complexity:** The use of sophisticated stabilizers and coatings can increase the cost and complexity of nanomaterial production.
- **Long-Term Stability:** While stabilizers and coatings improve stability, their long-term effects and potential degradation over time must be thoroughly investigated.

The use of stabilizers and coatings is a crucial aspect of enhancing the stability of nanomaterials. By carefully selecting and applying appropriate stabilizers and coatings, researchers can ensure that nanomaterials maintain their desired properties and performance over extended periods, enabling their successful application in various fields.